W9-BVK-308

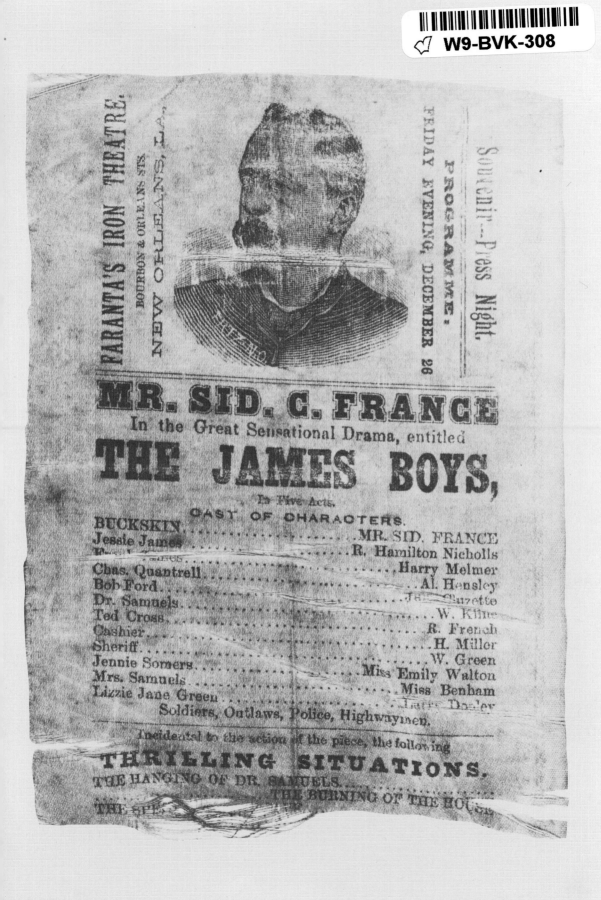

FARANTA'S IRON THEATRE.

BOURBON & ORLEANS STS.

NEW ORLEANS, LA.,

PROGRAMME:

FRIDAY EVENING, DECEMBER 26

Souvenir—Press Night.

MR. SID. C. FRANCE

In the Great Sensational Drama, entitled

THE JAMES BOYS,

In Five Acts.

CAST OF CHARACTERS.

BUCKSKIN,
Jessie James .... MR. SID. FRANCE
.... R. Hamilton Nicholls
Chas. Quantrell .... Harry Melmer
Bob Ford .... Al. Hensley
Dr. Samuels .... J. .. Guzette
Ted Cross .... W. Kline
Cashier .... R. French
Sheriff .... H. Miller
Jennie Somers .... W. Green
Mrs. Samuels .... Miss Emily Walton
Lizzie Jane Green .... Miss Benham
Soldiers, Outlaws, Police, Highwaymen.

Incidental to the action of the piece, the following

THRILLING SITUATIONS.

THE HANGING OF DR. SAMUELS.
THE BURNING OF THE HOUSE
THE SP

DISCARD

SIGNOR FARANTA'S IRON THEATRE

F.W. Faranta. Ca. 1905.
Courtesy Robert C. Stempel.

SIGNOR FARANTA'S IRON THEATRE

Boyd Cruise and Merle Harton

792.0232
St41
BC888s

PUBLISHED BY
THE HISTORIC NEW ORLEANS COLLECTION
NEW ORLEANS, LOUISIANA

International Standard Book Number: 0-917860-13-6
Library of Congress Catalog Card Number: 82-083592
The Historic New Orleans Collection, New Orleans 70130
©1982 by The Historic New Orleans Collection
All rights reserved
First edition. 1000 copies
Printed in the United States of America

FOREWORD

As a non-native New Orleanian, albeit one who has fiercely adopted the city, I feel as though I have maintained some degree of objectivity in observing this potpourri of a city. There is one area, however, that even the coolest and most dispassionate of observers can rarely ignore: the theatrics of our fellow inhabitants. New Orleans is a living stage set with much of its life acted out in its streets. Parades, maskers, street vendors, mimes, pickup bands, jugglers and marching groups today continue the perennial New Orleans tradition of a vivid and theatrical way of life.

Formally-organized indoor theater began here in 1792, and the nineteenth century saw serious drama with internationally known stars presented at the city's many theaters. Signor Faranta and his Iron Theatre, however, played to a less cultivated audience, providing popular entertainment with few cultural pretensions. There were many variety theaters in New Orleans during the 1880s, but most were given to risqué entertainment, drunken patrons, and street brawls outside their doors. Signor Faranta always aimed to maintain a respectable family theater at which ladies and children were welcome.

The Iron Theatre was part of the national theatrical circuit that developed after the Civil War; the shows there were virtually identical to those seen in any other major American city of the period. Before the war, theaters had depended on resident stock companies with a limited repertoire. The completion of the nation's vast railroad system after the war allowed troupes of traveling entertainers to tour the country, appearing in each city for a week or two. These touring groups brought greater variety and higher levels of professionalism to local theaters.

The popular audience that Signor Faranta captured was jaded and demanding. Theatergoers were no longer satisfied with a simple minstrel show and a few songs. They expected increasingly more sensational shows with dozens of acts; ranging from minstrels to contortionists; from jugglers to trained animals; from melodramas to hypnotists. A performance was expected to last at least three hours. Any group not measuring up to the audience's expectations was quickly fired and replaced.

Signor Faranta was, for a time, a successful and innovative showman. I am pleased that the Historic New Orleans Collection is able to make a small contribution to the history of theater in New Orleans by publishing the story of "the cock of cheap shows," Signor Faranta, and his Iron Theatre.

Stanton Frazar, Director

ACKNOWLEDGMENTS

It is surely our pleasant duty to recognize the assistance of those who helped to make this book possible, as well as to acknowledge the aid of institutions that opened their doors to our labors and intellectual needs. We should like to thank Miss Rose Lambert and her staff of the Louisiana State Museum Library; the staff of the Louisiana Division of the New Orleans Public Library; the staff of the Special Collections Division of Tulane University's Howard Tilton Memorial Library; the staff of the Louisiana Division of the Troy H. Middleton Library, Louisiana State University, Baton Rouge; Miss Florence Jumonville and her staff of the Research Library of the Historic New Orleans Collection; and photographers Miss Jan White and Mr. Wesley Sandel.

We owe special thanks to Mr. Stanton M. Frazar, director of the Historic New Orleans Collection, for agreeing to undertake this publication; to the board of directors of the Kemper and Leila Williams Foundation for supporting our work; to Mr. Robert Clifford Stempel and Mr. Edward William Stempel, the grandsons of Signor Faranta, for allowing us access to, and the free use of, their memorabilia and remembrances; to Mrs. Kathy Haase Harton, who encouraged us to complete the book; and to Miss Maria Ybor, who read the page proofs.

Two people we cannot thank, because they are now deceased, but they justly deserve credit and recognition for their early help—Mr. Dan Leyrer, who kindly photographed newspaper articles and illustrations for us, and Mrs. Isabelle Marie Lagarosse Stempel, Faranta's daughter-in-law, who was kind enough to share with us her time and memories.

CONTENTS

PROLOGUE   1
    The India Rubber Man
CHAPTER I   9
    Faranta's Pavilion
CHAPTER II   29
    The Barnum of
    Ten Cent Shows
CHAPTER III   47
    The Iron Theatre
CHAPTER IV   71
    "A Real and
    Proper Theater"
CHAPTER V   99
    Encores

Notes   119
Bibliography   133
Index   137
List of Plays   141

PROLOGUE

Faranta in a Limber Pose.
Photograph by M.B. Brady & Co., Washington, D.C., 1864.
Courtesy Robert C. Stempel.

he minstrels of Sanford's Opera Troupe excited much interest and attention when they entered New Orleans in October of 1863. This was to be the first appearance of Samuel S. Sanford and his group in the Crescent City in eighteen years, and their debut in the Academy of Music seemed to promise—despite the continuing Civil War—a period of stable divertissement. Life for the citizens of New Orleans had not returned to normal, and there was little evidence that it would. "For nearly six months," complained the *Daily True Delta* on October 11, 1863, "our pleasure loving population have had no regular place of entertainment open." Then the base of military operations in Louisiana, New Orleans was occupied by Union soldiers, as it had been since its capture in April of the previous year, and martial law was still in effect. Major General Benjamin F. Butler, the "Beast," no longer ruled the city, however, and it was the more lenient regime of Butler's replacement, General Nathaniel P. Banks, that made it possible for David Bidwell to reopen his Academy of Music[1] without fear that some petty occurrence within the theater would cause his quick arrest by federal military authorities. Sanford's organization, advertised as the oldest and most complete of its kind, was said to be a troupe of genuine artists who made their perilous journey to the theater on St. Charles Avenue directly from Sanford's opera house in Philadelphia.

On the evening of October 7, the first performance of Sanford's Troupe in Burlesque Opera was given before a crowded and delighted audience. General admission was fifty cents, entry to the "colored gallery" cost twenty-five cents, and children and servants could attend a matinee for only a nickel. The Academy's outdoor balcony serenades were resumed, and both the theater-goer and the passer-by were attracted to the spot nightly to listen to the arias, patriotic and operatic, performed by Sanford's band. The activity gave to St. Charles Avenue an old and familiar look. It also bode well for the purses of the minstrels.

Sanford's burlesque shows, which proved to be a likable amusement, were met each night by a full theater and hardly a week had passed before General Banks and his formal retinue attended one of the performances.[2] In its second week the Academy advertised "An Entire Change of Performances Nightly, embracing Songs, Dances, Witticisms, Burlesques, Ballads, Comic Acts, etc.,"[3] and, as a rule, the stage presentations were changed frequently to ensure that returning admirers would behold fresh entertainment. In the group's third week was a "burlesque fete" that featured, in addition to "grand Miscellaneous Variety" from the minstrels, a farce entitled *The Black Statue* (an Ethiopian sketch that Sanford himself had written) and a burlesque "on Bellini's Opera of *La Sonnambula*." Despite the dark times, the Academy's new season had a fortuitous beginning.

Sanford continued to offer his audiences a varied show, including a pantomime of *The Four Lovers*, a scene from the "black-letter edition of Boucicault's Romeo and Juliet," further Ethiopian burlesque, and a "side-splitting farce," *The Mummy*. Even the successful return of the Varieties Theatre,[4] which opened on October 29 with three one-act comedies, did not diminish Sanford's popularity. By October 31, the Academy of Music was able to exact larger admission fees for presenting each night what the theater advertised as "all the Gems of Minstrelsy." Entry to the theater's dress circle, parquet, or family circle now cost fifty cents, while both black and white could gain admission to their designated galleries for twenty-five cents; quadroon boxes cost fifty cents; private boxes were available for prices ranging from two dollars to five dollars; and children and servants were charged twenty-five cents for the daily matinee.

On November 9, Sanford's feature was *The Spectre Guest,* a play whose principal performer was a ghost, the specter of a murdered woman. From its very first appearance, due to crowded and enthusiastic houses, the play's astonishing optical illusion became the reigning star in the New Orleans theatrical scene.[5] The next presentation, which also featured the ghost, was *The Doomed Bride; or, The Jealous Mute,* a terrifying little drama "written by a gentleman of this city." This played from November 16 through November 21, and it was followed two days later by a curious performance of *Richard III,* in which the ghosts of Henry VI, Lady Anne, Prince Edward, and the Duke of York were seen in the "Ghost Illusions." This spiritual contrivance appears to have had a prominent role in every remaining presentation by the minstrels of Sanford's organization. Not only did it come onstage again in *The Doomed Bride,* which returned on November 25, but it also loomed on November 27 in the "first original opera ever written in this country," an Ethiopian comedy entitled *Bone Squash.* During the interval, Mr. C. Villiers danced, Mr. F. Moralti displayed gymnastic and acrobatic feats, and "Mr. Stemple, the young American contortionist," appeared in his "great challenge act."[6]

The ghost was finally laid to rest in *The Haunted House of Lafayette,* the theater's feature of December 1 and 2, and with the play's last performance, which included a thrilling farewell by the well-known ghost, Sanford and his minstrels concluded their stay at the Academy of Music. At this terminal appearance of Sanford's Opera Troupe, Bidwell announced that he had succeeded in arranging with two great circuses—Sands, Nathan & Co. and George F. Bailey & Co.—to begin a short combined season on the following night. These two companies had but recently performed in combination in St. Louis, and their opening in Bidwell's theater on December 3, 1863, made it evident to the residents of New Orleans that their city would host its first equestrian event in three long years.[7]

The Academy was entirely renovated for the appearance of the combination circus, which changes were made during Sanford's visitation, and the removal of the stage at the minstrels' departure recreated "the most beautiful arena ever shown the public." The arrival of the "Great Circuses" drew a vast concourse of persons eager to witness the acrobatics, clowns, tumbling, holiday sports, hippodramatic scenes, pantomimes, and combination animal acts—a variety that encouraged Bidwell to label the Academy a "Temple of Olympic Games." So great was the immediate interest in this spectacle that the Academy could not seat all of its many patrons.[8] The circus performed nightly before a full house, and it was reported that "whole battalions" were unable to secure seats to the show. By the end of the first week, the demand for tickets was so large that Bidwell had to inaugurate two extra performances on Wednesdays and Saturdays for the pleasure of women, children, and servants. There seemed to be no limit to the popularity of the Academy, now the "most fashionable place of resort in

Faranta and Magician A.J.D. Wallace in Masonic Ceremony in Haiti.
Photograph by Oscar Ochon, Port au Prince, Haiti, ca. 1880.
Courtesy of Robert C. Stempel.

the city," and of its combination circus.[9] It was precisely this *succès d'estime*, however, that gave the *Daily True Delta* grounds for an unusual complaint—the newspaper's "vocabulary of commendation" was "well nigh exhausted by the heavy demand upon it which the extraordinary equestrian and gymnastic performances at the Academy have compelled us to make."[10]

By December 14, there was an entire change of acts, featuring the premier performance of the celebrated French equestrienne, Mlle. Lola Lehman. The residents of New Orleans continued to fill the Academy each night, but the number of interested theater patrons grew larger as Christmas approached. They were no doubt anxious to see the "side-splitting Christmas Pantomime" the Academy advertised for December 23; in this show the complete company of equestrians, gymnasts, acrobats, clowns, contortionists, and jugglers would appear in their best and most daring acts. Prominent among this talented group was "young Ferranti, 'the India Rubber Man,' in his wonderful iron ring performance."[11] The "young Ferranti" also displayed his skill on the day after Christmas. The ladies and children who attended the noon performance were astonished and pleased, noted the *Era*, "and the delight they manifested at the antics of the clown, the daring acts of the riders, the wonderful contortions of young Ferranti, the India Rubber man, and the amusing pantomime of the Cobbler's Frolic, was unbounded, and their mirth irrepressible."[12]

The young contortionist, Ferranti, was seventeen years old, and how he came to the circus is the least of the many mysteries about this man. As "Mr. Stemple, the young American contortionist," he first appeared on the New Orleans stage with the other members of Sanford's Opera Troupe. His separation from Sanford's organization and subsequent enlistment into Bailey's circus was a common and accepted practice in the profession, and it was one that he would follow many times in his lifetime. He was born Frederick William Stempel on October 30, 1846, in Buffalo, N.Y.[13] His father was a brewer, and both parents were immigrants from Strasbourg, France; he was the eldest of their nine children. Although his earliest years are unknown, it was sometime before 1860 that he moved with his family to Ottawa, Illinois, for it is from this place and at this time, according to the legend bequeathed to us, that the fourteen-year-old boy left his home and his school to join the circus and, under the name "Master Willie," entered the employ of a small tent show. In 1861, at the start of the Civil War, young Stempel joined the Union Army as a drummer[14] for what was to be an exceedingly brief career; he was soon taken prisoner by Confederates in Missouri, but was released within a few weeks. He then resumed his original plan and was taken into George Christy's minstrels as a contortionist. His limbs were naturally supple, and those acrobatic skills that the young man had not taught himself he acquired quickly, for the fraternity of the profession easily made teachers and students of its members. He toured the concert halls of the Midwest, later traveling down the Mississippi to New Orleans, where he joined Sanford's minstrels at the Academy of Music. His first friendship with David Bidwell, who took some interest in the fledgling contortionist, was a fortunate one. Sometime during his stay in the Academy—either with Sanford or with the combination circus—Bidwell suggested to him the name "Signor Faranta," for the simple reason that its Italian sound would make the young Stempel more conspicuous before the public and would add distinction to the show. It is likely that "Ferranti" was the young man's version of Bidwell's suggestion. Within a year we find him using "Signor Faranta" (and sometimes only "Faranta"), the *nom de guerre* he would continue to use both publicly and privately, and so consistently that it became better known than the name given to him at birth.

The success of the combination circus, with which young Ferranti had allied himself, was without parallel in the city, and its popularity continued even in the face of some interesting competition from the Varieties Theatre. After three weeks of the circus, the show still attracted patrons "like a mountain of load stones."[15] On December 28 Henry Cooke and his troupe of educated dogs and monkeys made their debut. This attraction from the Cirque Napoleon in Paris and Astley's Amphitheatre in London was joined two days later by jester, wit, and balladist Sam Long, who thus began a short engagement in the Academy and contributed to the good fortune of the theater's new season. Even the inclemency of the weather that ushered in the first few days of 1864 was powerless to stem the current of expectant visitors to the warm and brightly lit Academy.

On January 9, in addition to Henry Cooke's performing beasts and favorite acts by the entire circus troupe, Professor Nicolo and his pupil Robert, a father and son team from Havana, entertained the audience with their perilous act on the flying trapeze. "The brilliant, startling, and mirthful arenic displays" continued for the many delighted people who entered the theater each night, and the *Daily True Delta* urged the populace to "take time by the forelock" and to profit from the few remaining performances of young Nicolo and the Academy's combined circuses. Ferranti was not mentioned again by the press, but he undoubtedly performed every day. The journalists' puffs usually went to the more established stars, like Mlle. Carolista, who was wont to ascend her tightrope from the rear of the stage to the dome of the theater, as she did on January 31. As the engagement of the circus neared its end, several benefit shows were held, one of the first being for Robert Nicolo, whose audience that night included Admiral Farragut and a great many Union military personnel. During the course of the evening, the show was interrupted long enough for a Major Bradley, representing both the Army and the Navy, to present the young aerialist with a gold medal as a mark of their appreciation of his skill and daring.[16]

On February 10, the Academy held a benefit performance for acrobats and gymnasts George Ross, William Carlo, Sam Shappee, and J.H. Whitney. During the show, Carlo and Ross were seen as the Comic Brothers, and Shappee and Whitney performed on the trapeze; all four made up an acrobatic ensemble; Carlo returned in an "impalement act," and Ross awed his spectators with his versatile horsemanship and somersaults over forty soldiers with fixed bayonets. These specialty acts were supported by the full strength of the combination circus.

It was also at this time that the Mardi Gras festivities began, and attempts were made to revive the old gaiety of the occasion. The Civil War could not prevent the approach of Lent, nor the city's carnivals, but it seemed to bid farewell to the merriment that had distinguished these days in New Orleans. What celebrations there were still bore the miserable signs of war and capture.[17]

The Academy's circuses fared better. A benefit for equestrians Le Jeune Burt, James De Mott, Lola Lehman, and George Sloman was held on February

11. In an added attraction they were to present to a member of any New Orleans fire department a massive silver goblet as a reward for the fastest time achieved in running around the circus ring a full fifteen times. All the local firemen were invited to compete for the elegant prize. A similar diversion took place on the following day, when the Academy presented a horse, saddle, and bridle to the person purchasing the largest number of tickets for the remaining days of the circus.

On Saturday, February 13, visitors saw the last performance of the combined circuses. The Academy's stage manager, Frank Rivers, announced that the theater had engaged a Baltimore group, George Lea's Variety Company, whose celebrated entertainers included black-face comedians, a roller skating acrobat, a ventriloquist, and a pantomimist.[18] This variety troupe, which opened in the Academy on February 17, was received with such enthusiasm that its stay was eventually extended to June 17. The great circuses left New Orleans on February 16.

With George F. Bailey & Co. went young Frederick William Stempel. He subsequently associated himself in 1866[?] with the Haight & Chambers Circus in Washington, D.C.; he later returned to Bailey's circus, where he remained for several years. During his early stay with these circuses, the youthful contortionist, Signor Faranta, would master his art and learn to twist and knot his body with an apparent ease that won him a reputation for grace; to his repertoire of acrobatic skills he would add handsprings and trick skating, both of which he could do until he was seventy years old. After leaving Bailey's employ, Signor Faranta is known to have been connected with the circus of Dan Rice[19] and with Howes' Great London Circus, and later (circa 1880) to have traveled with a small circus troupe to Brazil and through the West Indies. In Brazil he was made a Mason by a fellow performer on a boat trip along the Amazon River and contracted yellow fever in Rio de Janeiro. He was employed as an acrobat in the Boston Museum upon his return to the U.S. Sometime during these years he was married (allegedly to a countess) and divorced and married a second time.

Between April and September, 1882, Signor Faranta, then thirty-five years old, and his second wife, Alva Lowe, herself a stage performer, toured the eastern provinces of Canada with the Ryan & Robinson Circus. Five months later he returned with his wife to New Orleans. It is unlikely that the circumstances of his return would have given anyone reason to suspect the great success he would find in the Crescent City, or what fame he would attract to the iron theater he would build.

CHAPTER I

Faranta in Tights.
Inscribed "F.W. Faranta" and dated January 12, 1874.
Courtesy Robert C. Stempel.

Frederick William Stempel opened the first show of his first season as a New Orleans showman on the 18th of February, 1883, under cover of a borrowed "Mammoth Pavilion" at the corner of Orleans and Bourbon streets. The entrance was similar to that of a circus, but the mammoth tent was pitched inside a lot surrounded by a high fence, which was constructed, as was common in the city, of wide beveled boards. A gate "about as wide as the average carriage"[1] admitted visitors onto the lot and so into the pavilion. This shelter, in fact two tents joined to form a "stretch of canvas of eighty-foot round top and forty-foot middle piece,"[2] protected the patrons who came out of curiosity to see one of the two shows the new entrepreneur offered each day. The first of these, a matinee, took place at noon, while the second began at eight o'clock in the evening. The price of admission had been put within reach of all—a mere ten cents secured entry to the flapping tent and a position upon the rough boards of the benches that encircled the structure's interior. The proprietor of this inexpensive show was known to the public only as Signor Faranta, for that is how he presented himself, and soon even his friends would know him by this theatrical name alone.

Whether or not it was, as his newspaper advertisements proclaimed, "The Cheapest And Best Show On Earth" and true that "'Par Excellence!!'" was the public's verdict, Faranta's Summer Pavilion Theatre enjoyed a flourishing beginning. Faranta gave an assortment of names to his new show, intriguing potential customers with such titles as "Faranta's All Star Specialties," "Faranta's All Star Combination Novelty Company, Under a Mammoth Summer Pavilion," "Faranta's Specialties," and "Faranta's Great 10 Cents Show," but he was careful to point out that what he offered was an "entertainment for the people of a highly pleasing, strictly moral and intellectual nature, organized for the special edification of the Ladies and Children."[3] What his patrons could expect, and what they received, was "refined" vaudeville for the family, a heterogeneous program with a wild diversity of amusements, but nevertheless an entertainment unlike its unrefined rival, also called vaudeville or burlesque, in the nightclubs and dance halls of the West and the saloons of the East.

Not for nothing was vaudeville often labelled "variety" entertainment. Anything capable of presentation on a stage might find its way into a vaudeville show, and if the variety of the entertainment offered was exhausted by an amusement's classification, there was still the style of its presentation to give it its variety: a simple feat such as a dance (whether it be the cakewalk, ballet, hula, march, or folk dance) could easily be combined with a particular kind of music (ethnic, patriotic, topical tunes and songs), special shoes (taps, clogs, skates, snowshoes), various accessories (stairs, chairs, a cane and hat, guns, rope), and special clothing (uniforms, formal wear, folk costumes, the short dress of the soubrette)—any one of these possible combinations would alter the delivery of the dance. Among the diverse elements of the variety show were, in addition to dances, light dramatics, comedy, pantomime, dialogues, songs, magic, ventriloquism, animal acts, innumerable circus features, roller skating, club-swinging, acrobatics, gymnastics, juggling, black-face comedy, and recitations. These might be brought together in an "olio," a miscellaneous arrangement of these acts, but more often than not they were assembled in the program around short pieces of comedy—or

11

"sketches"—that served to separate one element of the program from another, which it introduced. An actor might be asked to bring to this sketch a specific talent, identified as his "specialty," and yet he might be given a role only because he was available for a part in the sketch. Vaudeville could make up an entire show, thus comprising sketches and specialty acts, but it could also be used briefly to divide the acts of dramatic plays or other stage presentations.

All of the variety of vaudeville could be found in Faranta's pavilion. The *Daily States* took note of Faranta's diverse presentations when, during the show-man's first week under canvas, the newspaper honored Faranta's show by placing on its list of amusements "Faranta's Combination—Variety Performance," along-side the stalwart and respectable Academy of Music, St. Charles Theatre, and Grand Opera House.[4] What is significant about Faranta's early success, however, is that he had arrived penniless in New Orleans a few weeks earlier, after misfortune put an end to his first attempt to run a show of his own.

Late in January of 1882 Faranta had advertised through the *New York Clipper* for work as a contortionist and tumbler.[5] He and his wife were subsequently engaged by the Ryan & Robinson Circus,[6] which played in Albany, N.Y., on June 12 and then throughout the summer in four Canadian provinces—Ontario, Quebec, Nova Scotia, and New Brunswick—returning to New York to exhibit on Pleasure Island during the first week of September.[7] The circus wintered in Albany, where it was purchased before the end of September,[8] thereby leaving Faranta unattached to any amusement organization and free to deliberate about his entrance into the new career that, though apparently well planned and executed, would yield only destitution to its architect.

During October and the first two weeks of November, Faranta managed to gather under the name "Combination Fraternal" a group of specialty entertainers whose collective aim was to perform in South America. Among this miscellany were Faranta's wife, Alva Lowe, who was billed as an illusionist, Signor Carlo Benedetti, a sword swallower, Professor Wallace and Anathalia Wallace, magicians, Rocambole, a trapeze artist, Little Tony, a gymnast, and the group's agent, Ben A. Stempel, Faranta's younger brother.[9] The Combination Fraternal sailed on November 18 aboard the steamship *Commonwealth* for New Orleans. There they rendezvoused with other members of the group, sailing on December 2 on the steamship *City of Dallas* for tropical Belize, British Honduras.[10] From there they were to journey to South America for the extended tour that Faranta and his brother had arranged. It was sometime during this voyage that the majority of the entertainers contracted yellow fever. Ben Stempel returned to New Orleans, arriving on January 2, 1883.[11] Faranta, who was spared a second visit by the disease, was not spared its financial straits. He agreed to pay the victims' medical costs and return transportation, whether or not he had bound himself legally to the Combination Fraternal, and this consequently exhausted what monies the unseasoned showman had. When Faranta and his wife returned to New Orleans on January 30, he was without money and without credit, and their only possessions consisted of three trunks, a bag, a valise, and the circus tents borrowed originally for the trip to South America.[12]

Within two weeks, Faranta had leased the vacant lot on Bourbon Street, between Orleans and St. Ann streets, erected the borrowed pavilion, completed negotiations with his specialty performers, assembled a management staff,[13] among whom was probably younger brother Gus Stempel, who came to New Orleans in mid-March, and arranged for all the equipage necessary for the realization of his new project, paying for his location and accouterments with money provided by John H. Scott, an oil merchant of the city, who wished to supply the fuel for lighting the lamps in Faranta's canvas theater, and who made available to the showman sufficient sums for the payment of essential debts and claims against the entrepreneur. A steady supply of gasoline and inflammable oil was delivered thereafter, and Faranta "promised and bound himself to pay to Mr. Scott, from time to time, the one half part or share of all the net earnings or profits of the business or establishment known as 'Faranta's Summer Pavilion Theatre.'"[14]

Although Ben Stempel did not return to his brother's employ until late in March, the 28-year-old actor may well have assisted his brother in securing performers for the earliest shows. Among the first entertainers were Billy McCarty, the "Irish Comedian," Thomas Tandy, the "great Slack Wire Performer and Gymnast," Naoni, the "great juggler and plate spinner," the "beautiful and accomplished Miss Jennie Elkins, in gems of song," the Morris Brothers (the "Mobile Mokes"), the "most comic of the comic niggers in their comicalities," who appeared in "truthful delineations of plantation life," and Faranta's stage manager, Johnny Patterson, the "great Irish jester and clown" known best for his patriotic song "Bridget Donohue."

On February 27 the *Daily States* gave this review of one such show:

> The large summer pavilion of Faranta's, corner of Orleans and Bourbon streets, was again crowded last night by an audience to witness the good performance that is given nightly under the tent. The programme, which is varied and very interesting, opened with a sketch by Miss Jennie Elkins and Mr. Billy McCarty. This was followed by feats on the horizontal bar by the Lamont Brothers. Naoni, the famed Japanese Juggler, entertained the audience with some wonderful Chinese and Hindoo tricks.
>
> Mr. Johnnie Patterson, the late clown of Bachelor and Doris Circus of the "Bridget Donohue" fame, was present, and kept the audience in a continual roar of laughter.
>
> The Morris Brothers were good in their song and dance.

Also joining the talented group were skaters Charles and Carrie Moore "in entertaining feats on Parlor skates," and "Prof. Moore's trained Dogs, seven in number," one of which, a dog named Charley, was able to tell the time of day by looking—in his own eccentric manner, of course—at a watch. Foremost on this list of specialty acts was the "greatest contortionist living," Signor Faranta, who could be seen on stage in "Classical Posturing."[15]

At the close of the first week, following a fast increase in attendance at the Summer Pavilion, Faranta added a section of reserved seats, available for thirty-five cents, near the raised platform that served as a stage, and increased to fifteen cents the admission price to the matinees. General admission to the evening shows was kept at ten cents. On the one hand, Faranta's public estimate of these entertainments was that he gave to those entering his pavilion an "exhibition in which the advanced scholar may be interested, as well as the youthful student or ordinary observer."[16] There certainly seems to have been something for everyone at the Summer Pavilion. During the second week, in addition to the aforementioned performers, Faranta offered to his public "Le Fils Der Fer Aerian! The Human Wheel! The Impossible Ascension!" and "The Canine Wonders!" On the other hand, if we are to believe his advertisements, these intellectually alluring exhibitions were nightly greeted by "Cyclones of Laughter! Tempests of Applause!" and "Roaring Cataracts of Honest Applause" with "Foaming Oceans of Unpremeditated Screeches." The *Mascot*, having noticed that the "entertainments given at this place are well patronized," gave a more sober assessment of the Summer Pavilion: "For the price charged, there never has been anything of the kind equal to it, in this city."[17] The *Times-Democrat* came to a similar conclusion on March 11:

> Faranta continues to draw immense crowds to his spacious and neatly fitted up pavilion. This show is of an eminently respectable character, being conducted by efficient gentlemen, long residents of this city. Under their auspices it is proving an unprecedented success, and recommends itself to the patronage of the ladies and children. Excellent order is maintained, and nothing is tolerated upon the stage to offend the most fastidious. The price of admission is an innovation. For one dime an interesting, pleasing, novel and varied entertainment may be witnessed. Comfortable chairs may be indulged in at a slight augmentation to the price of entrance.

A fire occurred on March 18, exactly one month after Faranta opened the successful theater. For that Sunday evening show, it was later learned, 1772 persons (728 less than the pavilion's capacity) were there to be amused and entertained.[18] According to newspaper reports of the disaster,[19] the tent had been handsomely dressed with colorful banners and a number of American flags of various sizes, and the patrons sat watching with interest the roller skating exhibition of Charles and Carrie Moore. This presentation was lighted, as usual, by several oil lamps attached to the great wooden poles that supported the bulk of the canvas tent. John Scott had supplied the lamps in Faranta's Summer Pavilion Theatre, and it was his responsibility to maintain them. That afternoon, in fact, he had inspected and filled the lamps with oil, finding them in satisfactory condition.

It was nine-thirty, and the show was advancing as usual. The Moores had just finished their complicated gyrations on skates and were enjoying the enthusiastic applause of the audience, when one of the lamps attached to the tent pole to the left of the stage overflowed and a small quantity of oil trickled down the pole. The applause for the Moores died abruptly as the trickle of oil ignited and a thin finger of flame hurried to the ground. The tent support was situated beside a decorative curtain that masked the area beneath the stage; when the flame reached this painted fabric, it too caught fire. George Clark, Faranta's canvas man, rushed onto the stage to turn off the lamp, which was operated by a cock switch, as on a gas jet, but before he could reach the lamp an excited gentleman grasped the post and tried to shake the lamp from its position there. This scattered the flaming oil over the stage and burned Clark's forearm. The flying droplets ignited the American flag above the lamp, and within seconds the canvas pavilion was aflame.

Emile Drespar, a young man who was seated near the post, saw the lamp fall to the ground; he sprang forward and attempted to smother the flames with

14

his coat. Others, the more excitable of Faranta's patrons, began to hurl chairs at the offending flames. Joe Allen, the banjoist scheduled to appear next on the evening's program, came forward and with a bucket of water succeeded, despite the flying chairs, in extinguishing the burning lamp.

Someone shouted "Fire! Fire!" and the audience rushed toward the main entrance. Many were trampled in the wild fight to escape the tent. One man was pushed to the floor, where he lay crying "For God's sake save me!" Some sailors from the man-of-war *Tennessee* used knives to cut slits in the tent, allowing several women and children to pass through the pavilion. During this activity, the property man, Theodore Martum, who was only a boy, climbed the tent pole and extinguished the burning canvas with his hat. The audience was too intent on escape to notice his action or the smoking black-rimmed hole, some five feet in diameter, that the flames had burned in the canvas enclosure.

Officer Edward Ryan, the policeman on duty that evening at the pavilion, sent word to Charity Hospital to send wagons for the injured. He then stationed himself at the entrance and, seeing that the fire posed little danger to the audience, attempted to stop the people scurrying past him. The policeman was buffeted and knocked down, and was kept prostrate as the mob hurried over him. The wooden fence that surrounded the pavilion, the last obstacle to the frantic multitude, was pushed down and broken. Shortly thereafter, Sergeant Thomas Dorsey, Corporal Timothy Driscoll, Acting Corporal Thomas Byrnes, and several other policemen arrived and were able to restore some order, if not calm, to the scene. On orders from Johnny Patterson, Faranta's stage manager, the musicians began to play a buoyant melody.

Wagons from Charity Hospital arrived, and the attendants began the removal of those persons requiring medical attention. Among the first to enter the vehicles were a twenty-two-year-old Austrian, who suffered a spinal injury, and a twenty-three-year-old steamship oiler, who was hurt about the head, leg, and groin. Several children were injured in the melee, as well as a number of women, two of whom later died as a result. Other women in the audience had, upon discovering safety in the open air on the banquettes, promptly fainted, but apparently needed only resuscitation and comfort. Six-year-old Willie Zengle and Joe Maximillian, an eight-year-old negro, were taken to M.T. Breslin's drug store, on St. Peter Street, where every attention that science could suggest was paid to them. Willie was later taken home, but Joe, who had internal injuries, was moved to the Third Precinct Station, where Deputy Coroner Paul Archinard attended him. The largest portion of the crowd, intent on leaving the area, moved to Royal Street, where many entered Anthony Labarbera's confectionary in quest of some stimulating libation. It was discovered on the following day that the evening's excitement left the modest supply of glassware on Labarbera's bar shelves greatly depleted.

When a measure of quiet had been restored to the neighborhood, Faranta commenced the remainder of the show. Corporal Byrnes ordered him to desist. Faranta declined to do so, and the policeman, fearing another disturbance, withdrew. Sergeant Dorsey went to the dressing rooms and there held a conversation with Faranta, who then agreed to discontinue the performance for the night. Patterson disagreed with the decision, though, and, after the sergeant left, urged the performers on to the stage to continue the show. Just as the program was about to recommence, Sergeant Dorsey arrested Faranta and transported him to the Third Precinct Station, where he was jailed.

On the following morning, March 19, Judge Thomas Ford entertained the case against Faranta in a courtroom full of spectators from the Summer Pavilion. Faranta's arrest had already raised much public outrage and criticism. After some deliberation, the judge decreed that the only charge that could be brought against the showman was that of failing to keep the entrance to his pavilion free from obstructions. He was released under a two hundred and fifty dollar bond and ordered to appear again on Thursday to "answer any charge that might be made against him."[20] The legal matter seems to have ended here.

Joseph Livesey, author of "Bridget Magee's Society Notes,"[21] one of the most popular columns in the weekly *Mascot,* had this to say about Faranta's recent adventure:

> Signor Faranta complains bitterly av Sargeant Dorsey's tratement av him, both at the toime av the arrist an' durin' his sourjurn at the police cill. "Be this an' be that," (all froightful oaths). "I'll run yez to the frunt," sed the Sargeant, shakin' his fist at the Signor. Whin they arrived at the dungeons the circus proprietor objicted to racline on the dhirty flure av the cill. "Gimme a blanket," sed the prisoner. "We've none but lousey blankets," sed the cops, an' the burnt out showman had to stand shiverin' in the could all noight. Whiniver they had an opportunity Dorsey an' his pals taunted an' abused the prisoner an' refused to git him the commonest nacissities that his unfortunate condishion raquired, without pay. Dorsey had worked himsilf up into a wild excitement against Faranta, because he had carried on his performances while the people in the tent were rushin' madly into the sthrates. The showman tuk the course av mosht performers who have bin in similar pradicamints, he continued his antics to show the peple, there was no danger, if they would kape quiet. He naturally feels indignant that his intintions have been mish-construed. Many av the palers are too frish an' too fond av goin' off half-cocked on peple that have no perlitical influence an' they should be promptly re-adjusted wid a brick, if the authorities are too lazy to luck afther thim.[22]

The *Daily Picayune,* on the other hand, while it helped to dignify Faranta's position with "The Troubles of a Showman," an editorial concerning his arrest and incarceration, found no injustice in the legal actions against him:

> [W]hen Mr. Faranta, the proprietor of the Varieties Show on the corner of Orleans and Bourbon streets, was arrested on last Sunday night, a too captious public sentiment entered an indignant protest. An accident had oc-curred. Only a bucket of water had saved the circus tent which covered Mr. Faranta's stage and auditorium from speedy reduction to smoke and ashes. Nobody suspected, it seems, that there might be some means of checking the progress of the flames about the place, and the consequence was a panic more dreadful than the fire itself. . . . How was a well-disposed policeman to meet an exigency like that? Something had to be done, and it was obviously impossible to arrest the mob. But Mr. Faranta was available. He had not run away, and, moreover, it was his tent that had caught on fire. It was, therefore, at once feasible and proper to take him in charge.[23]

After the trial, hundreds of persons visited the corner of Orleans and Bourbon to view the aftermath and the newly made skylight in the mammoth pavilion.

In order that the canvas theater might be reopened as soon as possible, workers engaged themselves in repairing the many damages and in bringing order to the area. In the company of Mrs. Faranta the proprietor of this public attraction visited all of those injured during the panic and so attempted to bring them some small relief.[24] With a compassion to which his public would become accustomed Faranta offered to pay the medical bills of the wounded and arranged to bear the cost of burying the two who died. He pressed the sum of fifty dollars upon John Eckert, husband of Louise Strader, who died on the night of her injuries.[25] Mrs. Delia Jenkin Vila, the second fatality, died on March 23.

The property clerk was kept busy caring for and attempting to return to their owners at least a part of the articles left in the tent and on the grounds after the fire. Included in this lot of wayward possessions were: nine ladies' hats, the hats of three gentlemen, ten children's shoes, ten assorted shoes, one skirt, two coats, three shawls, two rings, and a pair of enameled bracelets. Many persons reported the loss of valuable jewelry. Two young girls called at the office of the property clerk, inquiring whether their sister's black hair had been found, and were reported to be quite piqued to learn that it was not resting safely on his shelf.[26]

Under Faranta's personal direction, the damage to his establishment was repaired within four days, and the Summer Pavilion Theatre was set to reopen on March 22. On this date "Faranta's Card to the Public" appeared in the local newspapers. In this open letter the showman declared: "At the time of the accident, seeing the audience completely terrified, I did everything in my power to protect them from harm, actuated by motives inspired from a twenty years' experience as a performer and director of public amusements, having witnessed, during that time, many such scenes." The event in question was "simply one of those inexplicable and uncontrollable panics which occur at times in armies, churches, schools and theatres." He assured his public that their return to his pavilion would be a safe one, and he announced that, as a preventive measure against the recurrence of fire in his tent, he had replaced the oil lamps with new electric lights. He set the time of his matinees at noon on Wednesdays, Saturdays, and Sundays, and further promised to host a benefit performance for all who had been hurt in the March 18 mishap.[27]

For the reopening of his popular show on March 22, Faranta had secured at "immense cost" the services of Black Lily Long-Tree, who would perform an aerial suspension act wearing the costume of her native country, which was never identified. Also billed was Johnny Patterson as Professor Patterson in a piece of burlesque with the curious title "Prince Awaitin, Cats-notion," but the feature of the show was a sketch entitled "The Black Jersey Lily's Recreation," of which Mme. Long-Tree (or her caricature of professional beauty Lily Langtry) was the main attraction. The entertainment, Faranta advertised, was greeted by a crowded house that made the pavilion ring with "avalances of solidified laughter and equinoctial hurricanes of mirth," and ladies were duly cautioned to provide themselves with extra corset cords before attending.[28]

Said the *Daily States* of the variety show's return:

> Faranta's show is under full headway at the corner of Orleans and Bourbon streets, and the tent is crowded nightly with pleased people. The pavilion is

now illuminated by electric lights, and everything moves smoothly and safely. Faranta has struck a bonanza in his cheap entertainment, and he is literally coining money.[29]

On Saturday, March 24, the entire city was forced to contend with the high winds and heavy rains of a tropical storm that uprooted trees and blew down large signs in the commercial district. Under the influence of this eastward gale, which prevailed for most of the day, the Mississippi River was raised against the levees and driven through the planks of the wharves, doing considerable damage to the freight stored there. The rain raised the river nine inches above the last and highest mark, and there was "too much water overhead and underfoot for the show at Faranta's Pavilion," but many expected the city to have dried out enough to allow a matinee on Easter Sunday, March 25.[30]

Mme. Long-Tree continued to perform in the Summer Pavilion until, it seems, March 28, when a new bill was announced. On the evening of March 30 Faranta gave his benefit performance for victims of the recent excitement, as he had pledged to do, and, under the supervision of a Committee of Friends of the Beneficiaries, placed at the entrance to his pavilion a donation box into which each patron was expected to drop his contribution toward the relief of the injured. This was a small measure of Faranta's concern for the ill-used and underprivileged. March 13 had been "Newsboys' Night," the first of many benefits. At this performance "the little folks were given free admission to the show and plyed liberally with lemonade and presents."[31] It was a special treat for these youngsters, often uncared for and barefoot, and it was long remembered. "Despite accidents, storms, Lent and other antagonisms," he now advertised, believing these to be behind him, "Faranta is Still Triumphant with his popular company of first-class specialty artists."

The "other antagonisms" mentioned in Faranta's advertisement may well have included the unexpected competition of Eugene Gorman at Clay Square. This gentleman had been successful during the previous summer as manager of theatrical entertainments at Spanish Fort, the summer theater and resort on Bayou St. John, at Lake Pontchartrain. He was not, as had been noted in the *New York Clipper* of March 10, the "director of Amusement" for Faranta's Summer Pavilion Theatre, but had recently returned from New York, bringing with him "a splendid and ample pavilion capable of seating 3,000 persons."[32] The size of this tent— its top was one hundred feet in diameter, its center pole reaching forty feet in height—far exceeded that of Faranta's. Upon his arrival in New Orleans on March 22, 1883, Gorman secured a lot on the corner of Chippewa and Third streets, opposite Clay Square, and perfected his arrangements for the opening of a large tent show in the predominantly English part of the city. Gorman's show began on April 1 with "Gorman's Standard Novelty Company," which featured songs, dances, recitations, and exhibitions of skill on the horizontal bar and trapeze. This was to be followed by a series of light and comic operas similar to those that Gorman had presented at Spanish Fort. The price of admission to these performances matched Signor Faranta's, for general admission cost only ten cents and reserved seats were available for thirty-five cents. Faranta could not know that this was only one of innumerable competitors who would appear in New Orleans within the next few months.

Alva Lowe, Faranta's Second Wife.
Photograph by Robinson and Roe, Chicago, 1886.
Courtesy Robert C. Stempel.

Faranta had designed his theater for the family; it was his published intention not to play the pander for vulgar amusements, and he was careful to ensure that any gentleman could take or send his family to the Summer Pavilion for respectable entertainments at a price that anyone could pay. This meant, of course, that persons from a wide variety of professions and trades, regardless of color, could be found together in Faranta's pavilion at any one time, and it meant that there were few, if any, class barriers to guard the more sensitive patrons of his establishment. Faranta could not fail to notice this, especially when temperatures began to rise at the start of April, and so he added to his auditorium an automatic perfumed fountain that dispensed its scented spray for the comfort and pleasure of the fortunate occupants within the semicircle of reserved seats. To add to the new elegance of his pavilion, Faranta also arranged with local scenic artist Harry Dressel to paint "a proscenium and a Garden Scene."[33]

The range of talent presented in the Summer Pavilion during the start of April is not known, but then neither the advertisements nor the press notices of these performances were designed for the historian. Despite copious announcements that Faranta was at this time presenting "New Faces" and "New Features," and that visitors would find "New Talent coming all the time," we are able to discover, besides Johnny Patterson, only the names of a Miss Levanion, J.E. Gay, and James Lefevre, all of whom performed during the first week of April. Concerned with Faranta's own activities, one interested party did note that the showman had his eye on a riding club recently formed in New Orleans and that he proposed to exhibit the riders throughout the South after they finished amusing the citizens of this locale. He further suggested that, if Faranta could keep Bridget Donohue, *i.e.*, Johnny Patterson, sober during the summer and could secure a few more entertainers, by the end of the season he would have "bloomed into a bloated capitalist and we shall hear eventually that the Boneless Man of the Boundless Prairie has once more 'struck ile.'"[34]

A second rain fell on Saturday, April 7, and for a few days reduced the size of Faranta's audiences considerably. The first few drops fell at 5:40 in the morning, and from that time on it rained steadily. It was the heaviest rainfall in the city in a decade, dropping a foot of water within three days.[35] Within a half-hour many of the city's thoroughfares resembled lakes. The Mississippi overflowed at the foot of St. Ann and St. Peter streets and required nearly seven thousand sandbags and seven hundred feet of temporary levee to stop its flow.[36] The rain stopped on Monday, but the river continued to rise and poured over these barriers and rushed through St. Anthony's Alley, flooding nearby streets and banquettes.[37] On Tuesday, April 10, the sun shown again, and the river fell. There were no reports that rain or flood had forced Faranta to end or delay any performance in the Summer Pavilion, although Eugene Gorman was reported to have postponed his show on April 7 because the ground inside and outside his mammoth tent was largely under water.[38]

By mid-April, Johnny Patterson had concluded his stay with the Summer Pavilion, and on April 14 Faranta announced the first appearance of Forstell, the "Musical Prodigy and Dutch Clown," who played thirty-six instruments during his act, and "Russian Phenomenon" and "Scientific Wonder" Antonio Gofre. Both remained with Faranta's variety troupe for the rest of April.

By this time, too, news of fire and panic in Faranta's pavilion had made its way to the European press. The following extract from a German newspaper shows the embellishments one "Report of a Catastrophe in New Orleans, America" received during its journey:

A traveling circus, under a tent supported by poles, having the sides closed with sail duck, was performing in that city. Last Sunday, a week ago, the place was crowded, the audience being composed chiefly of workmen with their wives and children, the women and children being in the majority. The performance was opened by the 'lion tamer' who, while in the cage with his wild beasts, was exercising them in jumping through fiery hoops. While one of these hoops was being removed it accidentally set fire to a curtain at the entrance of the stables, and immediately desperate cries caused by the fire rang through the place. The audience, becoming crazed, rushed to the gates. The fire, however, was promptly extinguished by a courageous clown, who leaped upon the shoulders of one of his comrades and tore down the burning curtain. The people were intensely excited, and at the exits human masses were being pushed and smothered, and in their hurry to leave the place had recourse to their knives, and cut their way through the sail duck around the tent, and through these openings threw their wives and children into the street. At another point the pressure on the poles supporting the tent became so strong that they yielded and fell, carrying with them the largest portion of the tent, under which those who had not had time to leave were buried. Through the efforts of the people and the firemen 60 bodies, mostly women and children, were removed from under the debris, and about 100 other persons were wounded.[39]

"Edelweiss," the Tyrolean National Concert Company, comprised of "ladies and gentlemen from Alpine and Romantic Tyrol," appeared on Faranta's stage from April 21 to April 24, bringing picturesque costumes of the group's native land, "Charming Mountain Songs," and selections from popular operas. At the departure of Edelweiss, the "Senegambian Minstrels," a troupe of negro songsters, and "America's Greatest Gymnast," Frank Clifton, who would execute the most difficult of feats on three bars, joined Forstell and Gofre as Faranta's featured performers. Also on this bill was Alva Lowe (Mrs. Faranta), who appeared on stage in a playlet entitled "Raphael's Dream, or the Sculptor's Studio."

The public endorsed Faranta's enterprise by filling his coffers with admission money. On April 24, the *Daily States* noticed that "the popularity of Faranta's All Star Novelty Show increases perceptibly" and that his pavilion is "thronged week in and week out with cultured audiences, who like a show because it's cheap and good." The longevity of such popularity was still an open question. The proscenium that Harry Dressel had been engaged to design and paint was finished and installed in Faranta's tent during the first week of May, and the refined drop curtain, upon which was depicted a Louisiana scene of old plantation days,[40] brought forth high praise from visitors to Faranta's show. Eugene Gorman, however, had a similar drop curtain, painted by Dressel and [William J.] West,[41] placed in his tent on April 22. Edelweiss did not return to Austria immediately after leaving Faranta's stage, but instead appeared in Gorman's larger tent on April 25. Like Faranta, Gorman offered "One Dollar's Worth of Fun for 10 Cents," "A Specially Selected Corps of the Best Artists in America," and "A

Strictly Moral Entertainment."[42] If this was flattery, it was also serious rivalry between two very similar amusements.

Despite the success of his theatrical ventures, Faranta was once again embarrassed by the law. In the press of his multiple duties, or perhaps because he blamed the oil merchant for the disaster in his Summer Pavilion, Faranta neglected to fulfill his part of the bargain with John Scott. On April 30, 1883, the sheriff seized the pavilion's contents after Scott caused a writ of attachment to be served upon the seemingly remiss proprietor, contending that Faranta's Summer Pavilion Theatre had earned at least a net sum of three thousand dollars since February 18 and that, while the showman had invested a considerable amount in furniture and appliances, he kept the balance of these profits and refused to pay or even to account to Scott, who consequently hired attorney Charles S. Rice to settle the issue.[43] Assisted by local shoe merchant Emile Angaud, who had been in the pavilion with his family on the night of the fire, Faranta posted a $2,250 bond. He also enlisted the firm of Braughn, Buck & Dinkelspiel as his legal counsel. On June 5, the date on which the matter was adjudicated, the showman opened his financial records to the court and presented a list of items purchased (for a total of $457.95) for use in his pavilion.[44] According to Faranta's records, the theater's gross receipts totaled $6,608.30, of which $4,822.12 had been expended for general salaries and current expenses, leaving a sum of $1,786.18. Of this remainder Faranta laid claim to $1,708.25 for salaries to himself and his wife ($600, for 10 weeks at $60), Gus Stempel ($72, for 6 weeks at $12), and Ben Stempel ($45, for 30 days at $1.50), and for the use and rent of the Bourbon Street property ($991.25, or 15% of the gross receipts). Still due Scott was $212.37 for oil and maintenance, leaving a total indebtedness of $134.44, one half of which the oil merchant was liable for. The court's decision, however, fell in Scott's favor, although the sum awarded was only $333.66, with court costs being borne equally by both Scott and Faranta.

After this legal unpleasantness, Faranta was anxious to remove the site of his operations from the corner of Orleans and Bourbon, and for this end selected a vacant lot at the corner of Canal and Villere streets. He did not complete this move until June 10, when he first advertised his new location, and did not actually open his show until June 14. In the meantime, from the last few days of April to the end of May, when, unfortunately, he did not advertise many of his featured performers, the following entertainers were added to Faranta's show: Frank Le Roy, a female impersonator, singer Celia Rexford, comic singer G. Renaud, and Jerry Keating and Eva Ross, a song and dance pair; also performing during May were Professor Davidson, the "Hero of the High Rope," vocalist Dixie Garland, dancer Clara Boyle, negro and Irish comedians James and Thomas Dalton, and Joseph Francis, a one-legged dancer. Admission to any seat during a matinee was now ten cents; this was a pecuniary change that Faranta made in mid-May, and it was continued after his relocation.

Newly named (and no longer connected with John Scott), Faranta's New Summer Pavilion Theatre was opened in a smaller tent, its capacity being 500 less than his last; it boasted "a regular stage, electric lights, a good orchestra, a fair variety company and everything in good style and proper form."[45] Because the summer's heat had begun, the large pavilion was elevated to improve the circulation of air inside.

Added the *Daily Picayune* on the day after his reopening: "Faranta represents amusements in town, and he is doing his best for those who visit his place." During the first week at this new location, and perhaps with an eye toward increased patronage, Faranta would appear on stage in the graceful contortion act for which he had become well known. He was followed on stage by gymnasts Frank Clifton and Moncayo, and then by Essex and Williams, two character artists who presented a negro comedy act. Chief among the new performers in June were Herr and Fräulein Ulm (the "Ulms"), formerly of the Pappenheim German Opera, who captured Faranta's audiences with their operatic selections. Master Hofer and Forstell were also featured during June, as was Mrs. Faranta, who posed in artistic representations of famous statues.

The performances continued apace at the corner of Canal and Villere streets, some eight blocks from Faranta's former location, and on July 1 George Castle's Celebrities, J.E. and T.H. Kennedy, the "World's Greatest Mesmerists," joined Billy Maloney and Mabel Gray under Faranta's new tent, where one could also find songs and character imitations by German comedian J.W. Hettinger and sketches by Mason (who stood six feet tall) and Ralston (who was only thirty-six inches high). At several of these shows, Miss Gray and Mr. Maloney donned boxing gloves and sparred with each other. The lady, reported one witness, "stands firmly on her pins, brushes back her bangs, and being nimble as a cat, gives blows right and left that worries her opponent."[46] This was a novelty in New Orleans, and it was recommended to all who were seeking a higher education in the matter of female muscle and form.[47]

The Kennedy Brothers and their mesmeric exhibitions also occasioned much interest. They were said to be capable of making a subject, once placed under their control, behave in any way they chose. Present at one of their incredible performances was a physician who agreed to test the Kennedys' skill at hypnosis. Pins were stuck promiscuously into selected subjects, the most delicate portions of the body being preferred, but this seemed not to awaken the slightest feeling of pain in the mesmerized volunteers; three of the people were then placed in a row and sewn together, the needle being passed through both cheeks and tongues of each, and yet even this test failed to evoke from them some indication of discomfort.[48] Unconvinced by what the newspaper considered humbuggery, the *Daily Picayune* called the Kennedy Brothers "prophets without honor in their own country."[49]

In mid-July Professor E.G. Johnson, the "World's Greatest Mesmerist," replaced the "World's Greatest Mesmerists," the Kennedy Brothers, as a featured performer with Castle's Celebrities. Johnson was about twenty years old, with reddish hair and a mustache of a similar color; his chin was weak and his general features indicated sensitivity rather than will power.[50] On Faranta's stage, however, he was able to throw himself into a "cataleptic state," as he called it, and with a few passes of his hand over his body could make himself so still and rigid that he could be lifted bodily and laid onto the backs of two chairs, where he proceeded to defy the weight of several persons sitting on him.[51] The *Daily Picayune*, no less skeptical about Johnson than about the Kennedys, remarked: "For the moment 'Professor' Johnson becomes the champion stiff, and any undertaker would delight in burying him."[52]

None the less, it was the educational nature of such performances that helped to earn Faranta's New Summer Pavilion Theatre a reputation as "the only moral place of amusement that has been seen in New Orleans for years."[53] Of course, the fact that Faranta proscribed the sale of liquor in his establishment and would not allow his patrons to go out between acts to support an industrious barkeeper also helped to make his canvas theater a model neighborhood show.[54]

Eugene Gorman, whose tent show was equally popular in his quarter of the city, was unable to attract the same esteem. One of Gorman's ingratiating efforts toward gaining more press notices resulted in this sour statement from "Bridget Magee":

> Little Gorman, the showman, danced up to me the other day an' sed, in his jirkey way, "The *Mascot* has not treated me well at all, at all. Bedad I've been advertisin' in it from the first, an' divil a notice kin I git for love or money. Be me own swate auburn hair, I want yez to kriticise me avin if I git hill." "Will," I raplied, "ye wear a wig an' pretind to be Frinch, whin ye know ye are a mick. For shame on yez, ye little spaleen, goin' back on yer country an' callin' yerself Eugane whin ye know ye were christened Paddy. Notice indade," sed I, shakin' me umbrella over his kranium. "I hear yez kape a brace av blayguards called Howard an' Alton, that shock the modesty av dacint paple be their filthy jokes. Go 'long, ye imp av the divil, an' don't ax me to minshun yer indacint show till I kin inter yer canvas widout blushin'."
> How will that do for a kriticism, Eugane, ma bouchal?[55]

Gorman closed his pavilion at the corner of Third and Chippewa streets on July 23, when he presented a wrestling match between Theodore George and John Hudson. The fashionable summer resort, West End, had opened its season on May 6, and Gorman made arrangements to manage the Criterion Opera Company again in a series of light and comic operas at West End. His pavilion, however, did not stand empty for long.

Without any prior notice, the following advertisement appeared in the local newspapers: "Moved, Sig. Faranta, Corner Third and Chippewa, has leased the tent of Mr. Gorman, and for a short season offers his great Castle's Celebrities, opening Monday, July 30, 1883." For Faranta's initial show at this new location, Gorman's more capacious tent was "packed from centre pole to the top row back" with an estimated 2,500 persons.[56] This overflowing audience was entertained by Mlle. Eugenia and her new character dances, Mason and Ralston, Maloney and Gray, Hettinger, who appeared in a Hebrew and Dutch sketch, and other members of Castle's Celebrities. Temporarily with Faranta's show was Professor Johnson, who, on the evening of August 1, was "taken with a spasm" as he made his entrance on the stage. It is not known whether his mesmeric art assisted him in this case, but Johnson did receive prompt medical attention and was later placed in the care of his friends.[57]

Faranta was forced to close his tent show in the first week of August. Normally the summer's heat required the closure of all permanently housed theaters in New Orleans, and, while this made a canvas theater more alluring, there were other reasons to flee the same structure at the height of summer, since those who sought entertainment in the cool air of a summer pavilion had still to struggle with mosquitoes and sundry other insects attracted by light and flesh at nightfall. Faranta's season at Clay Square was charmingly short, lasting as it did from July 30 through the performance of August 5—exactly one week. Except for two sentences in August, there were no further reports of Faranta's participation in either theatrical or social activities in New Orleans until September. The one exception was the mid-August notice by the *Daily Picayune* that he had just returned from Galveston, Texas, where he planned to take his variety troupe for a short season on the beach of that city.[58]

Suddenly, on September 9, we find Signor Faranta advertising the opening of his Roller Skating Rink in the casino at Spanish Fort. This amusement was begun on the following day and would offer parlor skating and instructions in the vehicular sport every afternoon and evening for a very short season, if the date of his last advertisement, September 16, is any indication of his venture's life span. On October 12 he proclaimed that he would be "At Home Again!" when Faranta's Summer Theatre returned to the corner of Bourbon and Orleans, reopening on Saturday, October 13.

Faranta's latest tent, newly christened and now under his ownership, was capable of housing three thousand people, and for the debut of his new season, remarked the *Daily Picayune*, it was "crowded in every space."[59] General admission to any of the seven evening shows was still a dime, reserved seats being available for thirty-five cents, and entry to any seat during a Saturday, Sunday, or Monday matinee was kept at ten cents. Faranta's choice of entertainment was a double dose of pantomime: *Humpty Dumpty's Picnic* and *Humpty Dumpty No. 2*. The first of these fantasy plays, which was seldom, if ever, performed in a tent, was said to be presented on Faranta's stage just as it had been at the Grand Opera House in San Francisco. Its principal performers included Andy Morris, "the best pantomime clown in the world," Ida Maussey, "the most graceful *Columbine* in America," Mrs. Faranta, "the beautiful Queen of Queens," and Fräulein Gretchen, "the Swiss Nightingale," who sang in French and German. *Humpty Dumpty No. 2*, which concluded the program, featured "Master Tootsey, the youngest living clown, but six years old, and yet perfect in the art of facial expression." Preceding each play were specialty acts, the staple fare of Faranta's previous season, featuring Signor Faranta himself in "his graceful plastic exercises," Frank Essex in Ethiopian business, Emil Myers on the trapeze, and Naoni in his juggling act. Patrons of the Summer Theatre were treated to "uproarious merriment"— or so promised Henry Rollande, Faranta's business manager and the manager of the "Humpty Dumpty Company," in advertisements circulated throughout the city.

Noted the *Daily States* at the end of the first week:

> If crowded houses are any criterion of a good performance, then surely "Humpty Dumpty's Picnic," performed under Faranta's mammoth pavilion, must be immense, and at every performance it is crowded to its fullest capacity; and everybody goes away with a determination to see the show again. The pavilion is situated at the corner of Orleans and Bourbon streets, and the price of admission is only ten cents.[60]

On October 25 Faranta was offering a variety of songs, acrobatic feats, a laughable pantomime, *The Magic Flute,* and a skit entitled "The Cooper's Frolic," whose setting was, of course, a cooper's shop. Besides Andy Morris, Miss Maussey, and Mrs. Faranta, a Miss Perry, formerly of West End's Criterion Opera Company, was added to Faranta's group of featured performers. At the start of November, Faranta was advertising a "host of specialties" and his program's newest pantomime, *The Brigands of Calabria,* which starred his clowns Andy Morris and Little Tootsey. Because he offered his patrons entertaining shows, changed his programs with a refreshing regularity, and kept his admission fee to the lowest possible figure, Faranta was rewarded with crowded houses at each and every one of his shows. Commented the *Daily States* with pointed reference to Faranta's theater: "Cheap shows in the French part of the town seem to catch on."[61]

The Brigands of Calabria opened on October 30 and was featured at Faranta's Summer Pavilion Theatre until November 11, when a new pantomime, *Robert Macaire,* took its place. In this latter program were the Harper Brothers, two one-legged acrobats, and gymnast and athlete Mabel Francis. Before this weekend performance, however, Faranta added his own personality to the new brand of advertising he had recently adopted. In his handsome four-in-hand, seated on his prancing steed, and attended by his band in red coats, which played a selection of light tunes then in vogue, Faranta and his entourage traversed the principal streets of the city distributing colored handbills and dispensing coppers and nickels to the hundred or more excited and unbelieving street urchins who soon made up his retinue. With a graver manner the Signor also handed out five hundred complimentary tickets to his new tent theater, which he had renamed Faranta's Pavilion on November 9, promising fresh and talented artists who were completely "up in their business."[62] His new performers may have included some from a combination company managed by A.J.D. Wallace, the magician who accompanied Faranta's small troupe on its short-lived venture in South America, who was negotiating just such an engagement with his friend at the start of November. Wallace and his entertainers had recently returned from Havana, Cuba, where they spent a short season in Jane's Iron Amphitheatre.[63]

On the evening of November 11 the French Opera House opened its season with a well-attended performance of *Faust*—a presentation that had been much discussed and anticipated by the eager musical connoisseurs of the city. Faranta's Pavilion, two blocks away, was nevertheless entirely full, moving the *Daily Picayune* to remark ungracefully that "it was evident that the opening of the French Opera House in the vicinity had not hurt his business."[64]

Faranta could expect more of this provincial commentary on New Orleans: On November 12, as his patrons assembled for an evening of entertainment, a man wearing a straw hat entered the tent and was promptly received with shouts of "Shoot the hat!" and "Sambola has fired the cannon!" and other taunting and discourteous reminders that Straw Hat Day, which signaled the city's annual change from straw to felt hats, had arrived on October 21.[65] This seasonal crusade against straw hats, achieved each year by the symbolic shooting of straw hats, was begun in 1880 by Anthony Sambola, then a captain in the Louisiana State National Guard and later Judge of the Third Recorder's Court, and it lasted until Sambola's last "straw hat salute" was fired on October 12, 1902, during which period the occasion usually brought trepidation to the hat-wearing public, but joy and money to the city's hatters.[66]

On Sunday, November 18, Adrienne and Blanche Lamothe, two New Orleans artists, were seen for the first time in Faranta's Pavilion with their songs, dances, and quick costume changes. The one-legged acrobats, the Harper Brothers, began the second week of their twenty-minute circus act, and Andy Morris, Ida Maussey, and Little Tootsey performed together in Morris's new pantomime, *Baked Alive*.

In the following week, beginning November 26, Faranta presented a new attraction in conjunction with his repertory of performers. The fresh group in question—"The Great Blitz Combination"—was headed by magician Signor Blitz, Jr., and included ventriloquist Orm Dixon, whose life-size figures spoke in a variety of voices, Mlle. Luie's trained canaries, tenor and dancer Frank Conway, and Charles Bixamos, the "Man of Iron," who would engage himself in a kind of tug-of-war with two powerful horses. The Harper Brothers, Mabel Francis, and the Lamothes were also featured, while Johnny Patterson was promised for the near future.

CHAPTER II

Faranta. Ca. 1874.
Photograph by M.B. Brady & Co., Washington, D.C.
Courtesy Robert C. Stempel.

aranta's return to New Orleans seemed now to presage a season of increased patronage, if only because the entertainers in his pavilion continued to play before large audiences, but the showman had nevertheless begun his second year in the face of much theatrical competition. There was, of course, David Bidwell's trinity of respectable establishments—the Academy of Music, the St. Charles Theatre, and the Grand Opera House on Canal Street, between Dauphine and Burgundy—as well as the elite *Théâtre de l'Opera,* or French Opera House, at the corner of Bourbon and Toulouse, two streets from Faranta's Pavilion, and the more common Wenger's Garden, a saloon and music hall managed by Henry Wenger, Jr., in the first block of Bourbon Street. New, however, was the Park Theatre on Royal Street, between Customhouse (now Iberville) and Bienville, which opened in the last week of September with Harry Guion's Female Minstrel Combinations; later offerings, available at prices comparable to Faranta's, included Mlle. Clarisse Ducantel and her "Corps of Parisian Dancers, in Original French Can-Can," boxing tournaments, and such mild erotica as "30 Models of Love and Loveliness" in "Costumes of the richest texture and fitting neatness." On October 7, the *Daily States* had observed that Eugene Gorman was constructing on his former site at the corner of Third and Chippewa a building "on the style of one of our summer theatres." Gorman held the grand opening of this "water proof pavilion" on December 15 and for this occasion advertised "Myriads of Novelties," including several acts previously seen on Faranta's stage, which were again available at Faranta's innovative prices. More significantly, though, New Orleans was now accommodating numberless new centers of amusement whose names and characteristics have not survived the ephemeral handbills and posters that advertised them. Indicative of this late trend is the discovery in early December that "Canal Street, from Basin Street out, is lined on both sides with museums and tent shows."[1]

The decision to hold the World's Industrial and Cotton Centenial Exposition in New Orleans had been announced at the end of April, 1883.[2] The exposition's construction upon the 249 acres of Upper City Park (now Audubon Park) was not begun until December, therefore leaving only twelve months to complete the ambitious project. Apparently there was a fortune to be made in this, and, whether or not carnivals and minstrelsy would in fact yield this end, there was no dearth of entrepreneurs determined to establish themselves early in the city and thus find a vantage point from which to seize this expected fortune. Signor Faranta was in an advantageous position. Ten months earlier he was stranded in New Orleans with a vacant tent and an empty purse, but within half of that time he had filled both and had made Faranta's dime show a popular custom in the city. If, during this time, he pondered leaving the city to relocate his show or travel with it, the planned exposition no doubt decided the issue for him. There was success in what he was doing in New Orleans; the forthcoming exposition, and the visitors it was expected to attract, would increase his prosperity—but only if he competed with equal success with the many newly arrived pretenders to his throne of cheap family shows.

So, despite the array of available competition, Faranta continued to follow his formula for appealing vaudeville. On December 2, in newspaper advertisements adorned with a wood-engraved portrait of the showman, the "Barnum of Ten Cent Shows" announced a new program and additions to the team of performers kept over from late November. On December 3, a minstrel pair, Frazer and Allen, introduced fifteen different musical instruments into their sketch of the "Arrival of Cousin Cal" and Johnny Patterson was back with "a budget of New Songs." The Irish clown's return was warmly welcomed, and his singing of "Pat Mealy" elicited long applause, but the appreciative audience would not be satisfied until he exhausted himself by singing "Bridget Donohue," the song for which he had become famous, over and over again.[3] On the previous night hundreds of persons were turned away from the entrance, and the sale of tickets was curtailed long before the curtain was raised on what proved to be one of the most entertaining of Faranta's presentations.[4]

Three days later, because of the crowds, the chief of police instructed his officers to clear the banquettes in front of Faranta's Pavilion as soon as possible after the rise of the curtain.[5] At the close of the week, 2,800 school children witnessed Faranta's show; each was charged five cents upon presentation of a "Scholar's Ticket," and all were later discharged through the three spacious exits arranged for this performance.[6]

For the week of December 9 Faranta's "Ten Cents Show Par Excellence" included Signor Blitz, Jr., Frank Conway, Frazer and Allen, Johnny Patterson, and Mlle. Luie and her talented birds; *Humpty Dumpty* was brought back collectively by Andy Morris, six-year-old clown Little Tootsey, Ida Maussey, and Mrs. Faranta; joining this group were Lew Delmore and Fred Wilson, who concocted their sketch entitled "The Surprise Birthday Party," and (from New York) J.W. Sheppard, the "Tonawanda favorite." This program seems not to have changed until December 16, when Charles Bixamos returned to Faranta's stage and Leon, the "Silent Clown" from Barnum's Circus, joined the troupe of performers.

At this time, however, Faranta found that he had engaged more performers than he could use in his tent show, and arranged to have some of his company present their variety acts in a hall in Algiers, across the Mississippi River.[7] Notwithstanding this excess of talent, he was still advertising for additional artists: On December 22, he announced in the *New York Clipper* his need for performers in all branches of variety entertainment, including automaton-figures, character artists, and sundry specialties, but added that such performers must have acts suitable for lady audiences.

The Signor offered a double program during Christmas week, beginning Christmas Eve. The first part was given over to a minstrel concert by no less than twenty-five performers; the second part introduced a new specialty company, although the members were not named. Faranta also prepared 3,700 baskets filled with fruits and candies for distribution among those attending the noon performance on Christmas Eve (the "Santa Clause Matinee"), but he soon found that he had more enthusiasm than patrons; he gave the remaining baskets to the neighborhood children and to the Sisters of Mercy for distribution among their charges.[8]

At the Sunday matinee, December 30, Faranta's "Extra," held under the sponsorship of the St. Ann Shoe Store, was a lottery drawing for "Beautiful Dolls." On this date, in conjunction with Faranta's new specialty company, French strong man Charles Bixamos again exhibited his physical powers in the tent. Two days before, following articles of agreement he had signed in Faranta's Pavilion on December 20,[9] Bixamos engaged in a Graeco-Roman wrestling match with French wrestler André Christol, but on January 10, 1884, lost to his compatriot in a rematch in the Baronne Street Cock Pit (between Common and Gravier streets);[10] Bixamos did, however, win their return bout on January 31.[11]

On January 2, the weather turned disagreeably cold and deflected audiences from Faranta's well-used tent and this "Grand New Program," which he had arranged for the week of January 6:

> Mr. Faranta announces to his patrons the engagement of Four of the Leading Musicians of the late Defossez French Opera Orchestra, who, in addition to his Celebrated Band, will perform Choice Selections. Musical critics are invited to hear them. Also will appear: Miss Marie Dearing, the celebrated Vocalist; Blanche and Adrienne Lamothe, the French Comiques; J.V. De Paul, the great Solo Trombonist, late of the Defossez French Opera in operatic selections; Connors and Barron, in their great act, "Commotion."[12]

He had improved the quality of his music, and, noticed the *Daily Picayune*, he was "making unusual exertions to keep his family resort up to the highest mark of excellence in the way of performances,"[13] but Faranta was quick to realize that his patrons desired a warmer show spot and would prefer to remain in their homes than to brave an evening in what had become his enormous, drafty tent. He found in the cold a good reason to replace his pavilion with "a much finer one," it was announced on January 9. "The new canvas is now on the way here from New York. It will be weather-proof, and will be put up in a week, ready for the opening with a new company."[14]

Faranta suspended his productions in order to prepare his lot for the new structure. The tent was indeed on its way to New Orleans, but was delayed in transit, playing havoc with his plan to reopen his show on Saturday, January 12, as he declared he would do. Instead the "Best Ten Cents Show in the World!" held its grand reopening on January 13 with "talented specialty artists in new acts, songs, dances and sketches," including William Barron as "The Black Momus" and acrobats (or "Kings of the Bar") Loto and Valido. Unfortunately the show also took place in Faranta's old pavilion, for the new weatherproof enclosure had not yet arrived.

The bad weather "has told against Faranta," commented the *Daily Picayune* on January 18: "but he is still in the ring, though his tent is somewhat battered. His brand new waterproof canvas will be here tomorrow from New York and goes up immediately. Charley Howard, the original of all the darkey business done by men of the Milt-Barlow stripe, arrived yesterday. He joins Faranta with a new company." This new combination was advertised for Sunday, January 20, and featured, in addition to negro impersonator Charles Howard, the "Eccentric Comedians" Cort and Murphy (as "The Editors") and the "Big Four"—John Connors, J.W. Sheppard, Billy Barron, and Burt Richardson. On this date the *Daily Picayune* again took notice of Faranta's new program, but remarked only that the "weather has not been kind to the under-canvas show for a week past" and failed to mention that the new company was forced to perform in the worn pavilion.

Not until January 27 is it announced that Faranta "has just received from New York and put up a magnificent new pavilion, and painted everything neat and new under it."[15] In vain do we search for a description of this new structure, instead learning only that it is a rectangular "Two-Centre Pole Tent" and "Wind and Water Proof!" At this time, character actor Joe Oliver and Marie Dearing, the "[Adelina] Patti of serio-comics," made their first appearance with Faranta's show, joining Charles Howard and the new company to make "a grand Pleasure Party" of twenty artists. This program continued until February 3, when magician and ventriloquist Clever Carrol, the Irish team Crimmins and Doyle, and Cora Henry, "the American Langtry, on the Trapeze," were moved to first position among the twenty-member company. On February 11 Faranta announced that Miss Lizzie Aldine, "Champion Lady Rifle Shot of the World," and Samuel Baughman, "Champion Trick and Fancy Shot," would "positively appear" on Monday, February 18, but, until that time, he announced no further changes in his show.

The *Daily Picayune* announced on February 17:

> Signor Faranta, always on the lookout for something new at the Pavilion at the corner of Bourbon and Orleans streets, has engaged Marlande Clarke, a leading man from the London Theatres, and Florence Gerald, a star actress, and with a good supporting company they will play a drama called "A Friend," localized to show New Orleans by gaslight. Lizzie Alden, the champion female shot, with Sam Baughman, and several specialty artists, will appear in an olio. This makes a wonderful ten cent show.

Faranta's house could now seat four thousand persons comfortably, and the stage, which was extended beyond the tent itself, had been enlarged to accommodate the professionally produced plays, of a finer quality than sketches and pantomime, that would occupy the bulk of Faranta's new theatrical fare. Bringing the first of this talent to the pavilion was "A Friend Dramatic Company," owned and managed by English elocutionist Marlande Clarke, Florence Gerald, a Southern poetess and actress, and W.B. Page, the group's treasurer. Originally set in northern Italy, *A Friend* concerns a woman who marries for money and becomes the mistress of a Russian exile, a disguised nihilist, who stabs her to death, kills a trusted servant, and is marched off the stage in handcuffs. Comedy parts were supplied by a lady of uncertain age, a lawyer's clerk, an amateur photographer, and a French waiter; Clarke and Gerald, the play's co-authors, were cast in the leading roles.[16] The melodrama was in New Orleans on a Southern tour that began on September 29 in St. Louis, Mo., and then traveled through cities in Missouri, Kansas, Arkansas, and Texas.[17] The company was dissolved after presenting its play in Faranta's Pavilion, and in June one of its players, Nellie Billings, was successful in her court suit to recover her unpaid salary of $100.[18] Both Clarke and Gerald remained active in theatrical matters in the city for several months after the collapse of their drama troupe.

A Friend was Faranta's daily feature until February 24, when *The Lights of New Orleans,* a drama about the scenes and life in the Crescent City, opened to a well-attended house. This was replaced on March 2 by *Fun in a Boarding School,* a two-act musical comedy, although not before Faranta warned his visitors to look out for the "New Museum," about which nothing more is said, and purchased a sea lion, an "electric woman," and several painted automaton figures.[19] What plot there was to *Fun in a Boarding School* was subservient to fun and amusement. The deaf professor, who used an ear trumpet to read aloud and was fond of repeating the phrase "Come again" whenever he missed the meaning of words meant for his ear, was a favorite character of Charles P. Brown's play,[20] in which both Marlande Clarke and Florence Gerald held important roles.

On March 10, the comedy was replaced by *The Lucky Ranche*, a romantic drama. Presented by the W.M. Paul Company, a casual collection of entertainers that included Maggie Morgan, Thomas Morris, William Barron, and Larry Dooley, *The Lucky Ranche* was brought to Faranta's from Gorman's Pavilion, where it was produced in January by E.R. Dalton, W.M. Paul, their wives, Maggie Morgan, and Horace Cone. In April, *Fun in a Boarding School* was presented at Gorman's by E.R. Dalton's Sterling Comedy Company, another temporary assemblage of performers; Nellie Billings and William Page, freed from their association with Clarke and Gerald, joined Dalton, Lizzie Haywood, and Harry Gleason in this production. This apparently generous use of the word "company" was not unusual; it is no less common to find stage performers adopting stage names than it is to find them banding together, often for a short time only, and adding distinction to their confederacy by calling themselves a "company." This made it easier for a theater's repertory to seem fresh to the public.

By mid-March Faranta had opened his new "museum," which was nothing more than a side show designed, of course, for the diversion of his patrons, and in it he displayed, among other things, a giant ox and his recently purchased sea lion, valued at two thousand dollars. The seal's name was Harry. According to contemporary reports,[21] Harry lived with Faranta and his wife in their rented accommodations on the corner of St. Ann and Bourbon, although he slept in a water tank fitted for him in the courtyard adjoining Faranta's pavilion and residence. Harry, it was said, knew the voice of Mrs. Faranta, who served him his meals (mostly raw fish) and was so attached to his mistress that he would follow her about the house and obey all of her commands like a pet dog. When the Signor would pat him on the head, the seal answered this affection with a sound that resembled a human's. Harry vanished on one occasion, but a thorough search of the premises discovered the creature asleep in Faranta's bed. He was fond of buggy rides and at least once rode with the showman to visit the newspaper offices in the city. During matinees in Faranta's Pavilion Theatre, as it was renamed on March 9, Harry was allowed on stage to delight and entertain the children.

On March 17, Faranta's attraction was a comedy, *Joshua Whitcomb*, concerned with life in rural New England, in which the members of W.M. Paul's company were again participants. The Valdez Brothers, in their first appearance together since one of the brothers lost a leg eleven months earlier,[22] introduced the play with an exhibition of their talent on the trapeze. The premier of this program was met by a relentless rainfall. Faranta cancelled the performance and closed the pavilion until Thursday, March 20, on this day presenting the belated *Joshua Whitcomb*. The combination of rain and Lent had a noticeable effect on all theatrical attendance in the city.

Hattie Adams, the "Queen of the Kehoe Clubs,"[23] was the headliner of the variety show in the following week, beginning March 24. She was assisted on stage by the "Black Senator," Frank Vendetta, in addition to Clifford and Kelly, Larry Dooley, and Horace Cone. The play of the week, authored by W.M. Paul, was a comedy-thriller entitled *The Phantom Avenger,* whose story and style were drawn from the genre of dime novels. Faranta's next show was on March 31. Featured in the olio were three pairs of entertainers: Mendoza and Victoria ("Emperor and Empress of the air"), Noone and Gentry, and Vendetta and Adams. The evening's drama was Paul's rendition of Lester Wallack's *Rosedale; or, The Rifle Ball,* a military drama whose plot turned upon the exchange of two infant children and the supposed theft of one by gypsies. Horace Cone, Maggie Morgan, and Paul and his wife held the principal roles in this production. *Rosedale* remained Faranta's feature for nearly a week; on the night of its last scheduled performance another presentation of *Joshua Whitcomb* was given "by request" instead.

On April 7, *Lafitte; or, The Pirates of the Gulf,* Paul's "Great Historical Nautical Drama," opened for the week and was introduced nightly by variety acts by Frank Vendetta, Hattie Adams, the team Noone and Gentry, and gymnasts Moncayo, Davidson, and Meyer. Like *The Phantom Avenger* before it, the nautical drama was earlier seen in Gorman's Pavilion under Paul's direction. For Faranta's show, Mrs. Paul held the part of Maraquita, the pirate queen, opposite Horace Cone's Lafitte, and together they helped the drama to "set the boys wild with delight."[24]

Faranta's next attraction elicited a greater response from his public. *Pluto; or, The Seven Daughters of Satan,* which had been rehearsed by Paul's group during the run of *Lafitte,* began on April 14, the Monday after Easter. Also titled *The Seven Daughters of Satan,* although often produced as *The Seven Sisters,* this play was given elaborate scenery, luxurious costumes, and a ballet, whose many female members also appeared in a grand Amazon march. The larger charm of this piece was its plot: Pluto, King of Hades, ill-treats his wife, Mrs. Pluto, while their seven daughters, Diavoline, Flutella, Tartarine, Sulpherine, Fasanella, Satanella, and Cantabella, demand permission to visit Earth. Pluto refuses to grant the visit, but with their mother's assistance the seven sisters travel to New York City, where they first try their hands at acting, but eventually turn to vending peanuts, candies, and apples, and even take turns at blacking boots. Pluto later takes back all of his daughters except two, who remain on Earth as mortals.[25] As an added feature of this grand production, which was so successful that a lack of seating and standing room often forced Faranta to disappoint patrons at the front entrance to his pavilion, the showman used gas lamps to illuminate the stage pictures.

The local press was so captivated by the play that the variety artists who introduced it were overlooked entirely. This neglect was partly corrected at the end of the week when an advertisement in the *Times-Democrat* numbered among the performers Edward and Minnie Hart, T. Hunter, and Frank Budworth.[26] Since there was an obvious demand for it, Faranta kept *The Seven Daughters of Satan* for another profitable week, beginning April 21, and not even the heavy rain on its closing performance was able to diminish the size of the audience. Faranta's only regret at the time was perhaps that his giant ox, whose height was set at seven feet, had sickened and died.[27]

Signor Faranta (holding dog) with friends at Fair Grounds race track.
Photograph by Charles H. Adams.
Courtesy Robert C. Stempel.

Engraving of Faranta.
New Orleans *Daily States*, October 25, 1885.

Oliver Twist had its initial presentation on Monday, April 28. Mr. Paul, playing Fagin in his version of the play, was joined in the story by his wife, who appeared as Nancy Sykes. Their daughter, Maggie Morgan, was Oliver, while Horace Cone and T.D. Morris were cast in supporting roles. Neil Price sang the new motto of the New Orleans firemen in the variety performance preceding the play's premier. There was also a rumor circulating at this time that a Mr. McIntyre was Faranta's partner in the pavilion, but the *New York Clipper* of April 26 was able to straighten this out. McIntyre had an interest with the Signor only in a saloon on Bourbon Street (in the building on the corner of Bourbon and St. Ann), which was also the front of Faranta's residence. The saloon was called "Tween the Acts," and was located on the same site as Faranta's Pavilion Theatre so that he might exploit more completely his investment in the leased Bourbon Street property and no doubt exhaust the available and valuable space, wasting little, for a remunerative end. The saloon was open to visitors of the pavilion before and after shows, but never—as was his firm policy—between the acts. The saloon remained at this location until it was incorporated into Faranta's Iron Theatre in 1887.

On the sixth night of *Oliver Twist* a familiar accident occurred in the pavilion. At about midnight the canvas was discovered to be on fire, later said to have been caused by a lighted cigar thrown into the folds of the tent, and the alarm was sounded.[28] The flames were extinguished, the damage was small (estimated at one hundred dollars), and the tent was repaired in time for the last performance of Dickens's tale and Faranta's new feature for the week of May 5, *Peril, or Life by the Sea Side*, acted by the W.M. Paul Comedy Company, and an olio with clog dancing by Master Hogney and other specialty acts, whose modest popularity is implied by this compliment from the *Daily Picayune* of May 2: "Faranta's Pavilion is the only legitimate place of amusement open in the city, and it is quite the thing to go down there."

Paul's comedy troupe continued with *The Dumb Man of Manchester; or, The Murder at the Mill* in the following week. Sometimes produced under the title *The Factory Assistant*, B.F. Rayner's amusing murder story revolves about a dumb boy named Tom, who is falsely accused of knifing to death a kindly dowager, the aunt of mustachioed Edward Wilton, who was the real murderer at the mill and who was secretly married to his aunt's ward, the sister of the speechless Tom. To these stock figures were added a comic milkmaid, her boot-maker husband, a rising young barrister, and a pompous chief justice.

Mrs. Faranta was away during most of these performances, having left on May 8 for a short stay in New York, while her husband was enjoying a four-day trip to Memphis and a visit to friends in Philadelphia.[29] Faranta was back in New Orleans by May 12, for on this day he visited one of his entertainers, Frank Warwick, who was convalescing in a local hospital.[30] We have no way of knowing whether these separate vacations have any significance for their later divorce.

On May 19, the W.M. Paul Dramatic Company brought *Jack Sheppard* to the canvas theater. Larry Dooley, Frank Budworth, Neil Price, and strong man James Messenger were featured in the grand olio preceding the period drama. The story of *Jack Sheppard*, for which Faranta promised new scenery, "correct costumes," and original music, concerns the adventures of a highwayman and burglar whose young life and avocation are ended by execution in London. It was a plot that had been reworked several times and by several playwrights, who thereby spawned such "Jack Sheppard" plays as *Jack Ketch, the London Apprentice, The Idle Apprentice, The Young Housebreaker, The Boy Burglar, Thomas Darrell, The Storm in the Thames,* and *Old London.*[31] Maggie Morgan was cast as young Jack in Faranta's version of the story. The *Daily Picayune* of May 21 reported that about two thousand people attended the play's second performance, but we are given no other indications of the drama's popularity or merits.

On May 26, and for the following two weeks, Faranta's Pavilion Theatre devoted its programs primarily to vaudeville. Among those featured were the "Famous Criterion Two," Larkins and Kelly, in songs and dances, and Mlle. Jeanne Delorme, the "Queen of French Opera Bouffe," with serio-comic songs. Professor Harry Stapp, a "staff-bell performer" from Antwerp, proved to be a competent musician, and the Spanish Señorita Estelle DeCapo made her debut with a selection of songs from her native land. Included in the week's fare was a performance of *Muldoon's Picnic,* a comedy about parsons who give Muldoon his just deserts for maligning their profession. This program was changed slightly on June 3 to include "the finest comedy ever presented in New Orleans." The play, *Casey, the Piper,* was an adjunct to the previous week's featured entertainers and Faranta's "Star Specialty Corps," in addition to the seal, Master Harry, who was engaged for the matinees to "speak to the children as they pass by."[32]

The Signor held a "Grand Show" for the week of June 10, on this day announcing the engagement of Professor W.H. Davison, a high wire performer and "hero of the most daring feat ever accomplished." Professor Davison was said to have outdone Charles Blondin, the famous French equilibrist, "when he crossed at an immense height from one peak of the Sierras to the other, 8000 feet above [sea] level," and would "positively appear during the whole week and at matinees."[33] Also in this show were "premier danseuse M'lle Watson," who had been employed for the previous week, the Malcom Brothers in feats on the double trapeze, and *Going to the Ball,* a "laughable effervescent comedy." As a special treat, "His highness Mast. Harry, the Fur Sea Lion, at urgent request of the Governor and Mayor, consented to give the ladies and children a chance to see his beautiful fur sealskin coat."[34]

This grand show gave way to less imposing entertainments in the following weeks. Featured for the week of June 17 were Irish clog dancing and costume artistry by Adrienne and Blanche Lamothe, comedy by Daveney and Reed, serio-comedy by Lizzie Haywood, highwire feats by Professor Davison, acrobatics by the Malcom Brothers, and "the old favorites of the regular company." On June 23 was the first appearance of John Coburn and his "Irish specialties." Included in the week's variety show were gymnasts Victoria and Mendoza and an untitled comedy.

On June 18, Faranta renewed the lease on his Bourbon Street property, between Orleans and St. Ann. By signing his name beneath that of Mary A. Roberts, owner of the site, he extended his lease for two years, beginning June 15, 1884. According to the signed agreement, the Signor bound himself to pay Miss Roberts the sum of $350, broken into monthly payments of $29.17. In the second year the entire rental fee was to amount to $325, with monthly payments at $27.09. The document also accorded Faranta the right to renew the lease, if he chose to, for a second period of two years and at the same pay scale as the second year of the first lease. Faranta's agreement with Miss Roberts permitted him "to erect on said premises buildings and other structures of any kind or character whatever as he may see fit, and same shall always be his exclusive property."[35] When his lease was terminated, Faranta was to have the right to purchase the lot at a value then to be agreed upon by the two parties.

In the first week of July, drama was again available in Faranta's Pavilion Theatre. Mr. and Mrs. E.R. Dalton, formerly with Gorman's Pavilion, presented the romantic *Fanchon, the Cricket,* a dramatization of a novelette by George Sand. Heading an entirely new company, the Daltons followed this with a military drama, *The French Spy; or, The Fall of Algiers,* complete with special costumes, disguises, Arab dances, sword encounters, and startling combats, for the week of July 7. On the evening of July 9 the "coolest and most comfortable theatre in the South" presented this French story in a gala performance for the benefit of the "Faranta Base Ball Club," tickets for this show costing twenty-five cents.[36] At ten o'clock, while *The French Spy* was underway, thirty-four-year-old Frank Budworth, who was cast as a king, fell insensible on the stage. He was taken to Charity Hospital, where, suffering from heat prostration, he lay in critical condition until his death at 12:30 in the afternoon of the next day; on July 11, after a funeral cortège consisting of twenty-five carriages headed by Faranta's brass band of twenty musicians. he was buried.[37]

The Faranta Base Ball Club, the beneficiary of Budworth's fatal performance, had been organized in the previous month with the election of six officers and with Signor Faranta, the club's sponsor and benefactor, as its honorary president.[38] On June 8, the club's seventeen players, none of whom was connected by occupation with Faranta's theatrical establishments, were scheduled to play the Crescent Base Ball Club for a prize of twenty-five dollars.

On August 3, 1884, after two months of the sport, the New Orleans Amateur League issued a list of the twelve teams under its direction and the number of games to the credit of each: Faranta's club was last on the list with six losses and no wins.[39] On August 27, his club met for the purpose of restructuring and making a permanent organization of the club, and, in addition to electing three delegates to the New Orleans Amateur League, designated three new officers.[40] Faranta then issued the club his ultimatum—the team would either win more games or disband altogether.[41] The New Orleans Amateur League was reorganized on the evening of October 8; later in the same month, it seems, the league was dissolved, but not before noting that Faranta's club had a record of six games won to nine lost.[42]

Apparently because of this small accomplishment, Faranta withdrew his sponsorship of the club, but only until January, 1885, when the team was again reorganized for a final year of activity in the sport, held under the auspices of a revived New Orleans Amateur League. There are no reports on the Signor Faranta Junior Club after 1885. This club, formed during the first reorganization of its adult counterpart, was Faranta's baseball team for boys under the age of fifteen, an age limit that was raised to sixteen in the first week of September,

1884. Its final record is not known, and it seems not to have survived the demise of its senior club.

Theatrical entertainments at Faranta's Pavilion Theatre continued without a break during the summer, except for one day, July 14, when the tent remained dark in honor of the city's French citizenry and their celebration of Bastille Day. On the following night Faranta presented a French drama, *The Two Orphans*, acted in English by the E.R. Dalton Drama Company, with E.R. Dalton, his wife Kate, Neil Price, and Lizzie Haywood holding the principal roles in this production. Adolphe D'Ennery's story concerns two Norman foster-sisters, Henriette and blind Louise, who travel to Paris in quest of relatives. They arrive in a snowstorm and are quickly separated: Henriette is abducted by a scoundrel of noble birth, and Louise is ensnared by an old hag who forces her to go begging in the streets of the city. Henriette is rescued by a gallant chevalier, and she is then able to locate Louise in the old hag's hovel. Before she can leave, the hag's pickpocket son intervenes, but his crippled brother summons a reserve of strength and dies fighting his brother as the blind girl escapes. The play ends as Louise finds her mother (a countess), a physician promises to restore her sight, and Henriette finds happiness with the gallant chevalier.[43] An estimated two thousand persons witnessed the opening performance, which was such a success, it was noted, that it would "be given red hot to the boys, for one dime, until further notice."[44]

Fraud and Its Victims, whose four acts included several scenes set in New Orleans, was Faranta's feature for the week of July 21. Adding interest to the play was its star, accomplished actor Louis Warwick, who was supported in this production by Neil Price, Mose Morgan, E.W.B. Page, Clara Beaumont, Mamie Freely, W.B. Myers, and E.R. and Kate Dalton. The play was well received, and the only obvious dark moment of Faranta's week came during the Friday night performance—at about seven o'clock, it was learned, Harry the sea lion died. Mrs. Faranta was said to be saddened to tears.[45]

Mr. Warwick's availability resulted in his engagement in *Davy Crockett*, which was Faranta's principal show for the week of July 29. W.M. Paul's company was back in the pavilion for this production of Frank Murdock's four-act play. With the exception of the Crockett motto, "Be sure you're right, then go ahead," there was little of the historical Davy Crockett in the story. As both an idyll of the backwoods and a romance, it concerns young Davy's love for the orphan Eleanor, once his childhood playmate, who is betrothed to the nephew of her guardian, a man blackmailed into arranging the marriage for the control of his ward's fortune. Davy rescues Eleanor from a storm, and they spend a tender moment over a volume of Scott's poems before Davy struggles with a pack of hungry wolves. Having recovered from his maiming by wolves, Davy liberates Eleanor from the marriage ceremony, burns the incriminating documents, marries his beloved, and is congratulated by the cast while the villain cries for revenge. The *Daily Picayune* judged that Faranta's drama was acted at least as well as it had been lately in the city's "regular" theaters.[46]

Tom Taylor's English drama, *The Ticket-of-Leave Man*, was the pavilion's next attraction, beginning August 4, with members of the W.M. Paul Combination in all roles. The *Daily Picayune* again found an audience of two thousand assembling on opening night to view the celebrated work, distinguished for one of its characters, Detective Hawkshaw, whose facility with make-up engendered a string of successors with more impenetrable disguises. The play's remaining characters include the ticket-of-leave man himself, Bob Brierly, an ingenuous youth from Lancashire, two veteran criminals, James Dalton and Melter Moss, and the pretty heroine, May Edwards, initially a strolling guitar player.

The plot hinges on Bob Brierly's arrival in London and his descent into the hands of Dalton and Moss, whose most recent criminal plan is to pass some forged notes with the naive hero's assistance. Bob makes friends with the heroine, passes the notes, and is dispatched to prison, after which he and May, who knows of his innocence, exchange letters and fall in love. Employed as a seamstress, May saves her money with an eye toward matrimony. Bob is released on parole, *i.e.*, with a ticket of leave, and, under an assumed name, begins work for a Mr. Gibson's brokerage firm, where he is soon raised to a trusted post. The villains recognize Bob in his new situation and plot to use the hero to get Gibson's coffer. Bob refuses, but for his honesty he is denounced to Gibson as a "ticket-of-leave man" and is dismissed on the day of his marriage to May. The hero secures work in a rowdy music hall. Again the villains find him and approach him with threats and their plan to take Gibson's money. In apparent desperation the young man falls in with the scheme, but later pens a warning to Gibson. Disguised as a man flustered with drink, Detective Hawkshaw overhears the plot and then reveals himself to Bob before taking the note to the broker. The denouement takes place in a churchyard, where the malefactors have taken flight and are apprehended. Bob is wounded, and in May's embrace rebukes his former employer for his unjust mistrust, and Hawkshaw claps the handcuffs on Dalton, crying "I've done it at last."

Of the leads in this melodrama Mrs. Paul was mentioned by the press as being "garrulous and lively,"[47] Miss Morgan was "splendid,"[48] Neil Price had "become a favorite,"[49] and Mr. McDonald was "a good exponent of his character,"[50] while Faranta's orchestra performed very smoothly under the "beautifully trained Professor W. Weldon."[51] As Bob Brierly, however, Mr. Paul was treated with less kindness: He "lacks a young wig, a good quantity of Lancashire dialect, and should give more attention to his general make-up. It is true the boys only pay ten cents to see him act, but they know what acting is—and so does Mr. Paul, for he is an old actor—and whatever is worth doing at all is worth doing well."[52]

Faranta's Pavilion, its name again altered, was taken down on the night of August 11, 1884. It was moved to the corner of Congress and Dauphine streets, a site nearly two miles away, where it was set up in time for the next evening's performance of *The Ticket-of-Leave Man*, which continued to play to large audiences. There was neither secrecy nor surprise to this move. Faranta announced it in his daily advertisements, and one month earlier it was rumored that the showman was prepared to take down his tent and erect in its place an "iron frame building," an amphitheater in which he planned to present circus performances at his usual prices, thus establishing in New Orleans the world's first ten-cent circus.[53] Faranta, who may well have started the rumor, did not comment publicly on the move to the new location and said nothing about the future of his leased lot on Bourbon Street, which he was preparing for the foundation of a new structure.

During this activity, *The Ticket-of-Leave Man* did not miss a single performance, even though all necessary scenery was not delivered to the new show place until August 14, when *The Lucky Ranche*, again under the command of Mr. Paul's company, returned to Faranta's Pavilion for a second series of performances. It was on this day that Signor Faranta, using the name Frederick W. Faranta, signed a building contract with local builders John A. Sicard & Son to erect the woodwork of a large building on Bourbon Street, between Orleans and St. Ann.[54] The work was to be completed on or before October 20, 1884, at a cost to Faranta of $5,050, a sum that was broken into six allotments and paid to the builders at specific intervals, the last being due ninety days after the building's completion. On August 26, the city council was given Faranta's petition for the erection of a corrugated iron building for theatrical purposes, and it was then pointed out to the council that the citizens in the vicinity of the site favored the opening of a new playhouse.[55] A committee held the petition until the council meeting of September 2. After some discussion, which has not survived this meeting, a vote was cast and twenty-two councilmen were found in favor of Faranta's petition; none was opposed, although seven members of the council were absent from this assembly.[56]

While the Sicards went to work on the iron building's foundation, Faranta's show, still active at the corner of Congress and Dauphine, continued with a new program. *The Lucky Ranche* was replaced on August 22 by a vaudeville show with Neil Price, Kate Hastings, Al Hensley, an "Olio of Fun," and the return of *The Phantom Avenger*, as interpreted by Maggie Morgan, Mr. and Mrs. Paul, and the Paul Combination. In the week of August 26 the new program included vaudeville, a "Grand Olio of Specialties," and a repeat of *Joshua Whitcomb*, the "pretty celebrated American Comedy in three acts," with Mr. Paul in the titular role, Maggie Morgan, and the rest of the Paul Combination. Lafitte and piracy returned in another nautical drama, *Lafitte, The Pirate*, which was presented for the week of August 29, in addition to vaudeville and the usual "grand olio."

On September 2, Faranta brought only vaudeville to his pavilion. Included in the week's bill were appearances by Mr. and Mrs. Paul, Kate Hastings, C.H. McDonald, Al Hensley, and other members of the Paul Combination, a variety sketch entitled "The Ladder of Fame," songs by Neil Price and Maggie Morgan, the "Great One Leg and Two Crutch Song and Dance Artist" Joseph Francis, and a short farce, "The Limerick Boy," which brought the show to a close. Faranta's stage show for this week carried the only change in the style of his programs until the first week of October.

For the remainder of September we find three returning plays. Beginning September 8, Jack Sheppard was back in *Jack Sheppard*, with Maggie Morgan again playing the young robber. This was followed by *Oliver Twist*, performed (as in April) by Mr. Paul's troupe, although added to this show were new performers Charles A. Frazer, Mae Harris, and M. Reed, a singer and acrobatic dancer. A repeat of *The Two Orphans*, complete with seven elaborate tableaux,[57] was Faranta's feature for the last week of September.

During the return of *Oliver Twist*, Faranta entered into a contract with the Cincinnati Corrugating Company of Ohio to supply him with enough "corrugated iron" and "ridge cap" to sheathe the wooden skeleton of the building the Sicards were erecting on Bourbon Street. This iron covering cost the showman $1,450. He paid George M. Gibson, the local representative of the Cincinnati Corrugating Company, eight hundred dollars when he placed his order, and mortgaged his expected theater for the remaining six hundred and fifty dollars, a sum that Faranta was expected to turn over to Mr. Gibson on the first day of January, 1885, after Faranta's Iron Theatre was completed.[58]

CHAPTER III

Signor Faranta in New Orleans. Ca. September 9, 1886.
Photograph by Gustave Moses, New Orleans.
Boyd Cruise Collection.

The Vieux Carré of New Orleans was the original *Nouvelle Orléans*, the colonial city established on the east bank of the Mississippi River by the French in 1718. The divisional spine of this small city—now bounded on three sides by Canal, Rampart, and Esplanade, and the river on its fourth—was Orleans Street, stretching from Royal Street, behind St. Louis Cathedral, to Rampart. Almost at its source, facing this early arterial thoroughfare, was once the *Théâtre d'Orléans*, or Orleans Theatre, renowned for the quality of its French opera and for its proximity to the famous Orleans Ballroom, a wing of the theater and, during its half-century of existence, the site of elegant dances, the source of many tales, and the meeting place of duelists, dance hall girls, and elect society.

Two buildings bore the name "Théâtre d'Orléans."[1] The first of these was the child of Louis-Blaise Tabary, an *émigré* from Saint-Domingue (now Haiti).[2] In 1805 Tabary was unsuccessful in his attempt to build a theater on city property, and this project was abandoned. In 1806 Tabary's new prospectus called for the erection of a theater on Orleans Street, between Royal and Bourbon, extending in depth to St. Ann Street. The property was purchased, Hyacinthe Laclotte was the theater's architect, and the cornerstone of the new building was duly laid on the 6th of October, 1806, in a ceremony attended by William C.C. Claiborne, then Governor of the Territory of Orleans.[3] The venture became a financial burden upon Tabary, however, and the theater was later completed by its stockholders, its earliest performances being held at irregular intervals during 1809 and 1810. It did not open in 1811 and remained inactive for four more years. In 1812, because the theater had become a monetary liability to its stockholders and their creditors, the sheriff seized the building and sold it to another group of men,[4] who took possession of it under a financial depression that delayed its operation until the start of 1815. The first Orleans Theatre was destroyed by fire in the following year.

In February of 1816, the theater's shareholders sold it to John Davis, a local entrepreneur and, like Tabary, a French *émigré* from Saint-Domingue, who in 1815 had purchased the property on the river side of the theater for the construction of a ballroom.[5] It was on September 28 of this year that both the theater and the ballroom, then being built, were burned down.[6] In November Davis published a prospectus for the rebuilding of the Orleans Theatre, in which he proposed to "rebuild it in the shortest space of time possible, on the same plan, but with the alterations necessary for rendering it more elegant, more vast, and more commodious, alterations pointed out by people of taste, who have had leisure to examine its defects."[7] He pledged to employ select French performers from Europe, and, underscoring the expense of this undertaking, advertised a tontine, an investment scheme in accordance with which Davis sold shares in the theater at a value of $150 each, forming a capital of $70,050; Davis would have exclusive use of the Orleans Theatre for at least five years, and would relinquish all rights to theater and property when and if the number of shareholders diminished in size to ten.

Davis's ballroom was completed by November 16, 1817, when it opened with a grand ball. He was still publishing notices of his tontine policy at the time, hoping to have the Orleans Theatre rebuilt by January of 1819, but it was not opened until later in the year, and then only with the aid of a $12,000 loan from the City of New Orleans.[8] Davis's Orleans Theatre opened on November 27, 1819, with a two-act opera, *Jean de Paris*, and an opera in one act, *The Married Bachelors*. The completed structure, a complex comprised of the two-story theater and adjoining hotel and ball and supper rooms, faced Orleans Street, extending at a right angle down Bourbon Street, and occupied nearly half of the square bounded by Bourbon, Orleans, Royal, and St. Ann.

Davis's theater was an immediate success. By the 1822-1823 season, he had made the Orleans Theatre the center for French opera in America and had kept his pledge to import his performers from Europe; his French Opera Company of New Orleans went beyond merely local praise to win wide critical acclaim when it toured the major cities of the east coast during the summer months from 1827 to 1833.

In 1836, three years before Davis's death, ownership of theater and ballroom was passed to the Company of the Orleans Theatre, and in 1849 to philanthropist John McDonogh, but the theater was still operated as an opera house through the Civil War period, although a declining interest in opera with growing competition from the city's newest theaters—most notably the St. Charles Theatre, the Varieties, and the Academy of Music—did force the management to widen the scope of its fare to include more pedestrian dramatic forms. We find, at the start of 1861, that "the ancient home of the opera has been converted into a regular dramatic theatre," whose presentations now include Spanish and German drama.[9]

After the war, the building was dilapidated and condemned. It was repaired and decorated for the 1866-1867 season, but its new series of productions proved to be unsuccessful. On December 7, the morning after a performance of a tragic opera, *La Tour de Nesle*, the Orleans Theatre was destroyed by an arsonist's flames. The structure on the corner of Orleans and Bourbon was in ruins, and the ballroom was all that remained in the aftermath, although the fire had so burned its upper story that its reconstruction was later required. Later, in November of the next year, the owner of the Louisa Street Cemetery purchased the theater's wreckage and used its bricks to make burial ovens.[10]

Until Faranta's Iron Theatre occupied the site in 1884, the corner of Bourbon and Orleans held no permanent structure of any kind.[11] Henry Parlange acquired the site in 1859; in 1873 it was passed to John H. O'Connor and then to the Roman Catholic Church, which owned the lot until it was purchased by Mary A. Roberts in 1881.[12] Its size and location made it an ideal spot for itinerant tent and circus shows, and these seem to have been the lot's most prominent, if not exclusive, tenants for the fourteen years following the destruction of the Orleans Theatre. During this time, in 1872, the repaired Orleans Ballroom became the Civil District Court, and still later, in 1881, it was the Convent of the Sisters of the Holy Family, a Catholic order of negro nuns, and Faranta's neighbor for the short lives of his pavilion and Iron Theatre.

It was not a fear of fire that lay behind Faranta's decision to build an iron-sheathed edifice, but it was this fear that made such a building possible in New Orleans. The city suffered two great conflagrations in the eighteenth century—the first was in 1788, when nine hundred houses and public buildings were consumed before the fire was extinguished, and the second, which destroyed a considerable portion of the city, occurred in 1794. By the nineteenth century, because fire was still a real threat to the city and its citizens, a municipal ordinance was enacted disallowing any wooden structure larger than ten feet square to be erected within the city's fire limits.

One means of evading this fire code, noted the *Daily States* of October 20, 1884, was to erect an iron building, whose chief advantage over masonry was that it could be built more quickly, if not more cheaply; the city council had to rule on many requests for permits to construct these ironclad buildings, and the newspaper suggested that the police commission look into the situation before these permits were granted, since the iron exterior would resist the efforts of firemen to reach the source of interior flames.

A similar issue had been raised two years before this. Combustible interiors and impediments to the fire department's attempts to reach fires inside buildings were the reasons for Chief Thomas O'Connor's letter to the City of New Orleans in March, 1882, asking that an ordinance be passed controlling the use of iron shutters on buildings, because, he said, "The evil of securing a building on all sides with iron shutters has caused incalculable amounts of loss and serious accidents to our men."[13] The mayor, members of the city council, and a representative of the local insurance companies all agreed that, if legal, such an ordinance should be created, although the ordinances that were later created did not ban this use of iron.[14] Beyond its brief mention by the *Daily States*, the use of sheet iron as a main building material seems not to have been much discussed or contested.

Faranta's Iron Theatre was the first of nine iron buildings to be built in the years 1884 and 1885. Three of these, constructed in 1884, were exhibition buildings in the World's Industrial and Cotton Centennial Exposition; the exposition's Art Gallery, built "wholly of iron" and said to be "thoroughly fire-proof," was 250 feet long and 100 feet wide.[15] Still larger, at 540 feet by 125 feet, was the iron Factories and Mills Building, erected as an extension to the exposition's Main Building.[16] The Mexican Government sponsored the remaining one—an octagonal building, designed by Mexican architect Señor de Ybarrola, that measured 78 feet in diameter, supported a dome 30 feet high, and was constructed of intricately patterned iron for the Mexican Government's mineral display.[17]

Situated outside the exposition's main entrance, but also constructed in 1884, were the iron Burke Hotel, at the corner of Ferdinand and Walnut streets;[18] and a circular, "castle-like" structure of corrugated iron at the corner of Exposition Boulevard and Magazine Street, built at a cost of $30,000 by the International Panorama Company of Chicago to exhibit Professor Louis Braun's panorama "The Battle of Sedan," which was opened to the public on December 30, 1884.[19]

The Temple of Art, at the corner of Canal and Dauphine, was another building erected to display a large painting. Constructed in a French Renaissance style, this fort-like building (complete with tower dome and five stories of "particolored iron sheathing") was put on the foundation laid for the later Mercier Building, which preceded the present Maison Blanche Building. It was built to exhibit "The Last Sortie and Battle of Paris," a diorama by Felix Philippoteaux, father of Paul Philippoteaux, who collaborated with him in painting the 24,000 feet of canvas.[20] The Temple of Art was opened on November 4, 1885, and closed on April 30 of 1886.

Constructed in 1885 on St. Charles Avenue and Exposition Boulevard, close to the exposition, was a second iron hotel, known as the Hotel Windsor.[21] In December of that year a second corrugated iron theater, the Avenue Theatre, which was also held to be "fire-proof," opened on St. Charles and Calliope.[22]

By mid-September, 1884, the wooden frame of Faranta's new theater was ready for its iron covering. The showman expected the corrugated sheets to be in New Orleans by the last week of September and hoped to have his theater finished and ready for an opening on November 10, but the burning of the bridge over Lake Pontchartrain delayed the delivery of iron from Cincinnati. The Northeastern Railroad's great Pontchartrain bridge and trestle, twenty-five miles long, burned on September 25, severing the city's rail connection with the hamlet of Slidell and losing 3,390 feet of bridge.[23] On September 29 approximately three hundred men, divided into two equal shifts, began to undo the damage and to replace lost steel rails with new ones.

By Saturday, October 4, the work was finished and Faranta's shipment of corrugated iron arrived in New Orleans.[24] The sheet iron was unloaded from railroad cars and carted by wagon to the theater site on the evening of its arrival. Faranta's workers began immediately to remove the scantling material that protected the theater's framework from weather and vandals and to nail the corrugated iron in its place.[25] The *New Orleans Bee* found the promised completion of Faranta's theater interesting enough to devote a well-mannered editorial to "Un nouveau theatre" and to "a Signor Faranta, about whom little is known," remarking that the iron theater "has been impatiently awaited by the public, and from all indications will be greeted with the same enthusiasm as the Pavilion presented at the old Orleans Theatre."[26]

As his new theater neared completion, Faranta made preparations for its gala opening, having engaged star equestrienne Zoe Gayton and her white horse, Gypsy, who were expected in the city by the week of October 19; but he nevertheless continued to operate the removed pavilion on Congress and Dauphine streets. A series of variety shows was begun on September 30 for a week or two on his distant stage; this included dramatic and musical performances by the W.M. Paul Combination, tightrope walking by El Niño Eddie, minstrelsy by Ethiopian delineator J. Kelly, and certain deception by female impersonator Jules Luminat, who was presented with several bouquets by recognized "dudes" after a few nights of his act.[27] These specialty acts and performances by the twenty members of the Paul Combination were continued in a "Monster Program" scheduled for Saturday and Sunday, October 11 and 12. Preceded by El Niño Eddie's evolutions on the tightrope and Jules Luminat's female "statues," among other acts, the program's dramatic offering was *The Long Strike*, Dion Boucicault's tale of proletarian dissent, murder, and suspense.

The setting of *The Long Strike* is Manchester, England, where a long strike in the manufacturing center leads to extreme measures by both parties of the dispute. Dick Readley, mill-owner and chairman of the manufacturers, refuses to make concessions to the striking workers, who are represented by Noah Learoyd, and promises them punishment. Readley is met in the street by a threatening mob, but he escapes to Noah's house and is secreted there by Noah's daughter, Jane, who loves Readley. Readley overhears her father plotting with others to incinerate the mills and later has the conspirators arrested, sparing only Noah because he is Jane's father. Noah then learns that Readley's interest in his daughter is not matrimonial and kills the mill-owner with a shot from his pistol. The blame is put on Jane's former suitor, Jem Starkee, who at the time of the killing was on the road to Liverpool with John Reilly, a sailor whose ship is sailing away. A lawyer freely aids Jane in telegraphing Reilly, who must jump ship and swim ashore, but arrives in court in time to save Jem's life. The two advertised performances of *The Long Strike* were well received, and the entire program was held over until the evening of October 22, after which the pavilion was apparently taken down.

A more homely drama had been played off stage. On the night of October 12, as William Paul was on his way to Faranta's Pavilion, a young man handed him a letter from a Mr. Sands, an elderly actor in Faranta's theater, challenging him to a duel. Paul wrote on the back of the letter, "Sands, don't make an ass of yourself," and handed it back to the messenger. Nothing further happened until Tuesday, October 14, when Paul was insulted and abused on the corner of Independence and Dauphine streets by a J. Armstrong, a member of a party that included Sands, who then came forward and accused Paul of owing him three dollars. Paul, who denied this, refused to part with any amount of money, but Tom Weldon, the leader of Faranta's brass band, intervened and gave the correct sum to Armstrong. This caused Sands to shout obscenities at Paul; he started to strike Paul, but William Weldon, Faranta's musical director, moved Sands into the street. The boisterous crowd attracted the attention of policeman G.H. Early, who quickly dispersed the principals.[28]

Faranta's Iron Theatre was completed by mid-October. It was a simple building, all on one floor, with its main entrance situated directly on the corner of the two streets it faced, Orleans and Bourbon. There were seven exits—two on Orleans, three on Bourbon, and two on St. Ann, one of which was designed for the sole use of performers and stage hands—and over each opening soared a five-foot transom for ventilation. The building was 35 feet high, an altitude exceeded only by a skylight that ascended five feet above the corrugated iron roof; it was completely ironclad, with the exception of the main entrance. Emblazoned on at least one of the theater's two forward sides was the word "FARANTA'S." Whether by daylight or by means of the electric lights that adorned the building's facade, visitors to Faranta's Iron Theatre could see that the corrugated iron surface was painstakingly painted to resemble granite.[29]

Of the 166 feet by 137 feet of the site, Faranta's theater occupied its entirety, incorporating his former bar and residence on the corner of Bourbon and St. Ann, which was now put to use as the theater's storeroom. Beside it on Bourbon Street was a new saloon and dining area for the exclusive use of his white patrons; a smaller saloon for black patrons was placed on Orleans Street, beside the main entrance. Also facing Bourbon was a band balcony, said to be one of the largest in the country.[30]

Inside the theater was a small triangular office where tickets and dimes changed hands. Past the hall was an auditorium designed to hold 4,500 persons, all of whom could be seated on comfortable patent chairs and benches. The floor of the auditorium was earthen and extended to an elevated stage, forty feet wide and fifty-eight feet in depth; this was bounded on two sides by dressing rooms and was illuminated by gas footlights and by electric lights that remained on, especially when the gas lights were turned down during stage performances, so that any of the six sets of scenery could be moved about. Adding elegance to the interior of the theater, crowned by a "frescoed" ceiling, was a handsome drop curtain, forty-two feet in width, that was painted to look like "a green plush curtain, with fancy touches and elegant draperies."[31] This *objet d'art* was the creation of Louis Philastre, the scenic artist for the French Opera House.[32]

The estimated value of Faranta's new theater, decorations, and appurtenances, which would include three Babcock chemical fire extinguishers, was later set at thirty-five thousand dollars.[33] Faranta insured all of this for a mere nine thousand dollars, a sum that he would regrettably find later to be seriously inadequate.[34]

Faranta and his wife remained in their home at the corner of Bourbon and St. Ann, now a part of the Iron Theatre itself, where they were joined by three of the showman's brothers—Gus, Frank, and Henry Stempel—who now assisted him in operating the theater. Ben Stempel did not appear to have connected himself with his brother's venture until 1887, when he helped Edward Stempel, the youngest of the brothers, operate the saloon and its several concessions.[35]

Faranta's Iron Theatre was ready for its premier performance, but this maiden effort was not theatrical, or at least was not billed as such. Being both a showman and a Democrat, the Signor offered his new edifice for the public meeting to ratify the nominations of Grover Cleveland and Thomas H. Hendricks for the U.S. presidency and vice-presidency; and General Leon Jastremski, chairman of the Louisiana State Central Committee, accepted the offer.

Said the *Mascot* of this occasion: "There is much in common between Chairman Jastremski's State Central Committee and a dime show. Also Faranta's seal is dead. He wants a new attraction, and will admit that from a ten cent point of view a live Jastremski is better than a dead seal."[36]

The evening of October 28 was selected for the meeting, and Faranta's new auditorium was decorated accordingly. The front of the stage, the posts, the rafters, and even the newly frescoed ceiling were all bespangled with garlands, wreaths of flowers, flags, and banners. Around the walls were the names of Cleveland and Hendricks, obvious amid the festoons of bunting, entwined with particolored stripes, that were stretched across the auditorium to display the shield of the United States and various other designs. Not even the torrents of rain that fell from afternoon till late at night kept the convening members from filling the Iron Theater to attend the ceremony and to hear speeches by Governor Samuel D. McEnery, Senator R.L. Gibson, General Jastremski, and others.[37]

Faranta advertised that the Iron Theatre would open on the following Monday, November 3. *Mazeppa; or, The Wild Horse of Tartary* was the production chosen to inaugurate the theater's new beginning, and the "talented World Renowned Equestrian Actress" Zoe Gayton, assisted by her "highly trained Arabian Steed *Gypsy*," was to appear in the lead. This was said to be Miss Gayton's first visit to New Orleans since her recent return from a successful tour of Europe, but she was no stranger to the part she would play, having appeared as Mazeppa opposite another splendid horse for a two-week period at the National Theatre in New York City in 1881.[38] Faranta's "fireproof" theater was prepared for her performance in his first presentation, and the chosen drama had a reputation that promised a respectable record of attendance. It did not matter, apparently, that Miss Gayton tipped the scales at two hundred or more pounds.[39]

"The entrance is spacious and everything about the place is on a grand scale," the *Daily Picayune* discovered on opening night, "and the establishment is likely to create a revolution in the way of cheap amusements." Not only was the theater "full of human beings, men, women and children," but it "was a regular circus jam, and there was given on the stage the best performance ever seen in New Orleans for ten cents."[40]

H.M. Milner's stage version of Lord Byron's poem remained a popular romantic drama on both sides of the Atlantic for several decades, and it was presented in New Orleans many times—both before and after it was made memorable by the New Orleans-born Adah Isaacs Menken in Albany, N.Y., in 1860.[41] The equestrian play concerns the love of Mazeppa, the grandson of the Tartar hordes's chief, for Olinska, the daughter of a Polish lord, who has chosen another suitor for her. The intended husband, a villainous member of the Polish nobility, inevitably devises a singular punishment for his rival: Mazeppa is stripped and bound fast to an untamed steed, who then hurries through the wilds, exposing his helpless rider to its many dangers, until the beast is exhausted and Mazeppa's body is broken. Mazeppa recovers from his wounds and, reunited with his grandfather, is proclaimed King of the Tartars. He later mounts an expedition to Poland and there reclaims his bride.

Mazeppa first came to New Orleans via the Camp Street Theatre in 1832, one year after its English inauguration, with J.M. Field in the title role and changes that made the play more suitable to an American audience.[42] No doubt there were changes made in the play for its presentation in Faranta's new theater, but it is not likely that there were enough to warrant the claim that his *Mazeppa* was in America for "the first time," as he advertised. The multitudinous details necessary for this production, as well as the numerous demands of Zoe Gayton, the temperamental star, were handled by her personal manager, W.J. Marshall, who was proclaimed a veteran in the business and the one who first introduced Adah Isaacs Menken to the public as Mazeppa.[43] It was his job to ensure that Faranta's version duplicated the one that brought fame to Miss Menken. All of the original music, we are told, was used in this show, which was made more splendid by the scenery and the effective costumes of the period, filled out by the twenty-five attractive ladies brought by William Paul to complete the *corps de ballet*. With a full cast, each performance of *Mazeppa* collected enthusiastic audiences to Faranta's Iron Theatre.

Faranta still charged only a dime for admission to his shows, which were usually three hours in length. His new policy, though, was to refuse the giving of checks for readmission to those of his patrons who went outside the theater between acts, whether or not their sole purpose in doing so was to breathe fresh air. The new system was introduced "so as to keep the sidewalks clear of boys and other hangers-on who annoy people by begging for checks" during intermissions.[44] Of course, this policy also kept a patron's search for refreshments confined to the two barrooms inside the theater. The *Mascot* took notice of this, but found it compensatory that his theater was "the home of legitimate drama" and was "now a recognized institution."[45] It is uncertain whether Faranta permitted the sale of liquor during or between performances.

Matinees, which were begun again on the afternoon of November 13, were regularly scheduled for Saturday, Sunday, and Monday of each week. The earliest matinees in the new theater featured the Mexican Automaton Company, which delighted the patrons, mostly children, with scenes of a grand masquerade ball, trapeze acts, Mexican combats from bull ring and cock pit, native dances, and vignettes of the daily lives of the Mexican people.

Zoe Gayton's engagement with Faranta's theater had been extended for a second week, during which, it was announced, she would exhibit her talents in the romantic melodrama *Timour the Tartar; or, The Captive Prince*, Mathew Gregory Lewis's tale of an oppressive Tartar leader. This second "horse opera" began on November 17 and, though it had been in the city many times and as early as 1818,[46] was said to be presented "for the first time in New Orleans." Appearing in the play's lead as the Amazonian princess Zorilda, Miss Gayton was supported in her theatrical and equestrian efforts by W.M. Paul (as Timour) and Maggie Morgan (as the captive prince Agib), who essayed her first role on a horse. The remainder of the case included Mrs. Paul, Hamilton Nicholls, T.L. Hartman, Al Hensley, and, playing opposite Miss Gayton's white horse Gypsy, a steed named Midnight.[47]

Faranta's second drama was as successful as his first, but not all of the excitement was on stage. In "catching a *Mazeppa*," said the *Mascot*, known to be less than charitable on occasion, Faranta had also "caught a Tartar." Sometime during the first few days of *Timour the Tartar*, William Paul was retired from the Iron Theatre. The stage manager had allegedly slapped a young boy, and appealed to Faranta to sanction his action after Miss Gayton intervened. "Faranta refused, as became a member of the society for the prevention of cruelty to children. Then Paul threatened to leave, and carry off his performing family with him. Faranta wished him good luck and goodbye. The show goes on as usual."[48] Hamilton Nicholls was named Paul's replacement and took up his work immediately, but was later reported to be carrying his "forefinger in a sling." It was also rumored that several others in Faranta's employ were "marked for life" and that Miss Gayton, who had made these marks, was much better versed in the use of her heels than her horse Gypsy.[49]

These backstage quarrels had no noticeable effect on Miss Gayton's popularity. She and her four-footed partner were engaged for a third week, beginning Monday, November 4, in another melodrama, *The French Spy*, much earlier a feature in Faranta's pavilion. Here she was cast as a young girl who is enlisted as a spy and master of disguise for the French army. The play, set in Morocco, included white-robed Moors, uniformed soldiers, and beggars in rags; Miss Gayton's wardrobe was said to consist of a "man's undershirt and drawers."[50] Matinees in Faranta's theater still featured the popular Mexican Automaton Company.

When W.M. Paul severed his connections with Faranta and the Iron Theatre, Paul's family and several members of his company departed as well. William Weldon, Faranta's musical director and Paul's friend, was among this group. Shortly after concluding his relationship with the theater, Weldon and some accomplices began to attend performances of *Timour the Tartar* with the purpose of "setting up howls and disturbing the peace."[51] On Sunday, November 22, after one such display, Faranta was obliged to appear on stage to quiet the audience, and the offenders were warned not to return.

On November 27, during a performance of *The French Spy*, Weldon returned in an intoxicated state. Witnesses claimed that he was abusive, cursed the door-keeper, and then disturbed the performers on stage until Faranta had him ejected.[52] Both Weldon and Faranta were called before the Second Recorder's Court on the following morning to explain the situation, which Weldon attributed to "jealousy" between them; Faranta denied this, then making clear his intention to protect visitors to the Iron Theatre from the kind of disturbances brought by the bitter Weldon, and the matter was ended, if not resolved.[53]

During the same day, Zoe Gayton, who was finishing her last week with Faranta's theater, was issued a writ of attachment for her unpaid account with the City Hotel. The sheriff was ordered to hold the mare Gypsy until the following bill was paid: Board and three rooms for 31 days at $7 per day, $217; fire, $1; meals in room, $1; bar, $36; bath, 50 cents; the account of Dr. Samuel Logan, $18; cash paid by agent W.J. Marshall, $1; bringing the total to $274.50. Of this account $145 had been paid, leaving a balance of $129.50 still due.[54] Further details of this episode have not come to light.

December 1 was the start of the week's new feature—Joaquin Miller's *Mexico*, preceded by specialty acts that included aerialists Lamont and Scorr, Charles Harding, an acrobatic clown, and serio-comedienne Lottie Dyercourt. Miller's drama, which revolves about Mexican and American life during the final stages of Emperor Maximilian's reign, centers on a young and beautiful Mexican noblewoman, her paramour (an American mercenary), and her cousin, who desires her and the death of his rival, and includes humor by an American consul and an Irish emigrant and his sweetheart.

When *Mexico* was first performed at New York's Grand Opera House in 1879, the *Dramatic Mirror* found it to be "one of the most pitiable, puerile and most inherently worthless pieces of dramatic claptrap which has encumbered the stage of that popular theatre for some time." The "serious interest of the piece," claimed its critic, "is evolved from constant references to the American flag and to the mountains of Mexico. There is no pretense of construction, as the piece and characters wander to and fro on the stage without apparent reason."[55] The play was not reviewed when it appeared on Faranta's stage, but its quality had no noticeable effect upon the size of his audiences.

Early in December Faranta again concerned himself with matters other than professional drama. December 7 was set aside for the formal installation of Lodge No. 30 of the Benevolent and Protective Order of Elks (B.P.O.E.). A planning meeting had been held on November 7, 1884, in the parlor of the Hotel

Chalmette on St. Charles Avenue, during which the invited participants each signed an application for a charter. Frederick Warde, who assumed the chair, discussed the beauty, advantages, and purpose of the organization, which was founded in New York on February 22, 1868, by tragedian Thomas W. Keene. After the business portion of the meeting was concluded, a series of recitations was given, followed by songs, skits, and more recitations. Both Faranta and William Paul, then still friends, contributed their talents to this part of the meeting.[56]

A second congregation was held in the assembly rooms of Grunewald Hall at noon on November 16, when the final arrangements for the founding of the lodge in New Orleans were consummated. Following Harry S. Meyers's suggestion, the group elected Colonel J.W. Coleman their chairman and affixed signatures to the application for dispensation and charter. The company adjourned and then lunched at the St. Charles Hotel, being assured that Meyers would soon be in New York with the application and would return with the supplies necessary for the lodge's installation before the arrival of Thomas Keene, Deputy Grand Exalted Ruler, who was expected in the city within the month.[57]

Keene arrived in New Orleans on November 30. He was met at the train station by a committee from the proposed lodge, after which he performed at the Grand Opera House in a presentation of *Richard III*, one of the many from his vast repertoire that he would appear in before December 7.[58] On this date, from ten o'clock until five, Keene, his manager, and other prominent Elks presided over the installation, initiation, and conferment of degrees. Lodge No. 30 was begun with a total of fifty members.[59] Of this number the following were selected to serve as the lodge's first officers: Colonel A.S. Graham, Exalted Ruler; Harry S. Meyers, Esteemed Leading Knight; Lionel Adams, Esteemed Loyal Knight; Edward Curtis, Esteemed Lecturing Knight; Marsh H. Redon, Treasurer; and, as Trustees, J.W. Coleman, E. Lilienthal, and Frederick W. Stempel (Faranta).

A committee of three was chosen to search for permanent rooms for the lodge, but no inquiries were made before the group repaired to the St. Charles Hotel for a sumptuous feast. Three of the participating showmen—Faranta, Eugene Robinson, the manager of Grunewald Hall and Robinson's Dime Museum, and William F. Cody (Buffalo Bill), who was in New Orleans with his "Wild West Show"—offered their establishments for benefit performances to profit the new lodge.[60]

Faranta returned to the activities of his iron theater on the following day, December 8, when his new repertory company, "Castle's Comic Opera Company," began appearing in Jacques Offenbach's comic opera *The Princess of Trebizonde*, scheduled to play until December 14, during which time, among other alterations then made to his theater, proscenium boxes were added to the sides of the stage.[61] For this production Faranta was able to lure from the Grunewald Opera House (Grunewald Hall) actress M.E. Benham and, as his new stage manager, Frank Haight, the business manager of Henri Laurent, whose Comic Opera Company presented *The Princess of Trebizonde* in the Grunewald from November 30 to December 10.[62]

Offenbach's *opéra bouffe* opens in view of a village square, the location of a juggler's show and a lottery booth. Here the audience is introduced to Cabriolo, the proprietor of the show, his two daughters, Regina and Zanetta, and his assistants,

FARANTA'S NEW THEATRE.

Corner Bourbon and Orleans Streets.

MONDAY EVENING, NOV. 17, AND DURING
THE WEEK,
First production of the Great Spectacular
Equestrian Drama,

TIMOUR THE TARTAR
—WITH—
MISS ZOE GAYTON,
As the Amazonian Princess
ZORILDA,
Supported by a full dramatic company, and
introducing the highly trained Arabian
Mare
GIPSY.
And the celebrated Broncho
MIDNIGHT.
Gorgeous Costumes, Grand Amazonian Marches,
Thrilling Tableaux and new and beautiful
Scenic Effects.

Our Timour and Tartar Matinee—SATURDAY,
SUNDAY and MONDAY.

Prices as Usual: Ten Cents.

FARANTA'S NEW IRON THEATRE.

SPECIAL NOTICE.

The Great Mexican Automaton
TROUPE.
Will Appear in Their Wonderful and
Pleasing Entertainments AT MATINEES
ONLY, on TUESDAYS, WEDNESDAYS,
THURSDAYS and FRIDAYS, and on SAT-
URDAY AND SUNDAY MORNINGS AT 10
O'CLOCK.

Admission - - 10 Cents.

Newspaper Advertisement of Faranta's New Iron Theatre.
The Historic New Orleans Collection.

Faranta's Iron Theatre.
From a Scene of Orleans Street.
The Historic New Orleans Collection.

Tremolini and Paola. The young Prince Raphael and his tutor, Sparadrap, are there to witness the juggling performance. Raphael sneaks into the tent, while Sparadrap is detained in conversation with Paola, who believes herself to be a lost princess, but the prince returns from the show to praise the beauty of a wax figure of the Princess of Trebizonde. This is really Zanetta, who took the place of the original statue after it was defaced earlier in an accident. Cabriolo's jugglers soon become mountebanks; having acquired the winning lottery ticket, which entitles them to an elegant castle on an estate, they resolve to take possession of their prize and live in accordance with their elevated station. While the jugglers dine on the terrace of their new home, they are interrupted by a party of hunters led by Raphael's father, Prince Casimir. Raphael is reunited with Zanetta, who is not impersonating a wax figure; they fall in love, and Raphael, seeking a way to secure his father's consent to their courtship, introduces her as the principal gem of a collection of waxworks owned by "Baron" Cabriolo. The father agrees to purchase the collection and appoints Cabriolo to superintend it, but later returns from a hunting expedition to find his son making merry with the jugglers. He forgives Raphael and agrees to his union with Zanetta, and Paola, discovering that her sister was Raphael's mother, learns that she is very nearly a princess after all. Among the cast in Faranta's stage production were Little Emma Rice, the star of the show, Lottie Dyercourt, Miss M.E. Benham, Hamilton Nicholls, T.L. Hartman, and Al Hensley.[63]

Faranta took the opportunity to introduce several specialty acts between the opera's first and second parts. Presented in a lavish style were a "Troupe of Genuine English Acrobats," a "Golden Chariot 'Carry-All,' drawn by Twelve Fiery Untamed Steeds," the "Three Wise Men of Gretna," who had ventured into Faranta's show from their burgh across the Mississippi, and a three-legged man "Captured in the Wilds of Algiers [also across the river], in his Sacred Song and Dance." Also included in this group of specialties was "The Sacred White Elephant 'Sunlight of Asia,' kindly loaned Mr. Faranta by the King of Siam for this truly great production." Unfortunately, nothing beyond Faranta's own advertisements is known about this amazing "loan." The elephant was owned by the Sells Brothers and was featured in their "Monster 50-Cage Menagerie and Great Quadruple Circus," which had arrived in New Orleans on November 30. During their second week in the city, and before returning to Columbus, Ohio, for the winter, they included the white elephant in their second parade.[64]

The Princess of Trebizonde was replaced on December 15 by Frank Dumont's "highly substantial drama," *Marked for Life,* with Sid C. France reprising his role as Skid, the play's popular negro character. Quite apparently the melodrama had all the necessary elements of a successful show, for Faranta's theater was reported to be crowded at each performance.

Originally written for Mr. France,[65] *Marked for Life* concerns Hiram Whitby and his daughter Dora, who moved from a Southern town to the West, where Whitby became a successful banker—but not before forging some bills of exchange for his daughter's future financial security. Whitby managed to take over these bills before their maturity, so there were no victims of his small crime, but he preserved the forged bills in a safe in his home, and all of this is known to Jack Blake, Dora's suitor before he was discharged from the bank for embezzlement.

Blake is now both the elected sheriff and the covert leader of a band of outlaws. Willie Harkins, once Dora's childhood playmate, arrives in town with his faithful servant Skid; he fills the vacant clerkship and soon becomes Dora's new suitor. Pretending to show the new bank clerk about the town, Blake traps his rival in a cellar, vowing that Harkins will never wed Dora. With Skid's aid Harkins escapes, but Blake resolves to steal Whitby's forged bills and extort his daughter's hand in marriage. Blake enters the house, removes the bills from the safe, stabs the alerted Whitby, and escapes through an open window. Skid shoots off one of Blake's fingers—Blake is thus "marked for life"—and pursues the fleeing figure, while Harkins enters through the window, discovers the prostrate banker, and is caught with knife in hand by "Sheriff" Blake, who charges him with murder. Skid releases Dora from the outlaws' cave, where she was imprisoned by Blake and his gang, and she is put in the care of a Dr. Horton (alias Whitby, who recovered from his wounds, learned that the bills were stolen, and donned a disguise to prevent exposure of his crime). Harkins, however, is sentenced to death for Whitby's murder. Skid travels two hundred miles to secure his pardon, outmaneuvers Blake's criminal band, and returns with the pardon, thus ensuring Harkins's release. Skid then recognizes Blake's mutilated hand and charges him with murder. He overtakes the fugitive sheriff on the cliff of a roaring waterfall; they struggle, both fall into the cataract, and the faithful servant Skid is drawn ashore by friends as the curtain descends.[66]

The day after the start of *Marked for Life* was a historic one for the citizens of New Orleans; it was on this day that the World's Industrial and Cotton Centennial Exposition officially opened its doors to an anticipatory deluge of visitors. Signor Faranta, knowing that the city would be crowded with people for most of the coming year, continued to search for one seductive amusement after another.

On December 12, he signed a contract with William Munroe to supply him with the services of a circus, performances of which would be available to Faranta for four weeks, beginning January 12, 1885, with the option for an additional six weeks.[67] Munroe agreed to supply Faranta with the services of Mrs. Munroe, who was expected to perform her "menage act," a Mr. Shields, who would serve for two weeks as ringmaster, and Mrs. Shields, whose duties were not specified. Munroe also agreed to furnish Faranta with one pad horse, one trick horse, one menage horse, six entree horses, one riding dog, two goats, one riding monkey, all of their accessories—which included one band wagon, one dog cart and necessary harnesses, pads, leaping boards, banners, and balloons—and all other articles required for presenting a proper performance. The band wagon and four of the horses were to be under Faranta's control for any purpose he chose, including street parades, for the duration of the contract. Faranta agreed to share the cost of repairing the wagon, which was in poor condition, and to furnish feed and stabling for the four horses in his care. Munroe was to be paid one hundred and fifty dollars per week for the first four weeks of the contract and one hundred dollars weekly for five additional weeks, if Faranta decided to take the option, with no compensation for the final week. The salaries of the circus personnel were solely Munroe's responsibility.[68]

This was not the end of Faranta's interests. Three days after signing the contract with Munroe, the *Evening Chronicle* reported that the showman had purchased the Trans-Atlantic Circus and, on December 14, sent it to Brewton, Alabama.[69] According to another report, Faranta sold the circus to his stage manager, Frank Haight, before the end of the month.[70]

On December 22, "the people's favorite," Sid C. France, began his second week of a four-week engagement in the Iron Theatre, appearing as Buckskin in *The James Boys*, which also featured R. Hamilton Nicholls as Jesse James, ten other main characters, and soldiers, outlaws, policemen, and highwaymen. The story was familiar to the audience—hardworking, honest country folk are driven to crime by attacks upon their property and the murder of their mother, and later become leaders of a bandit gang, to whom holdups, gunfights, and pistol-brandishing are commonplace activities. The play, full of action and gunpowder, abounded in such "thrilling situations" as "The Hanging of Dr. Samuels," "The Burning of the House," "The Spectre in the Cave," "Robbery of the Russelville Bank," "The Death of the Cashier," "Stopping of the Train at Gad's Hill," and "Robbery of the Wells Fargo Safes."[71] Adding interest to the drama were Charger and Blue Devil, the stage horses of Frank and Jesse James, which were introduced at various times during the excitement on Faranta's stage. Since Sid France, the star of the drama and "red-hot from the Bowery," could draw four thousand persons each night, he need never, suggested the *Daily Picayune*, want to play "Hamlet."[72]

France's second drama continued to play through Christmas week, ending on December 28. To mark Christmas day, Faranta prepared a celebration he advertised as "Sig. Faranta Remembers the Journalists." With an eye toward a better rapport with the local press, Faranta issued several invitations to a feast in his home on Bourbon Street. The guests, numbering among them many journalists, gathered on Christmas day and, after a warm welcome and a few introductory remarks by B.E. Fanning of the *New York World*, were seated and urged to partake of the following meal, prepared by Mrs. Faranta and her assistants:

ENTREES
Oyster Soup, à la New York World.
Gumbo, à la Mascot.
Turkey with jelly, à la Picayune.
Roast Pig, à la L'Abeille.
Chicken Fricasse, à la States.
Fish, with mayonaise sauce, à la Item.
Chicken Salad, à la Southern Knight.
Green Peas, à la Times-Democrat
Asparagus, à la Chronicle.

DESSERT
Fruit, Cakes, Pies, Candy, and Nuts.

INTERMISSION
Coffee, Cake, and Cigars.[73]

After the ceremony, which included singing, recitations, and innumerable toasts to Faranta and his wife, the host conducted his guests to the Iron Theatre, where they were treated to a performance of *The James Boys* and France's interpretation of the role given to him. The honorees were seated in the front-row seats reserved for them, and each was given a souvenir program printed on heavy white satin. On December 26, the next evening, all representatives of the local and visiting press were invited to a performance of *The James Boys;* their press cards served them as admission tickets and each was given a reserved seat. Souvenir satin programs were distributed to all of the ladies in this group.[74]

The popular Sid France began his third week in the Iron Theatre on December 29, portraying a trio of characters in the melodrama *Dead to the World.* The four acts of Frank Dumont's play were set in the South, showing scenes along the banks of the Mississippi, life on a beautiful plantation, a steamboat explosion, and a view of a dismal swamp. The special feature of the drama was the ease and rapidity with which Mr. France changed from one of his three characters to another—Flip, a faithful negro servant, Philip Warwick, a judge's son, and Aunt Liza, an old negro housekeeper. Thirteen other characters completed the cast of this action-drama.[75]

The Iron Theatre's stage presentation for the week of January 5 was a comedy-drama, *In the Web,* again starring Sid France, who would appear, it was noted, for "positively his last week." On January 8, Faranta was again the host to visitors to his iron theater, entertaining on this date military officers of the U.S. and Mexican men-of-war then in port. This guest list was enlarged by many non-military invitees, all of whom were treated to a performance of *In the Web.*[76]

With the arrival of January 12, Faranta was able to put into one ring the circus he had secured from William Munroe. For this event the center of the floor in Faranta's auditorium was changed into a single regulation-size ring, forty-two feet in diameter. On either side of this ring, ascending in the style of an amphitheater, were the usual rows of benches, but facing the stage were stalls placed there, in the style of the Parisian stabling system, for the reception of horses that would perform in the ring. The system, which Faranta may have introduced into New Orleans, required that the stalls be arranged so that horses could be backed into them, thus guaranteeing their prompt entry into the ring.[77]

Prominent among the specialties he had assembled for the circus were Mrs. Nellie Munroe, who would guide one or more horses through various tricks in her menage act, Fred Barclay, a bareback rider, aerial artist Ida Van Amburg, Sam McFlinn, a negro clown, Ed Nealy, a knockabout and singing clown, and actor Larry Dooley as a Chinese clown. There were also J.H. Shields, the equestrian director, the Krest Brothers, proficient in the art of singing and dancing, and two returning features—the acrobatic Patterson Brothers and Frank Clifford on the horizontal bars. Not least of all were the riding dogs, performing monkeys, and ponies, a trick horse named Gilford, and Matamo, an East Indian who walked on a ladder of swords. In all, advertised the showman, there were forty performers in his circus.[78]

Both Faranta and Frank Haight, the circus's manager, were there to welcome the audience to the Iron Theatre, and a concert of singers and musicians followed each circus performance. The local newspapers, whose representatives were given the exclusive use of a viewing box, teemed with laudatory notices of the show and the large crowds the auditorium gathered for each performance. Faranta's circus was so remunerative that Colonel J.H. Mapleson, a theatrical manager who leased the St. Charles Theatre for a short but brilliant engagement by Adelina Patti in the first two weeks of 1885, was said to be envious of Faranta's prosperity and planned to open a competing circus on a neighboring corner, but this turned out to be a simple act of flattery.[79]

Faranta's circus remained a successful attraction for more than a month in the Iron Theatre—from January 12 to February 15—during which time he added to the show: Charles Diamond, the "Milanese Minstrel," Mary Milton, an accomplished vocalist and reel and jug dancer, and a "tame giant," who often loafed about the lobby of the theater to the fascination of visiting youngsters.[80]

On February 3, the showman presented elements of his circus in a long morning parade. From the theater the procession traveled, in the following order, to Chartres Street, Esplanade, Decatur, Mandeville, Royal, Ursuline, Decatur, St. Ann, Dauphine, Dumaine, Rampart, Canal, St. Charles, Poydras, Camp, Calliope, St. Charles, Julia, Carondelet, Poydras, Magazine, Canal, Camp, Girod, Carondelet, Canal, Chartres, St. Louis, and finally Bourbon Street, returning to the Iron Theatre after this fatiguing journey.[81] "Faranta," remarked the *Mascot*, "has given the people a genuine circus, more complete and thorough than they have become accustomed to witness."[82]

Faranta kept the circus in the Iron Theatre for five weeks, extending his contract with William Munroe one week beyond the original terms of their agreement; since he wanted to keep the lucrative circus active, and yet intended to keep the attractions in his new theater fresh, Faranta transferred the entire organization—now named "Faranta's New York and New Orleans Circus"—to Eugene Gorman's pavilion on the corner of Third and Chippewa streets, and leased the large tent until March 8.[83]

What became of the circus after this time is not known. During the time the circus was in his theater, and perhaps because of its success, Faranta was able to pay the mortgage on his iron building; on January 21, twenty days after the agreed date, he delivered six hundred and fifty dollars to William S. Ingram, a representative of the Cincinnati Corrugating Company of Ohio, who in turn released the signed mortgage papers to the Signor.[84]

On February 16, California soubrette Georgia Woodthorpe and comedian T.A. Cooper were next featured with the Georgia Woodthorpe Combination in a comedy-drama entitled *Little Butterfly*. Miss Woodthorpe portrayed the butterfly, a pretty waif of the wilds, and the comedian, Mr. Cooper, impersonated a Chinese. On February 23, following a week of these performances, the Georgia Woodthorpe Combination presented a dramatic translation of *Les Mystères de Paris*. Eugène Sue's *Mysteries of Paris* was first printed as a serial, telling the tale of a nobleman who would learn how the impoverished class lives, but it was very soon dramatized after it was published in multiple volumes in 1842-43. For the Iron Theatre's adaptation, claimed the *Mascot*, Faranta went "head over heels into the pure realms of the sensational and realistic drama, and dishes up 'The Mysteries of Paris,' with blood-and-thunder sauce, to large and appreciative audiences."[85]

On March 2, Faranta presented two large companies, each bringing to the theater a separate feature: The first, which contributed variety performances,

65

was a "Mammoth Double Company"; the second, a "Great Specialty Company," featured S.J. Wheeler, his "$10,000 Trained Bulldogs," and a play, *Sports of the Mines*. The play was designed as a realistic portrayal of the primitive life of miners in the West, and not the least adroit of the performers in the cast was a bulldog whose task in the drama was apparently to save as many lives as possible. In one notable episode, when the bulldog finds the hero bound helplessly in a cave, he unhesitatingly brings him a pistol and loosens his fetters; later, rescuing the hero from death on a sawmill carriage, he kept him from being sliced in half by a huge saw. Among the specialties that attended the play, Ed Neary's imitation of Adelina Patti received special mention by the press.[86]

The *Sports of the Mines* was followed on March 9 by other specialty acts and a drama entitled *Ace of Spades*, which featured S.J. Wheeler, Miss May Olive, and bulldogs Fred and Turk in leading roles. Wheeler and Miss Olive were re-engaged for a border drama, *The Outlaw Prince*, which opened on March 16 with Wheeler's dogs and his trained horse, Frank, as members of the cast. During the run of the play, these animals came under scrutiny by the "Society for the Protection of Dumb Animals." This organization was the early Louisiana State Society for the Prevention of Cruelty to Animals, which completed the formation of its group in New Orleans at meetings on March 18 and 24, 1885, in Tulane Hall.[87] Before these meetings, though, the members discovered that the principles upon which their society rested also formed the basis for the training of Wheeler's dogs and horses.[88]

Beginning March 23, Faranta's commodious stage was occupied by Professor Hawley's vaudeville group, the "Magnets," and two comedies, *Fogarty's Racket* and *Hauled Back*. The latter was a burlesque based on Hugh Conway's contemporary novel *Called Back*, or on a play by the same name.[89] In a separate event Professor Hawley himself dove one hundred feet through an aperture in the theater's roof to a net ten feet above the auditorium floor.[90]

For the following week Faranta's dime show offered a fresh but unnamed company in the cast of *A Tale of Enchantment*, an elaborate facsimile of Charles M. Borras's literary drama, *The Black Crook*, which itself owed much to Goethe's *Faust*. The special feature of *A Tale of Enchantment*, in addition to its spectacular transformation scenes and mechanical effects, was a grand "Amazon March," in which Blanche Webster, the play's fairy queen, portrayed a warrior chieftain and led twenty shapely young women through a lively marching maneuver. This activity was always connected with *The Black Crook*, an acknowledged forerunner of modern burlesque, in which the dancing girls' appearance on stage need not be integral to the play. Between the play's acts were several available diversions. Señorita Magdalena Puig, assisted by Señor Guirrez, executed dances of Spain, John Brace and Ed Neary added the comic element, Miss St. Clair sang, and Nora Allen enacted the part of a sweetheart of the past.[91] The popularity of Faranta's show kept *A Tale of Enchantment* on his stage for a two-week period. "Taken all in all," remarked the *Mascot*, "it was the most elaborate and enjoyable ten cents entertainment ever given here, or elsewhere."[92]

This was followed on April 13 by *The Seven Sisters*, a variation of *The Seven Daughters of Satan*, which had played in Faranta's tent in April of the previous year. With nineteen characters to portray, the cast of this production was far larger than the earlier group and included Mrs. Faranta as Plutella, one of the seven daughters of Pluto.

The *Mascot* said in its brief review of the play:

> The piece was decidedly pleasing and interesting to the large audiences who nightly gathered into the immense theatre; interesting from the fact that their whole attention was required to ascertain what it was all about, and pleasing because the utmost energies of the most energetic auditor failed to solve the problem. The scheme was a success, however, as the seven sisters and the imps and mortals who hovered about them, all earned their salaries, and Faranta is happy.[93]

For the following week Faranta retired *The Seven Sisters* in favor of *Uncle Tom's Cabin* and the Fisk Jubilee Singers and Plantation Shouters, who, along with a selected cast, supported Mr. and Mrs. E.R. Dalton, who had returned to Faranta's establishment after a year's absence from his stage.

Uncle Tom's Cabin was replaced on Monday, April 27, by Payne's Celebrities, a group of specialty artists who were led in their vaudeville performances by Billy Payne, a New Orleans native, and his wife Alice. The regular show was interrupted on May 1 for a benefit performance tendered to Faranta by a group of his friends. It was reported that 3,000 people were received at the Iron Theatre's door for a show that featured Payne's Celebrities and other specialty artists who had volunteered to appear in this benefit for the showman.[94] Among the notables who welcomed Faranta during the celebrations was Mayor Joseph V. Guillotte, who had chaired a committee of volunteers to ensure the success of the benefit.[95]

The Streets of New York was Faranta's next attraction, beginning May 4 and introducing scenery that included a spectacular fire and a fine view of Union Square by night in a heavy snowfall. A real fire engine, drawn by live horses, was used to good effect, and the fire sequence was made so realistic that at one performance, claimed the *Mascot*, "the audience fled the theatre in terror, thinking the iron establishment was on fire!"[96]

The drama was Dion Boucicault's version of *Les Pauvres de Paris*, a melodrama by Edouard Brisebarre and Eugène Nus and the same French work that J. Sterling Coyne turned into *Fraud and Its Victims*, itself a feature of Faranta's tent show in the summer of the previous year. Boucicault's play was first staged in the U.S. in 1857 under the title *The Poor of New York*, but was exported to England in the following year as *The Poor of London* and as *The Streets of London*. Its American version is set in New York during a commercial panic, and begins as Captain Fairweather deposits his entire fortune in an insolvent bank, whose banker, Gideon Bloodgood, is planning to abscond with the money. Fairweather's later attempt to retrieve his $100,000 is met with refusal and ends with the sea captain's collapse. Bloodgood and his clerk, Badger, move the body into the street, where the captain is discovered to have died of heart failure. Bloodgood has the money, Badger has the receipt, and the Fairweather family is reduced to the bleak life of beggary—these three topics involve the remainder of the story. Fairweather's widow attempts suicide with charcoal fumes, succeeding only in setting fire to the house, but the receipt is finally retrieved, the fortune is saved, and the villain is released to begin his life anew.[97]

On May 11, Boucicault's drama was replaced in the Iron Theatre by the Murphy and Mack Comedy Company of twenty artists. Their program was varied, beginning each night with selections from the orchestra, under the baton of Professor J.B. Volel: In addition to songs by Miss Irene Worrell, Mr. Shannon and Mr. Emerson appeared in a laughable German sketch, the "Irish delineators" Murphy and Mack appeared in a sketch, and aerialist John L. Manning performed on the trapeze and later appeared in a comedy sketch that featured his several character changes, with his "siamese twins" presentation being the most popular. A Mr. Spence and Miss Sartelle introduced lightning-fast crayon drawing into their musical sketch on musical artists, Beattie and Bentley exhibited acrobatic tricks and contortions, and Harry La Rose showed his club-swinging talent while balancing on a turning globe. "Murphy's Dream," another sketch by Murphy and Mack, closed the evening of vaudeville.[98]

Not only did the group attract three thousand patrons for its second show, but, said the *Mascot* of May 16: "The *beau monde,* the beaux, bums and buzzards from near and far have been thronging into the immense auditorium by the thousands and the universal cry is 'The Murphy and Mack Comedy Company takes the cake.'" The company was engaged for a second week in the Iron Theatre, which was now guarded by the two policemen Faranta had recently employed.[99] For the last week of May the showman presented a stage version of *Rip Van Winkle,* which cast W.O. Blake as the main character and put E.R. and Kate Dalton in supporting roles.

June 1 was the opening day of the Fostelle Company, which returned to Faranta's show to present a comedy entitled *Mrs. Partington.* As a female impersonator, Fostelle portrayed Mrs. Partington herself; he was assisted by Miss Marie Heath as Ike, Mrs. Partington's mischievous son, Barney Reynolds as Jonathan Tittquick, a judge who has trouble hearing, Jeppe Delano as Philander Ablebody, a tongue-tied deacon, Joseph E. Nagle, Jr., as Sorotis, the ideal lover, and Miss Clara Hastings as a Boston lily.[100] Because the play was not very long, the remainder of the company participated in a variety program to complete the evening's entertainment. The *Mascot,* reporting that the theater was "crowded nightly," judged the company to be "an excellent combination of performers."[101]

On June 8 the Fostelle Company began a series of performances in the comedy *Rooms to Rent,* whose three acts were laid in a boarding house, where the mistakes and adventures of the plot take place, but, on June 15, the company was replaced by the California Minstrels, a troupe that brought forty performers, its own orchestra, and a three-part show that included acrobatics, negro impersonations, and songs and dances.[102]

For the week of June 22 was Augustin Daly's successful *Under the Gaslight; or, Life and Love In These Times.* Playing the main characters in the drama, among a cast of fourteen, were J.R. Allen as Joe Snorkey, Harry Gleason as Ray Trafford, Al Hensley as Byke, Sara Coleman as Laura Courtland, Blanche Lamothe as Pearl Courtland, and Nora Allen as Peachblossom.[103]

As the play begins, Laura Courtland, a belle of select society, is snubbed by socially prominent Ray Trafford, who has learned from her cousin, Pearl, that Laura was once a lowly pickpocket. Laura flees her home and position to become a day laborer. She is cared for by Peachblossom, a girl of the streets, and Snorkey, a Civil War veteran, and yet finds herself being sought not only by a contrite Ray but also by Byke, the villain, who claims Laura as his child. The audience learns from Snorkey that it is Laura, and not Pearl, who is the real Courtland, learning also that Pearl, the real orphan, is engaged to marry Ray. Byke hunts for Laura, who has made plans to leave by train and has importuned the station master to lock her in the baggage shed until the train arrives. Through a window in the shed she sees Snorkey being pursued by Byke, who, angry that the veteran has upset his plans by revealing the secret of Laura's birth, ties him to the railroad tracks. As the express train approaches, Laura seizes an axe and chops her way out of the shed in time to save Snorkey's life. Laura, at last established as the true Courtland, is reunited with Ray, Snorkey and Peachblossom indicate their matrimonial intentions, and the villain, Byke, is magnanimously released.

Under the Gaslight, not the better of Faranta's stage ventures, was replaced on June 29 by a comedy, *Elsie, the Mountain Waif*, said to be a reconstructed version of *M'liss, Child of the Sierras*,[104] the story of the daughter of a drunken miner and her eventually successful efforts to regain her father's rich mine from a Mexican villain and to secure the release of her lover from wrongful imprisonment. The thirteen-member cast of this production included Kate Dalton as Elsie, Will A. Miller as Theopholis Legit, and Al Hensley as Rocky Mountain Jake.[105]

On July 6, Faranta presented *The Boarding School*, a musical comedy that the *Mascot* persisted in calling *Fun in a Boarding School*, formerly the feature in Faranta's tent in March of 1884. Despite any confusion over titles, the Howard & Whitney Ramblers, who brought the comedy to Faranta's new stage, turned it into a popular show, "introducing new songs, dances and specialties." The troupe presented a new bill for the week of July 13, beginning with a sketch entitled "Nemesis" and an olio to separate it from the evening's feature, *Muldoon's Picnic*, also a former production in Faranta's pavilion.

Muldoon's Picnic was replaced on Friday, July 17, by another comedy, *Confusion*, which was scheduled to end on Sunday evening, July 19, the official termination of Faranta's first season in the Iron Theatre. The three acts of Joseph Derrick's *Confusion* were constructed of simple material. Mrs. Mumbleford, who aspires to high society, purchases a fashionable pug dog, which she must hide in a closet because her husband, Mortimer, objects to such animals. Their butler and servant girl are secretly married, however, and keep this secret by hiding their child in another closet. Mortimer discovers the baby; later the hiding places of baby and dog are exchanged and Mortimer becomes confused. He hires a detective to solve the mystery, but his family, thinking him insane, hires a specialist. There are further complications before the puzzle is solved and the characters are reconciled. Both *Muldoon's Picnic* and *Confusion*, noted the *Mascot*, "took the house by storm."[106]

After the departure of *Confusion*, the Iron Theatre was closed for the remainder of the summer, and arrangements were made to floor the auditorium and furnish it with opera chairs. On July 26, Faranta and his wife left New Orleans for a trip to Cincinnati, and then to New York, during which they expected to find more entertainments for the coming season.[107]

Said the *Mascot* of Faranta's initial season in his new theater:

The season at this popular place has been an unusually profitable one and we doubt not the enterprising Signor can count dollars for all the dimes he took in at the little tent of three years ago, after he had walked and swam over here from Central America with nothing but a play bill printed in Spanish, and a suit of tights.[108]

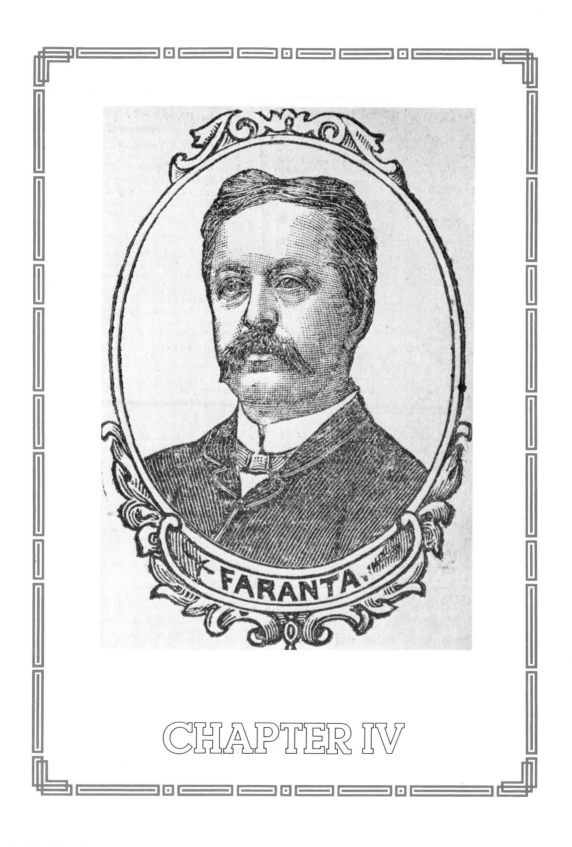

FARANTA

CHAPTER IV

Engraving of Faranta.
New Orleans *Daily States*, March 21, 1886.

ignor and Mrs. Faranta returned to New Orleans three weeks before the reopening of the Iron Theatre, scheduled for Saturday evening, September 19, 1885. The showman was soon inspecting his theater to see whether Gus Stempel, who had been placed in charge of its remodeling, had followed his directives. Faranta's brother had done a creditable job, said the local press, and many changes had been made since the theater's closure in July.

Covering the whole of the parquet was a heavy tongue-and-groove flooring; the entire area was slightly elevated to provide a gentle incline from the stage to the rear of the auditorium and the 900 reserved seats now situated there.[1] New mechanical appliances and scenery were added to the stage, electric lights inside the theater had been eliminated in favor of new gas fixtures, and all windows in the theater were colored to permit the darkening of the interior when performances demanded it.[2]

The ceiling had been covered with new canvas and "frescoes," the work of Joseph Piggott, who had recently completed a drop curtain for the Grand Opera House and was the artist responsible for the new stage scenery and all decorative painting in Faranta's theater.[3] His ceiling pictures were described as "a delightful combination of Moorish, German and Japanese styles of decoration."[4] The ceiling's center was "painted a very rich 'brindle' brown with blue and black borders and crossings; the edges turned out *a la Raphaelle,* the whole artistically blended with vermilion and gilt facings and trimming."[5] On top of the pillars separating the parquet from the dress circle were "paintings showing the country from New Orleans, La., through Arkansas, Kansas, Missouri and the East to the Atlantic coast."[6] Also the work of Piggott was a panoramic view of "An Overland Trip to the Pacific," which had been an exhibit in the World's Industrial and Cotton Centennial Exposition before being placed on the walls of Faranta's auditorium.[7] The cost of decorating the theater for its second season was set at five thousand dollars.[8]

Additional changes were not decorative. Ushers were now on hand during performances to assist patrons holding reserved seats, and Faranta had secured the services of an orchestra from Chicago, led by the theater's new musical director, Andrew[?] Bauer. He had delegated major responsibilities to a new staff: William A. Miller was named Faranta's business manager; Charles A. Aron was put in charge of the business office; Gus Stempel was now both a barkeeper and the theater's treasurer; Henry Stempel, whose other duties are not known, was the doorkeeper (a post he relinquished to William H. Connelly in 1886); Jules Luminat was the receiver of checks; and Mrs. Faranta sold tickets at the box office (a job that would go to Ben Stempel before the season's end) and also dispensed soda water at one of the concessions.[9] Saturdays, Sundays, and Wednesdays, were set aside for matinees, but performances were again available for ten cents and twenty-five cents, depending upon the availability of benches and reserved cane-bottom chairs.

The Riley and Fey Combination, headed by Richard J. Riley and Thomas Fey (or Fay), initiated the Iron Theatre's second season with a three-act drama, *Ragged Jack, the Vagabond,* preceded, as usual, by a display of vaudeville. Featured in the variety show were Irish songs and dances by Thomas White and

Edward Armstrong, Oscar Hall, a tumbler and contortionist, Kitty Wolf and Emma Harold, a song and dance team, Little Gertie (Gertie St. Vrain), a ten-year-old midget and songstress, and Edward Rush and William Gray, who opened the show with a sketch entitled "The Hebrew Senators."[10]

The main element of the program, however, was *Ragged Jack*, described by the *Mascot* as "a blood and thunder drama of the most pronounced lurid and sanguinary type," which included in its version of the Jack Sheppard story much gunpowder and free displays of deadly weapons, but which nevertheless attracted so many patrons that the Iron Theatre was "crowded such as our theatres are seldom crowded."[11] Indeed, the play's opening performance filled the theater's lobby with standees unable to see or hear the show but yet able to thwart the exertions of policemen who tried to remove them.[12] The next evening's performance also drew an overfull theater, despite a heavy rainfall, and many had to be turned away from the door.[13]

The popular Riley and Fey Combination remained for a second week, beginning September 28, with an equally likeable program, which opened with vaudeville and closed with a comedy entitled *The Travelers*. All performances were reported to be well attended.

These first two weeks also brought auxiliary excitements. The first was caused by some enterprising boys who, after being refused admission to the crowded theater, surreptitiously borrowed ladders from the neighborhood and, unbeknown to Faranta's personnel, placed them at the theater's transoms for a costless view of the program. Not unusually, though, the boys neglected to return the ladders. On Saturday morning, September 26, one provoked citizen spied the missing objects at the Iron Theatre and, following a conversation with Judge Sambola, confronted Faranta with the case, which was resolved by a young boy who explained the episode to them and laid the blame on "some other boys."[14]

On the previous day Richard Riley and another member of his vaudeville troupe, Thomas White, had involved themselves in an argument that grew so heated that Riley was stabbed by White, who was jailed for the wounding.[15] Finally, there was the smaller issue of August Jack, who, while visiting one of the last performances by the Riley and Fey Combination, was arrested for disturbing the peace.[16]

Despite signs that Faranta's inexpensive amusement would continue to be a successful venture in New Orleans, this was a period of challenge for the Iron Theatre. The first challenge was the closing of the World's Industrial and Cotton Centennial Exposition in June, 1885, for there would now be fewer people and thus fewer patrons in the city. On May 8, the idea of prolonging the exhibition under a new title was discussed by the exhibitors and representatives of twenty American cities, and on November 10, 1885, it was officially reopened as the North Central and South American Exposition. It soon faltered, encountering difficulties from its inception, and was permanently closed five months later, on March 31, 1886.

Of course, the loss of this great attraction also meant that Faranta would be faced with fewer competitors, a circumstance occasioned by the departure of the many tent shows, museums, and other amusements that entered the city primarily for the exposition and the people it attracted. But this too carried a perilous insecurity—whether or not he hoped to make his theater all things to all people, Faranta had to find a formula that would enable him, by following it, to keep the stature his theater had earned. His previous rule of thumb had been to provide his patrons with a balance of these three elements: consistency in low admission prices, manly entertainments a lady could enjoy and not find objectionable, but also of interest to children and youths, and a pleasant enclosure in which to enjoy them. For the next four years we find him adhering closely to this formula, which had been so successful, and resisting efforts to change it.

The Riley and Fey Combination was followed on October 5 by the Our Goblins Company, featuring William Gill's musical comedy *Fun on the Rhine*. The characters in this play are American tourists on a visit to a medieval German castle, where a ghost story is told to them; one of the group falls asleep, but is disturbed by a nightmare and rises from his sleep to take part in visions of the castle's former inhabitants.[17] Incorporated into this program were songs, dances, banjo music, tumbling, and pantomime, among other variety selections. Returning to Faranta's show for this production were actor Marlande Clarke and baritone singer J.C. Kline, who together helped "Our Goblins" to attract large audiences to the Iron Theatre.

"Our Goblins" remained for a second week, beginning October 12, with another comedy, *That Bad Boy; or, Fun in a Grocery*, whose plot revolved about the many pranks played by the Bad Boy, portrayed by Arthur Dunn. Commencing the program was an Ethiopian farce, followed by specialty performances, Irish humor, songs and operatic selections, and Leona Fountainbleau's "skipping rope dance." The entire production was a popular one, said the local press, although the *Mascot*, admitting that it was well worth the price of admission, did have a mixed opinion about the case.[18] Faranta's patrons seemed not at all critical in their judgments of the show, and each night large audiences attended his theater, which could still boast, remarked the *Daily Picayune*, that it attracted all classes of New Orleans society, from the "dudes and darlings of society, ladies and gentlemen, to the grinning darkies and the gamins of the market."[19] Unfortunately, some patrons brought with them poor social habits; at the opening of *That Bad Boy* Faranta was obliged, after whistling and stamping from the audience delayed the show's commencement, to step on stage to make a few remarks regarding proper behavior in his establishment.[20]

Sometime in mid-October Faranta was visited by a self-proclaimed agent for a new filter that could clear one hundred gallons of water per day; the agent asked that a filter be placed conspicuously in the theater's barroom, after which Faranta would receive it as a gift. The showman agreed, and it was installed on the following day. Less than a week later, though, the stranger returned to explain that he had dissolved his business partnership with the filter's inventor, and, after several more days, he came again to request a loan of six dollars; because the filter was worth that amount, the Signor gave him the money. Later still, the ex-partner and filter-inventor called upon Faranta and, after speaking disparagingly of the first stranger, inquired whether the water filter worked satisfactorily. Faranta said that it did, and the inventor then asked him to sign a "testimonial." Faranta insisted on reading the document and did so, finding that it was a declaration that he had purchased the filter and that legal action could be taken against him if he failed to pay any invoice sent to him. He told the man of the six-dollar transaction, and said that he could have the filter back if he returned that amount of money. The ex-partner left.[21]

"Barnum Outdone!" was the phrase Faranta used to introduce his public to the Iron Theatre's next attraction, the King, Burke & Co.'s Allied Shows, which brought to the theater a full and varied circus. The group opened to a large and enthusiastic audience on October 19, notwithstanding the inclement weather on this date. A farce, "Courting Under Difficulties," began the program, which continued with a troupe of five bicycle riders, A.C. Rigby and his banjo, exercises on the double bars, strongman Frank Burt with balancing feats and tests of physical exertion, Professor Andy Showers and his trained dogs and monkeys, four roller skating artists, magic by Professor Feggerter, trained Arabian horse Blondin and trick pony Pee Wee, character and quick-change artist John F. Stowe, a barrel-dancing act, Maude D'Almas, who juggled on a revolving globe, songs and dances, tumbling, high wire activities, and Lottie and John D'Almas in mid-air feats.[22] This versatile circus remained with Faranta's theater for two weeks.

Saturday, October 24, was Mrs. Faranta's twenty-second birthday. The matinee was made a benefit in her honor, and there she was presented with several elegant gifts, including a two-carat diamond ring, a pyramid of exotic fruits that stood four feet high, a set of hand-painted jars, silk hose, statuettes, and an English pug dog.[23] The last gift was no doubt intended to replace the Farantas' prize pug dog, Flo, which had died late in July.[24]

On the day before her birthday, though, Faranta gave away a gift of a different kind. "Respected Madam" began the letter he sent to the managers of every orphan asylum in the city:

> Having now at my theatre, corner of Orleans and Bourbon streets, an entertainment given by the King, Burke & Co.'s Allied Shows, which is especially pleasing to young people, introducing trained animals and many features of the circus, I take this opportunity, with my compliments, to invite the orphaned children of your excellent institution to visit my theatre in a body, admission free, with yourself, or in charge of any person deputized by you, on Monday, Tuesday, Wednesday, Thursday or Friday afternoon of next week.
>
> Day performances commencing at 1 P.M. Doors open at 12 m.—Respectfully yours, and the public's friend and servant, F.W. Faranta, Manager of Theatre.[25]

The offer was quickly accepted, if only by a few. The circus began its second week with a new program, and on October 30 two hundred orphans, from four of the city's sixteen orphan asylums, were Faranta's guests to the show, after which Mrs. Faranta dispensed cake and lemonade to the children, who were each given a stick of chewing gum upon leaving.[26] The date was also Faranta's birthday.

The King, Burke & Co.'s Allied Shows departed the iron building two days later, leaving behind Frank Clifton, who had leased a refreshment booth in the theater.[27] For the week of November 2 the new amusement was the Charles Gilday Comedy Company, which offered both vaudeville, whose principal attraction was jig and fancy dancer Kittie O'Neil, and a boarding house comedy,

Collars and Cuffs, with its playwright, Edward Chrisse, in a leading role. Three thousand persons were reported in attendance on opening night.[28]

Again Faranta had scheduled a very attractive series of performances, and again large audiences were drawn to the theater. The Gilday troupe remained in the Iron Theatre for a second week, bringing to the stage an olio of variety and a one-act play, *Worse and Worse*, another work by Edward Chrisse, who was again part of the cast. During the month, Faranta left New Orleans for a short trip to Chicago to procure one or two likely entertainments for the Iron Theatre. While in Chicago, he purchased 600 twenty-one-inch folding opera chairs, which were destined for the theater's parquet.[29] It was expected that the addition would raise the price of reserved seating, "but," judged the *Daily Picayune*, "the best people are now going to Faranta's, and they demand the best accommodations."[30]

During the week of November 16, the Iron Theatre hosted two dramas by the George W. and William J. Thompson Troupe. On the stage for the first half of the week (Monday-Thursday) was *The Gold King; or, The Life Prisoner*, while *For a Life*, written by the Thompsons, was scheduled for the remainder of the week (Friday-Saturday). Hector, a talented acting dog, played a leading role in both melodramas.

The Gold King proved to be the more popular of the plays presented by the Thompson group. The drama concerns an uncle who cheats his nephew out of some property and then murders the father of the nephew's betrothed and tries to fasten the crime upon the young man; the deed is undone, however, by the accused man's close friend, who takes the blame for the killing, escapes from prison, and becomes the "gold king" before righting all wrongs in the play.[31]

The *Mascot*, finding the tale to be excessively violent and morally corrupting, was "sorry to say that the mammoth theatre was packed every night" of the production.[32] "Even at the cheap prices," said the *Daily Picayune*, "the receipts seldom go below $400 per night."[33]

The second week of the Thompson Troupe was also to be a split week—beginning with *Yawcup; or, The Peddler's Story*, another work by the Thompsons, and concluding with *The Sightless Bride*—but the second feature was replaced instead by a requested series of the *Gold King*. Admitted the *Mascot* at the week's end: "The boom at Faranta's continues, and the audiences that nightly attend this mammoth theatre are unprecedented in amusement annals of this city. On several nights the past week the doors were closed before the curtain was rang up, it being physically impossible to admit any more people into the auditorium."[34] This was also the first week of "Faranta's Theatre"—the iron building's new and permanent title.

Faranta's attraction for the week of November 30 was the Acme Dramatic Combination in *Siskyon; or, For a Brother's Crime*, starring John B. Negrotto, a native of New Orleans and the director of the Acme group. Faranta was quickly taken to task for his choice. After witnessing the third appearance of *Siskyon*, the *Evening Chronicle* returned with this exhortation:

> The attendance at Faranta's Theatre last night was very small, and those people who were present yawned and groaned as the play progressed. If Signor Faranta expects to retain the clientelle he has secured, he should exercise more discretion in the selection of companies to cater to his patrons. The play of

"Siskiyon" is a bare-faced steal from "My Partner" and "M'liss," and would, perhaps, be pardonable if it were even passably acted. But a more finished and complete company of "sticks" has rarely been permitted to torture New Orleans theatre-goers. From first to last the play (?) is a weary drag, and the players an aggregation of incompetents. Faranta comes in for a big share of the blame in this case, and in all kindness the advice is given him to use more judgment in future. The people will not stand this sort of thing for any extended period of time.[35]

The "'Acme Hamfatic' aggregation" did not appear on Faranta's stage again. The *Mascot* reported that the Acme Dramatic Combination, "a band of itinerant barnstormers," was fired in the middle of its third performance and removed from the stage, and that Billy Kersands and his twenty negro minstrels, who were not scheduled to appear until December 14, finished the evening program.[36] All other reports are that the minstrels began their brief engagement on December 4, when, having survived this embarrassment, Faranta sent them to parade the streets in their colorful Zouave uniforms and found time to inspect, and eventually to purchase, the entire circus of Charles L. Davis, who had committed suicide.[37] Kersands and his troupe of minstrels continued through the remaining three days of the week.

On December 7, Faranta's stage was occupied by the Richardson Dramatic Combination, which appeared during the first half of the week in the four-act comedy *Our Bachelors* (a liberal appropriation of Joseph Bradford's comedy, said the *Daily Picayune* of December 8), centering on unmarried boardinghouse tenants sworn to the single state but apparently also desperate for marriage; during the second half of the week, the combination appeared in *The Danites*, Joaquin Miller's tale of a group of Mormons committed to avenging the violent opposition to polygamy and the Mormon faith. Both plays drew large audiences to the iron theater.

The Kersands Minstrels were strengthened to fifty black members for their engagement in the week of December 14, and Faranta's scenic artist, Joseph Piggott, had created for the occasion a new stage set that depicted exotic tropical flowers, plants, and birds.[38] The song-filled program, which included a large female chorus and thirty musicians, brought to the stage the Kersands Minstrels, the Madrigal Boys, the Tennessee Jubilee Singers, and Billy Kersands and Billy Wilson together in burnt-cork comedy.[39] On December 20, when the Kersands Minstrels ended their engagement with Faranta's Theatre, the program featured songs by the full company ("Swanee River"), Billy Kersands ("Pretty Lips"), and Billy Reynolds ("Old Plantation Home"), and included the "Black Zouaves" in a dress parade, a grand drill, bayonet exercises, and battlefield postures and scenes.[40]

On this date, too, the new opera chairs from Chicago were installed in the parquet circle.[41] According to the *Mascot*, these "patent automatic folding seats," each having a foot rest and a hat, overcoat, and umbrella rack, were unique in the city.[42] Each of the numbered chairs was available for 50 cents and could be reserved from one day to one week in advance.

Faranta had secured two circuses for the 1885-1886 season. The second of these, Lorrelaud's Circus, which included trapeze artists, slack-wire performers, and a trained giraffe, appeared during the Christmas week. On opening day, December 22, Faranta himself led his band, his red bandwagon, and Lorrelaud's Circus in a parade through the center of the city, and opened the theater to daily matinees for the duration of the circus's engagement. At the Christmas Day matinee a drawing was held for one of two prizes: an educated goat with a harness and miniature wagon, or, if the lucky child happened to be a girl, a magnificent French doll.[43]

This was also a time for adult charities. On Christmas morning, Faranta's friends Paul Lafaye, Richard Chantrey, and business manager William Miller surprised him with a silver set—a pitcher, two goblets, and a tray—from the showman's appreciative employees.[44] Faranta and his wife returned the kindness with a Christmas party and feast, which began late in the afternoon and lasted until 6:30 p.m., giving the 87 guests time to prepare for the circus's evening performance. Included in the cosmopolitan assembly of invitees were lawyers, doctors, theatrical performers, circus riders, employees of Faranta's Theatre, Faranta's five brothers, his sister Mamie B. Stempel and aged mother Rose Stempel, and Judge Anthony Sambola, who made a lengthy speech before the gala meal began.[45] Participants in the feast may have included visitors from Elks Lodge No. 30, now enlarged to 150 members, which had celebrated its first anniversary on December 23.[46]

Faranta's entertainments for the remainder of the 1885-1886 season consisted of the variety that his patrons had come to expect—comedy, drama, and vaudeville, which seemed to incorporate something of everything capable of stage presentation without incredulity. Starting the year 1886 was the Edwin Clifford Dramatic Combination, which brought *Monte Cristo* for the week of January 4. Edwin Clifford himself portrayed four characters in Dumas's tale, but the play attracted only small audiences because of cold weather.[47]

In the following week John W. Ransone and his company presented *Across the Atlantic,* a three-act play about the hero's efforts to marry his employer's daughter and the disguises he must don in order to be with her. For this production, which included songs and comedy, Ransone, an actor noted for his dialect imitations, also played four characters, appearing on stage as a black servant, a German guide, an Irish valet, and the hero.[48] For the week of January 18 Edwin Browne and Jennie Moore Browne presented *Good as Gold,* a four-act drama of mining life in Montana, which featured more new scenery from the hand of painter Joseph Piggott. I.W. Baird's Mammoth Minstrels next brought (for the week of January 25) a variety show of contortionism, dancing, feminine fashions, banjo music, trombone specialties, handbell ringing, and a comedy entitled *The American Abroad.*

Baird and his minstrels were replaced on February 1 by Jennie Calef and her "Little Muffets" Combination, presenting the *Little Muffets,* a vehicle for Miss Calef, who portrayed a waif (really a kidnapped heiress) found selling newspapers in New Jersey and New York while disguised in boys's clothes. The group appeared in two plays in its second week, February 8-14. The first, from Monday to Wednesday, was *Little Barefoot,* a Maggie Mitchell drama drawn from Berthold Auerbach's 1856 novella about Black Forest peasants, which again cast Miss Calef as a young girl, an orphan who must pass her early days as a goose girl until she is loved by, and marries, a wealthy young man; the second play, which concluded the group's engagement in Faranta's Theatre, was another version of *Fanchon, the Cricket*.

A similar group and a similar show were on Faranta's stage for the week of February 15: the Sisson & Cawthorn "Little Nuggets" Comedy Company in *Little Nuggets*, the story of a villain and a young girl who is unaware that she is the owner of a valuable estate. This production was highlighted by new scenery by Joseph Piggott and a parade, on February 19, by Faranta's band, whose members wore, in place of buttons, twelve silver dimes on each coat. His band "might get bursted on a note," remarked the *Daily States*, "but will always have a little cash on hand."[49] The last presentation in February was the Charles Sturgis Comedy Company in the musical comedy *Tourists in a Pullman Palace Car*, which brought to the stage a new and elegant parlor scene by Joseph Piggott and a large crystal chandelier.[50] The same company appeared during the first week of March in another comedy, *Up the Spout*, introducing it with variety performances.

Before the month of March, though, Faranta made two changes in the theater's operation. The first of these, noticed by the *Daily Picayune* on February 9, was a reduction in the price of the new opera chairs. While a bench seat was still available for ten cents, the general admission price, and a cane-bottom chair could be secured for twenty-five cents, an opera seat now cost only thirty-five cents. The second change was made on February 15, when Faranta altered the matinee days to Thursdays, Saturdays, and Sundays.

Mardi Gras in 1886 fell on March 9. Before the occasion, Faranta posted throughout the city what the *Daily Picayune* of March 4 called "one of the handsomest show bills ever put on a bill board in New Orleans." Each "three-sheet poster, worked in colors" announced a Mardi Gras Ball in his iron theater, for which event "the largest and the best floor in the city" had been laid. The ball was not free; at a dollar per gentleman's ticket, the dance netted the showman an estimated four hundred dollars.[51]

Performing during the week was Sargeant Aborn's Comedy Company, in John A. Stevens's *Unknown*, the melodramatic story of a young man who sails from Calcutta to New York to deliver important papers, which prove that his sister is the heir to a large fortune. However, he is shot and is thus made cross-eyed, insane, and "unknown"; he is cared for by his sister, who is poisoned, buried alive, and then rescued, after which her guardian, the villain of the piece, is thwarted, the important papers are delivered, and the "unknown" is restored to sight and sense on being shown a picture of his deceased mother. Lottie Church, wife of the play's author and formerly a performer in Faranta's show, starred in this production, as well as in the company's program for the week of March 15, Walter Fletcher's three-act comedy *Trix*, about a winsome and mischievous waif.

The week of March 22 brought vaudeville and drama by DeVere's Great Carnival of Novelties, a variety troupe that included in its repertory a circus of twenty-five performing dogs, the "Mastadon Dog Circus." If there were other discontented viewers of these novelties—a show that concluded each evening with Emma Harold as Champion Jack in a drama entitled *Champion Jack*—none complained louder than the splenetic *Mascot*:

Faranta, the irrepressible, the Solomon of his profession, has been "taken in," at last! He wanted to fill up a week's time and failing to secure Edwin Booth or Mary Anderson, he consented to permit Harry DeVere's heterogeneous combination of concert saloon talent, and peripatetic travelling mountebanks resting temporarily here under police surveillance, a chance to get shekels enough to get out of town. If his motive was really to assist them to get out of town he failed dismally, for a worse show was never seen on any stage since stages were first made of wood or Berny Shields began to recite Shamus O'Brien, and are so sticking they can never be moved except on a cattle boat. It was the bummest layout of bums, bummers, and bummeresses that ever escaped a brick-batting from an enraged audience, from the heavy villain, whose diseased mind conceived the direful plot, to the stage struck "boot black" who is seeking to win fame or famine under the invigorating title of *Champion Jack*. The rest of the company is so vile we won't particularize for less than forty cents a line prepaid in advance, no copies furnished.[52]

In the very next issue of the *Mascot* Faranta published his response, his wood engraved portrait, and these words: "This is the picture of the man who The Mascot, of the 27th, said had the worst show in the city. But come next week. Commencing Monday, April 5th. And The Mascot, must tell the truth that the Silbons are the greatest in the world."[53]

The Silbons and their Yellow Dwarf Company opened in Faranta's iron theater on March 29. The Silbons were aerialists and the main attraction of the troupe of thirty performing artists, whose program consisted of a comedy, *Under the Gas Pipes*, Little Pauline on the "silver wire," humor and songs by the coquettish Gilmore sisters, songs and dances by Madge Alston, a "Roman studio," *i.e.*, acrobats performing in Roman costumes, and the four Silbons in leaps, acts on the trapeze, and, of course, aerial feats. The entire company appeared in *The Yellow Dwarf*, a burlesque woven from the following elements: a yellow dwarf who protects a queen from magic lions on the condition that he be given her daughter's hand in marriage, the princess who loves a young king, the queen who does not keep her promise to the yellow dwarf, and a happy ending.

The *Mascot* did admit that the Silbons, "the wonderful artists and athletes," were "the best aerial artists and group athletes and tumblers we have ever seen on any stage,"[54] and that their combination "has proved to be the best paying card that appeared here this season, both artistically and financially, and Mr. Faranta may justly claim that they give one of the most unique, interesting and appreciative performances seen on the stage today."[55] The Silbons' combination was a successful entertainment in Faranta's theater, and it was continued in the week of April 5 with a program that featured numerous new specialties by members of the company, the Silbons in somersaults, feats on the trapeze, and flights from the theater's dome, concluding each evening with a play entitled *Adonis in Cupid*.

The Silbons and their group were replaced on April 12 by Will L. Smith's Swiss Bell Ringers, Comic Concert Company and Humpty Dumpty Combination, which supplied comical songs, musical glasses, one or more Swiss bell waltzes, stump oratory, character songs, a cornet solo, comical banjo songs, juggling, trained dogs, and the ghost of Humpty Dumpty.[56] Mr. Smith's company remained in the iron theater for one week. On Faranta's stage for the week of April 19 was

81

Davene's Allied Attraction and Capitola Forrest's Novelty and Burlesque Company, an amalgamation of talent that created a multitude of activities—a minstrel sketch called "Our Lawn Party," songs, dances, female impersonation, a singing dog, Miss Forrest's rope-skipping dance with a flaming hoop, aerial artists, Mlle. Lotta— the "Human Fly"—who threw herself through a paper balloon and leaped from the top of the theater to a net below, the Silver Cornet Band of ten female musicians, and, in conclusion, a burlesque entitled *Cast Steel Seminary.*[57] The joint attraction remained for a second week, beginning April 26, with a new program, which closed each night with *Zao*, another burlesque. The *Mascot*, in one more of its harsh assessments of Faranta's features, reported only modest attendance at the latter program.[58]

Within a month Faranta's second marriage was completely dissolved. In April "Bridget Magee" of the *Mascot* reported that Mrs. Faranta had departed New Orleans with the showman's friend Paul Lafaye, a bank clerk with the Louisiana National Bank and a husband and father.[59] Lafaye, "that deserted his home, wife and family and run away with that old hussie that used to sell hot peanuts in Faranta's show," returned to his home in September, but was turned away, according to later gossip from the *Mascot*.[60] However close to the facts the *Mascot* came in its attempt at a public service, the *New York Clipper*, at first considering that the issue of divorce was a rumor circulated to add spice to the theater's reputation, noted on May 15 that Faranta was granted an absolute divorce from Alva Lowe.[61]

Four companies appeared in Faranta's Theatre during May: Denier's Mammoth Humpty Dumpty Pantomime Troupe and European Specialty Company (May 3-9) in a variety show and the well-known pantomime; the Great World's Four Minstrels (May 10-16), bringing a program of youthful minstrelsy; Hume & Wesley's Big Specialty Company (May 17-30), which featured comedy, ventriloquism, musical sketches, fifteen-second crayon drawings, a muscular trapeze act and tests of strength by the Great Vim, the Wesley Brothers in a twenty-minute song and dance, for which they had to give eight encores on opening night, and the entire company in the comedy sketch "That Don't Go."[62] On May 31, Gus J. Heege and his company opened with a five-act comedy entitled *Brass Buttons*. They remained for a second week (June 7-13) with another comedy, *Heege's Bad Boy*, about the amount of fun a bad boy could get from the world in general, which the group was said to have presented over five hundred times in the principal cities of the U.S. and Canada.[63]

During the month, Faranta acquired the *Maid of Athens*, two tents, and several unnamed theatrical items—all purchased from a sheriff's sale.[64] The *Maid of Athens* was an enormous balloon that Faranta intended to use as an external attraction of his iron theater; unfortunately it was lost on June 5 at West End when it was overinflated and burst before it could be sent aloft.[65] Also obtained during the month was a large Babcock fire extinguisher. New and placed in a prominent place in the theater, the chemical extinguisher was mounted on wheels, fitted with brass fixtures, held sixty-two gallons of water, carried 350 feet of hose, and required at least two men to handle it effectively.[66] On May 12, Faranta renewed his lease with Mary Roberts for an additional two years.[67]

The last show of the season—the last performance of *Heege's Bad Boy*—was scheduled for June 13, but at least three other performances were given in Faranta's Theatre before this date. The first, a benefit for Gus Stempel and William Miller, was held on June 16; the second, held on June 18, was a benefit show for Faranta himself. During his benefit, which was attended by a full house, Faranta appeared on stage to accept a wreath of flowers from a young girl in the audience and then exhibited his skill as a contortionist in his "last" performance of the athletic art.[68] The third activity was a vocal and instrumental concert by the Excelsior Brass Band and Crescent Lodge of the Odd Fellows, after which the ironclad theater was closed to the public for the duration of the summer, giving Faranta the time needed to redecorate his establishment for its third season.[69]

Victoria Grace, known to her audiences as "Little Vic, Queen of the Air," died on August 4, 1886.[70] She was a trapeze artist, born about 1850 in Philadelphia, and had learned to swing on the trapeze while a child, later remaining on the trapeze in a career that connected her with many circuses. Faranta had known her in Mexico several years before. At the time she was considered quite wealthy, but a reversal of fortune took this from her, urging her into a world of opium and alcohol. She entered New Orleans at the start of August and became ill and delirious; having no one to care for her, she was taken to Charity Hospital, where she died. Learning that she had died and was to be buried in potter's field, Faranta visited the hospital and there defrayed the cost of her interment in Greenwood Cemetery.[71] Faranta and a few friends were present at her funeral.

Before Faranta's Theatre was opened for a third time, its proprietor made one more philanthropic gesture. An earthquake had demolished most of Charleston, S.C., on August 31, leaving fifty persons dead, over a hundred wounded, and property damage estimated at a high of ten million dollars.[72] As late as September 2, because the main office of the Western Union Telegraph Company had been destroyed by the quake, no messages could be delivered to the city. Another station was erected a mile away, and Faranta was then able to telegraph W.M. Huger, Mayor of Charleston, offering to dispatch his large circus tents to help house victims of the disaster. The War Department had sent one hundred tents, but more were needed, and the Mayor's reply was: "Thanks. Please send tents by first passenger train, if possible."[73] On the next train to Charleston were Faranta's five theatrical tents, capable of accommodating eight hundred people.[74]

Faranta's Theatre now seemed to be a real and proper theater. So discovered the *Daily Picayune*.[75] The dirt and sawdust floor had been replaced in the previous year by an inclined wood floor, and in the parquet circle were the numbered opera chairs for reserved accommodations, now set at 25 cents (or 15 cents during matinees); situated in front of these, and now available for the general admission fee, were rows of cane-bottom easy chairs; comfortable benches (as tier seats) lined the sides of the auditorium.[76]

For its 1886-1887 season the theater was again refurbished. Its interior had been repainted, papered, and varnished, and Joseph Piggott had produced more landscapes and a stock of new scenery. The subject matter of Piggott's new drop curtain was a panoramic view of Sorrento, Italy, in the evening—a nostalgic composition of ancient Italian buildings, native foliage, and a part of the Mediterranean. Lighting this curtain and the theater itself was a new electrical system of 175 Brush-Swan incandescent lights; among these 50 lighted the auditorium, 15 were footlights, 60 were used as border lights, 15 were placed in the dressing rooms, another 15 illuminated the business office and barrooms, and the remaining lights were used for the stage chandeliers and fixtures, when required.[77] The electricity was supplied by two separate circuits, as insurance against darkness if one of the circuits were lost.

The principal members of Faranta's staff had not changed, except Gus Stempel, who, though still a bartender in the theater, passed on his position as the theater's treasurer to Teddy Lefevre; at this time John Bowers was the stage carpenter, W. McPherson was the property man, Alex Mobery was the house officer, and John Luchasse was the theater's head usher.[78] The main addition to Faranta's staff was actor William A. Miller, who was appointed Manager of Faranta's Theatre for this and the next season.

The entertainment selected for the seasonal opening, and engaged for two weeks in the iron theater, was the Walter S. Sanford Dramatic Company, inaugurating the occasion with a melodrama, *Under the Lash*. September 18 was opening night. By eight o'clock the box office would sell no more tickets and William Connelly would admit no more patrons, since the theater was overfull and there was no more standing room left. Waiting for the curtain to rise was an audience of 4,200 people.[79] After a long wait, past the usual hour for the beginning of a performance in the theater, Faranta stepped onto the stage to explain that the play's cast had not arrived in New Orleans until 7:45, one hour earlier, but was expected on stage at any moment. Sanford's performers were further delayed in moving their luggage, which contained the accoutrements of their profession, and in settling into the dressing rooms. A few minutes before 9:00 the curtain went up on the first act of *Under the Lash*.[80]

The play revolves about the paternity of a blind girl, unknowingly the heir to a large fortune. The villain bribes the court to place her in the care of an Italian, who then proclaims her his daughter, enabling the villain to obtain her fortune through his accomplice. Not unusually, though, the villain's many plans are foiled by the continued efforts of a young German (W.S. Sanford), a negro domestic, a kind policeman, and two clever dogs.[81] When one of the dogs rushed onto the stage and seized the Italian by the throat, thus saving his master's life, "that part of the house surrounding the orchestra rose as a billow of a human sea and cheered the dog with a maddening delight until the overjoyed animal appeared before the curtain to make his bow."[82]

The audience, not sparing with its applause, was given many opportunities to express delight with *Under the Lash*. Faranta received compliments on the theater's new decorations, stage scenery, and drop curtain, but, unfortunately, he also faced complaints about the new opera chairs: their occupants had reserved the numbered seats expecting to retain them throughout the performance, but found, after brief periods away, that they were lost to interlopers. The *Daily States* suggested that the problem arose because Faranta's patrons were not given numbered coupons with their reservations.[83]

84

"Faranta's Show."
Mardi Gras Tableau of the Krewe of Olympians, January 26, 1946.
Courtesy Robert C. Stempel.

The second week of Walter Sanford's popular company featured *A Game of Life*, reported to be a thinly disguised version of the drama *Phoenix*, in which Sanford took top billing as Gerald Gray, a "Bohemian," and Joe Blossom, "right from California."[84] On October 4 the Riley and Fey Dramatic Company returned to Faranta's show with *Ragged Jack, the Vagabond*, and remained for a second week in *A Brother's Oath*, a "lurid drama of the wild West, abounding in war whoops, Indians, scalps, and heroes," and, said a newsboy after seeing the show, "it went great."[85]

The remainder of October was taken up by blonde May Adams and her Japanese Burlesque Company. The minstrel troupe's first week (October 18-24) brought to Faranta's stage a Japanese fete with Miss Adams and her group of girls in Mikado costumes, acrobatics by the Victorella brothers and a dog, songs, dances, black-face comedy, grotesque dancing and contortionism, and, in conclusion, a burlesque entitled *Robbers of the Devil's Gulch*.[86] In the last week of October the group was joined by the Gilfoil & Bush Specialty Company in a program that included a musical comedy, *Our School Girls*, and a farce entitled *Creme de la Creme of Ethiopia*, along with intervening variety entertainment.

November in the iron theater was devoted to two comedy companies and a drama company. The first of these companies, the Harry Le Clair and W.J. Russell Comedy Company, opened on November 1 in the three-act comedy, *A Practical Joke*, a "musical farcical absurdity" featuring Mr. Russell and female impersonator Le Clair. The target of the *Practical Joke* is an eccentric Yankee farmer who disapproves of marriage; the jokers are a nephew, financially dependent upon the farmer, and his new bride, an actress. The nephew invites his uncle to visit him in the city, not suspecting that the farmer, who knows nothing of the marriage, would agree to this; but he does, and upon arrival is met by the young actress (Harry Le Clair), who subsequently impersonates an Irish servant girl, a German prima donna, a Spanish *danseuse*, a demented young girl, and a Chinese beauty—all of whom the old uncle is eager to marry.[87]

The show was a critical and popular success in Faranta's Theatre, although it remained for only one week, moving aside on November 8 for Charles Gilday's Comedy Company, which returned in the three-act comedy *Collars and Cuffs*, whose chief attraction was songstress and dancer Fanny Beane. The comedy group stayed for a second week in *A Piece of Pie in 3 Slices*, another play by Edward Chrisse, who was again a member of the company. A special amusement during the group's last week was "The Vanishing Lady," an optical illusion imported from Paris. In the last week of November the Carrie Stanley Combination presented the only dramatic entertainments of the month—*The Collier's Daughter; or, A Coal Digger's Life in Pennsylvania Mines* and *Monte Cristo* (with Carrie Stanley in the lead) in a divided week of performances in Faranta's Theatre.

During November, Faranta bought more items known chiefly for their place in circuses, and still puzzling is what became of them. On the eve of its sale, November 21, the W.W. Cole Circus, which had previously appeared in New Orleans under Faranta's auspices, gave a farewell performance at its location on Canal Street. W.W. Cole was leaving the business he had entered in 1872, and within a few days the whole of his circus belonged to others.[88] One of these was Signor Faranta, who attended the two-day auction with representatives of the

Sells Brothers Circus, New York's Central Park Zoological Garden, the King, Burke & Company Circus, the Forepaugh Circus, and the Cincinnati Zoological Garden.[89] Faranta purchased a white buffalo yak ($200), three lions ($1,236), two white peacocks ($28), one female hippopotamus ($1,500), two white peacocks ($28), one female hippopotamus ($1,500), twenty-eight wax figures and twelve papier-mâché figures ($60), a collection of Mexican curiosities ($455), and four elephants: Jennie ($1,500), Laura ($950), Lizzie ($1,600), and Tom ($3,100). The showman's total expenditure was $10,629.[90] While he did exhibit the three lions (in their "den" with Harry George Coutlin, the Lion King) during the Carrie Stanley Combination's *Monte Cristo,* nothing further was made public about Faranta's large investment.

Faranta's theatrical features for December, 1886, began on November 29 with *Nip and Tuck,* a four-act detective story by the Harry Webber Combination. The plot of this comedy centers on the homicidal activities of a highborn adventurer who marries a rich young widow and then, after she makes out her will in his favor, feeds her slow poison and contends that her fatal trouble is due to con-sumption. The comedy of the play is provided by two detectives, Nicholas Nip (one of the four characters Harry Webber portrayed in this production) and Tracer Tuck, who solve the crime and bring a happy ending to the story.

The remainder of December was devoted to one comedy and two dramas. The first, by the J.C. Stewart Comedy Company, featured the company's fourteen performers as the twenty-two characters of *The Two Johns,* the comical tale of two fat look-alike cousins, Peter and Philip Johns, one of whom is a lover to every susceptible female and a debtor who outwits his creditors by leaving town and letting his double take the punishment.

On December 13, a new company, headed by Joseph J. Dowling and Sadie Hasson, began its two-week engagement in the iron theater with *Nobody's Claim,* a drama of the rough life in Western mining country, bringing together a wild mountain girl (unknowingly the heir to a fortune left by her late father), a heroic young army officer, and a desperado in search of the missing heir. During the week of the play, Faranta publicized the company's next scheduled feature by giving to each lady in the audience a small map of New Orleans, which indicated the location of his theater, and six pages of sheet music with a cover bearing the portraits of Dowling and Hasson, the stars of *Nobody's Claim* and the new at-traction, *Never Say Die.*[91] The second play opened on December 20, remaining through Christmas week with its combination of comedy, drama, colorful stage scenery, and incidental but conspicuous choral music. In keeping with a tradition in the theater, a purebred English pug dog was given away at the Christmas matinee.

On December 27, the German-American tragedian Daniel E. Bandman and his company began a successful two-week engagement in the theater. Presented on Faranta's stage was their repertoire of fourteen plays, a variety that required the entire two weeks to complete: *Hamlet* (Dec. 27), *The Merchant of Venice* (Dec. 28), *Richelieu* (Dec. 29), *The Lady of Lyons* (Dec. 30, matinee), *Romeo and Juliet* (Dec. 30, evening), *Othello* (Dec. 31), *East Lynne* (Jan. 1, matinee), *The Corsican Brothers; or, The Duel in the Snow* (Jan. 1, evening; Jan. 2, matinee and evening), *Macbeth* (Jan. 3), *Narcisse* (Jan. 4 and 5), *The Lady of Lyons* (Jan.

6, matinee), *Dead or Alive* (Jan. 6, evening), *Dora* and *Don Caesar de Bazan* (Jan. 7), *East Lynne* (Jan. 8, matinee), *Richard III* (Jan. 8, evening), *Othello* (Jan. 9, matinee), and again *Richard III* (Jan. 9, evening). The presentations were well attended—though not crowded—and all members of the local Shakespeare Club were reported to be in attendance at Mr. Bandman's dime performances.

The subject of admission fees brought forth Bandman's wrath, however, when the *Daily Picayune* insinuated that his acting (in *Hamlet*, in this case) was to be judged by the cost of admission to see him.[92] Responded Bandman, concluding a lengthy letter that revealed the educational purpose of his stagecraft and the many benefits in playing at Faranta's "popular prices": "I have provided myself with a lady of high culture and intelligence and a company of talent and refinement, and I can say conscientiously and without arrogance that I am doing good work and I therefore request your critic to put the knife of censure where it is deserved and praise when due, regardless of the price of admission."[93]

For the remainder of the 1886-1887 season Faranta turned back to a more familiar pattern. On January 10, and for a two-week engagement, I.W. Baird's Mammoth Minstrels returned to the iron theater in combination with the English Royal Hand-Bell Ringers. Beginning with five minstrel acts, and amid much black-face minstrelsy, their program included an original overture by the minstrels' orchestra, two songs—"Children, I'm Gwine to Shine" and "Rocked in the Cradle of the Deep"—a medley of songs, three solo singers (with "Home, Sweet Home," "Let Me Hear Thy Voice Again," and "Because She Ain't Built That Way"), seven members of the group in "Mania-Monia Cranks," the hand-bell ringers, a "Grand Terpsichorean Display," clog dancing, tumbling, and a comedy entitled *De Lillian's Duel*.[94] Adding interest to the group's stay were the several street parades by Baird's Silver Cornet Band. Faranta had planned to keep the minstrels in his theater for a week and then to bring back Harry Webber and his company in a drama, *Success*, but instead he was urged to retain Baird's minstrels for the additional week.[95]

For the week of January 24 was Charles Lee's Great London Circus, which featured athletic feats on the horizontal bars, clowns, a trick pony, the man with an "iron jaw," a "serpentine wonder," a comedy routine on the invisible wire, an Egyptian juggler in an act called "Oriental Pastimes," a riding dog, an Egyptian who did stunts with fire, Roman ladders, songs, activities with a "dancing barrel" and "magic cross," and a riding monkey.[96]

Melodrama returned to Faranta's on January 31, when the George W. and William J. Thompson Troupe presented *The Gold King* and *For a Life* in a divided week of performances, as the group had done in the previous season. The heroic acting dogs, Hector and Carlo, were popular stars of the group's dramas. Next, on February 7, was the Bayse-Davis Ideal Company in a romantic Irish drama, *Inshavogue; or, The Fenian Chief of '98*, which included the incidental but appropriate songs "Wearing of the Green" and "Barn-Door Jig." This was Faranta's show until Friday, February 11, when the company appeared in *New York by Gaslight*, the attraction for the remainder of the week.

The week of February 14 was also a divided week, featuring J.H. Hunter and John M. Gilbert and their "Huntley-Gilbert Company" in *Pink Dominos*, in combination with a short farce entitled *Turn Him Out*, until February 18. *Pink*

Dominos is the comic tale of wives who test the loyalty of their husbands by sending to each one and other gentlemen an invitation to a masquerade ball and a rendezvous with an unknown lady in a pink domino. The wives each plan to appear at the masquerade as the unknown lady; but then so does one mischievous wife's housegirl, who thus appears at the ball, complicating matters, in a pink domino. *The Streets of New York* occupied the company's talent for the remainder of the week.

On February 21, Harry and Eva Webber began a week of performances with three plays from their repertoire—*Confusion, The Whippoorwill,* and *The Thunderbolt.* George W. Thompson and his company returned to the iron theater on February 28 for a week of *Rip Van Winkle,* but, on March 7, Faranta's theatrical pendulum moved in another direction with his next attraction, "The Golden Bell Excelsior Cane Brake Hoe Downs, or The Mastodon Monarchs of the Plantation from Way Back," a negro minstrel group from Greenville, Miss., that was making its first appearance away from home. Despite encouraging words about a few of the minstrels, the *Daily Picayune* of March 8 reported plainly that the show was crude and below the accepted standards of minstrelsy, but the next issue of the newspaper had kind words for Faranta, who "bounced" the minstrels after a mere two days in his theater.[97]

The team was sent home and replaced, on March 9, with a vaudeville show by John B. Brace's All Star Specialty Combination. This well-received group remained in the iron theater for the rest of the week, during which the combination held a benefit performance for the Young Pelican Mutual Benevolent Association and, at the Sunday matinee, "the champion oyster shucker of the world," Baltimore's John Membriger, undertook to shuck 100 oysters in less than five minutes before the entire audience.[98]

Faranta's show for the week of March 14 was *Black Hawks,* a romantic border drama with wild horses, Mexican burros, trained dogs, and a company headed by shooting star Arizona Joe. It was a "red hot show," said the *Daily Picayune,* attributing this to Arizona Joe's skill with the pistol and rifle, and the four-act play's free gunplay and "imaginative gore."[99] Arizona Joe and his company remained for a second successful week in the four-act play *Wild Violet,* another romantic border drama. This was followed on March 28 by *Our Boarding House,* a "Comedy in Three Meals and a Luncheon". The cast for this version of Leonard Grover's popular comedy was supplied by the Palmer Company of Comics, who performed "well enough for the price," said the *Daily Picayune.*[100] The play continued until April 3, after which Faranta closed his theater for Easter week, reopening on April 10, the Easter matinee, with Frank Tannehill, Sr., and the Stranglers of Paris Company in *The Stranglers of Paris,* from Adolphe Belot's gruesome French tale.

The story line of *The Stranglers of Paris,* which takes up all of seven acts, concerns the rivalry between Jagon and Captain Guerin, an old sea captain, for the interests of their daughters. Jagon's daughter, Mathilda, is bequeathed a large fortune; Guerin contests the will. In the company of his accomplice, Lorenzo, Jagon visits the old captain and strangles him. With this obstacle gone Mathilda is endowed with her inheritance, but the captain's daughter, Jeanne, accuses Jagon of the crime, and he and an innocent man, Blanchard, are convicted and sent to prison for life. While at sea on a convict ship, the two men escape. Lorenzo, now living under an assumed name, marries Jagon's daughter and lives with her in a splendid style until Mathilda falls in love with Jeanne's suitor. Lorenzo accuses his wife of adulterous intimacy; she, in turn, reveals her knowledge of his crime and her plans to denounce him; he then strangles her. Lorenzo is acquitted of her murder, but Jagon appears in time to implicate them both and prove Blanchard innocent and is then shot as he attempts to escape.[101]

Between April 17 and May 8, there were no performances in Faranta's Theatre. On April 18, the *Times-Democrat* announced that the iron theater was closed for the summer season—a closing that therefore left the ironclad Avenue Theatre as the only theater open in the city—but, on May 8, Harry Webber, Wright Huntington, and Percy Plunkett moved with members of the Avenue Theatre Stock Company to Faranta's establishment for a two-week engagement, appearing first in a melodrama, *The Trail of Blood*. On Thursday, May 11, Faranta hosted a large delegation from the Order of Railway Conductors, who so enjoyed the drama and so quickly spread the word of their delight that the following evening found Faranta accommodating another large delegation from the order.[102] The Avenue Theatre concluded its season with benefit performances on May 12 and 14.

For its second week in Faranta's Theatre the Star Stock Company presented *Seeing the Elephant,* a comedy about a father who goes to London to correct the marital relations between his son and daughter-in-law, but ends up consenting to anything that will bring peace to the three of them. The play's title was probably derived from a cant expression used to convey that the speaker had reached his limit in sights and disappointments, and so had "seen the elephant." The play's last performance, the last event of Faranta's 1886-1887 theatrical season, was held on May 22, coinciding with the opening of the summer resort, West End.

While Faranta made plans to leave New Orleans for a short vacation in New York, he also arranged to have balcony boxes, each containing 140 opera seats, built on both sides of the theater's stage.[103] When he left for his summer vacation, returning to New Orleans on July 24, he was accompanied by his new wife, Rose Stempel née Marshall, from Chicago. This was Faranta's third and last marriage.

For the opening of the 1887-1888 season "The crowd was there in completeness, the wide amphitheatre of 10-cent seats filled tier upon tier with throngs of the unwashed, coatless men and boys in blue jumpers, women with babies in their arms, and over in one big corner the usual black cloud of enthusiastic colored attendants."[104]

> The patrons of Faranta's mammoth and complete temple of the drama would scarcely realize where they stood, if conveyed blind folded into the center of it and they be there permitted to look about them. An entire new, more perfect, and more easily regulated electric light plant has been introduced, a new and gorgeous drop curtain pleases the eye in front, and two new dress circles on either side containing a hundred and odd seats have been added to swell the already enormous seating capacity of the house. The entire building has been renovated, repainted and burnished up and when the doors open on Saturday night next everything will certainly look as the bills say: new, bright and attractive.[105]

These were kind words from the *Mascot*, but then there was nothing in the city, said the *Daily States*, like opening night at Faranta's Theatre, where one might "catch the full inspiration of the typical New Orleans crowd, its interest, as varied as its complexion, unimpaired by the uniformity of fashion, its freedom unrestrained by aught save its native good manners, its enjoyment unchecked by fastidious demands. Its phases are more attractive than the show even when it is a good one like last night."[106]

The Signor was reported to be in excellent health after his vacation.[107] His popular house had been refreshed by a coat of yellow paint on the building's corrugated iron, taking away the look of granite, while its interior was given new paint, a new drop curtain by "Johnson & Young," the two "private" boxes for 280 or more persons, and a reserved circle for black patrons; a system of Westinghouse incandescent lights and an additional exit, on St. Ann Street, were also new.[108] Faranta again offered three basic admission prices: the new boxes cost fifty cents, the opera chairs could still be reserved for twenty-five cents, and a cane-bottom easy chair was still available for the general admission fee—ten cents—the staple fare of his theater. The main changes in his staff concerned only Ed T. Adams's new position as the theater's treasurer and Professor Wood's replacement by new musical director Professor John J. Bush, who would direct his own eight-member orchestra.[109] Fred H. Quick now began his second season as Faranta's stage manager.

Faranta selected September 17 as the date for his theater's seasonal debut, managing to open seven days behind his uptown rival, the ironclad Avenue Theatre. In Faranta's Theatre for an early week of vaudeville was the newly formed Riley & Wolf Specialty Company, in combination with the Ramirez Troupe of Spanish Troubadours. The variety program began with a comedy, *The Five Black Noses*, whose plot turned upon the comical antics of a jealous husband, and then proceeded with Richard Riley and Kittie Wolf in character sketches and topical songs, Riley's burlesque of contemporary tragedians, jig-dancing by Lillian Hamilton, two sketches—"Stage Struck" and "The Crazy Actor"—a performance by the acting bulldog Jacko, "The Forge in the Forest" by Prof. Bush's orchestra, guitar and mandolin music by the four Ramirez Spanish Troubadours, and finally *The Black Statue*, an original comedy by Richard Riley.

During a break in the show, Faranta was beckoned on stage as the new drop curtain ascended to reveal a group of men from the Young Pelican Mutual Benevolent Association and the Protector Hook and Ladder Company Number 9. The chairman of the Pelican's board of directors, J.J. Weinfurter, then stepped forward and, with a few fitting remarks, presented Faranta with a gold medal that bore the recipient's monogram and depicted a pelican feeding her young; it was a token of their gratitude for the benefit performance he had given them during the previous season. Such was opening night at Faranta's Theatre, as it inaugurated the showman's sixth season in New Orleans.[110]

Faranta's patrons continued to fill his theater for variety performances by the Riley & Wolf Specialty Company and the Ramirez Spanish Troubadours, despite the cold and the rain that attended the first few days of the new season's first week.[111] Sunday evening, September 25, was the last date of the double attraction, and by the following evening the Riley & Wolf company was on the train to St. Louis—except Richard Riley, who had to spend the night in jail. Eugene Robinson, owner and manager of Robinson's Dime Museum on Canal Street, also owned a similar museum in Memphis, Tenn., and had employed Riley to manage the distant business. All the conditions had been agreed upon and the necessary papers were signed, but the apparent harmony between them ended on Monday, as the troupe gathered at the train depot to leave New Orleans for St. Louis. Robinson, who heard that Riley planned to breach their contract, confronted Riley as the group boarded the train; with hasty words he tried to convince Riley of the folly of his decision, but was stopped short when Riley suddenly punched him in the face. The pugnacious Riley was arrested, charged with assault and battery, locked in jail, and later placed under a bond of $250.[112]

Faranta's 1887-1888 season closely resembled the preceding seasons. His second feature of the year was the Hall and Devoy Comedy Company in *Fun in a Boarding School* (a "reconstructed version of the old-time screamer," said the *Daily Picayune* of September 27), which opened on September 26 and played to crowded houses until October 3. It was replaced by the Weston Brothers Combination in *The Way of the World,* a four-act comedy-drama with musical specialties, in which a villainous clerk fastens forgery charges upon the adopted son of a prominent banker and drives him from his home, murders the banker and abducts his daughter with matrimony in mind, and then is foiled by three characters—the banker's son, an ex-tragedian, and a black servant—who rescue the damsel and bring a happy ending to all but the villain.[113] Sam Weston was cast in two roles, the servant and a professional minstrel, while Morris Weston, the star of the play, portrayed the disgraced son, an Italian fiddler, and a Swiss boy.

In the next week, beginning October 10, Daniel A. Kelly and his company presented both *The Shadow Detective; or, Leonie the Waif* and *After Seven Years; or, The Mystery of the Willows* in a divided week of drama in Faranta's Theatre. Imported from the Avenue Theatre, where Mr. Kelly and his company had presented it in the previous week, *The Shadow Detective* concerns the disappearance of a well-known lady and the detective who searches for her, dons disguises, wends his way through the Italian dens of New York City, escapes death more than once, and eventually rescues both the lady and her daughter, who was also stolen.[114] Kelly displayed his thespian talents in four roles, appearing as the Shadow Detective, an Irish policeman, an Italian, and a Yankee friend. The company's second entertainment, *After Seven Years,* was a melodramatic tale of an unsolved murder in an ancestral home, the discovery of the murderer and proof of his crime seven years later, the search for the elusive criminal, and the deserved retribution.[115]

October 17 brought several amusements by a French group, the Berland Combination, featuring Victoria Berland, who performed feats of magic in a sleeveless costume, and Monsieur E. Berland, called "the man with thirty-six heads," who exhibited the facial characteristics of a man reading his newspaper, a dude, a drunkard, Napoleon III, Rochefort, Bismarck, Victor Hugo, and the Emperor William, among many others. It also included a troupe of acrobats,

Clarence Dietrich in a club-swinging act and on the horizontal bars with gymnast George Nagle, and an opera bouffe entitled *The Audition Parlor.*[116]

This program continued until October 24, when a new company appeared in *Storm Beaten,* T.H. Glenny's dramatization of Robert Buchanan's 1881 serial *God and Man. Storm Beaten* took six short acts and a prologue to recount the solemn story of hatred between two English families, seduction and a broken promise of marriage, a journey to America on an emigrant ship bearing the guiltless lover and a revenge-seeking brother, reciprocal attempts at murder, castaways on an icy Arctic island, repentance and compassion, and a return to England for atonement, marriage, and renewed love.[117]

On the last day of October, and for the first week of November, Faranta gave his patrons *The World,* a drama about mistaken identities, a villain in need of another's fortune, and much spectacular scenery. The five-act play was presented by the J.Z. Little Combination and starred J.Z. Little as sailor Jack Rover, unknowingly Rose Elliston's brother, Harry Elliston, who saves his sister and her friend from being drowned by villain Deveraux Powers and his ally. Powers is Rose's guardian; he wants his ward's fortune and enlists the aid of a third villain to prevent sister and brother from learning the fact of their relationship. The villains sink the ship they are all traveling on, but the hero saves the girls again by casting them off in a raft he constructed from the ship's ladder. The three are rescued, but Powers kidnaps Rose and incarcerates Jack in a lunatic asylum, where he remains until the final act, in which all is explained and settled.[118]

The press was informed that ten thousand dollars had been spent on scenic and mechanical effects for this production of *The World,* which, according to the manager of Little's troupe, was the original version of the play and was thus different in many ways from other versions offered in New Orleans.[119] Notable among the play's scenic effects was the trio's hasty retreat on the raft as the ship sinks on stage. As this raft scene was depicted on Faranta's advertising posters, however, "There are two horrid women represented as being cast away in company with the hero and more horrid specimens of the female sex would be hard to find." The *Lantern,* which expressed this judgment, considered the pictures to be "revolting to the intelligent mind" and recommended that they be torn down.[120] Neither the posters nor the *Lantern* is known to have affected the attendance at Faranta's attraction.

Faranta's theatrical entertainment for the week of November 7 was actress and vocalist Minnie Sartelle and a specialty company in *A Plum Pudding.* Proclaimed the handbills for this musical-comedy: "This is called 'A Plum Pudding' for the simple reason that the 'Plum Pudding' is a luxury and is supposed to contain things that are palatable and pleasing to the senses. This play is not a comic opera, neither is it a melodrama, and it cannot be called a tragedy, but it is a jolly concoction of mirth, music, pretty songs, choruses and seasonable novelties, free from all objectionable features."[121]

It was followed on November 14 by an elaborate production of *Around the World in Eighty Days,* Jules Verne's tale of Englishman Phileas Fogg and the wager he accepts to journey the world in eighty days. Under the management of William J. Fleming, and led by the star of the seven-act play, James P. Fleming, the company behind this production, rendered spectacular by its scenery and nine tableaux, was composed of forty persons, including the fifteen principal members of the cast and the "Gigantic Array" of ladies who appeared in the play's grand Amazonian marches. The *Daily Picayune* discovered this presentation to be "the grandest that has been seen in Faranta's Theater."[122]

Also in November was "The King Bees," or the Richards and Pringle Georgia Minstrels, led by Billy Kersands. Kersands had frequented Faranta's show before. He was a very large man who possessed an uncommonly large mouth, and he used both attributes to his advantage in his minstrel acts. Things occasionally went into his mouth when he appeared on stage; the earliest of these known props were billiard balls, but later in his career he would put five large soda crackers and a coffee cup and saucer in his mouth as he danced.[123] Kersands and his company began their performances on November 21 and heralded the occasion with a street parade by the group's two cornet bands that helped to lure patrons into the crowded theater for the negro minstrel show. Featured on stage were J.A. Watts in female impersonations, George Jackson ("the somewhat different comedian") in an eccentric stump speech, a vocal quartet, comedy by the "Grotesque Four," which included Kersands and Jackson, and, in conclusion, a sketch by W.H. Fletcher, "The Lawn Party," in which most of the minstrel troupe appeared.[124] For this week's engagement Faranta reserved one side of the auditorium for his many black patrons.[125]

The minstrels were replaced on November 28 by a company headed by E.T. Stetson, who portrayed twin brothers in *Neck and Neck*, the story of a man who is unjustly accused or murder and sentenced to death on the strength of curious (but apparently conclusive) circumstantial evidence, and then is hanged, cut from the gallows before the deadly instant, and hunted by police until he regains his freedom. Those attending *Neck and Neck* were treated to a warm enclosure, the result of several new heaters that Faranta had placed in his iron theater so that his patrons were protected from the cold weather outside.[126]

In December Faranta offered three distinct entertainments: melodrama, traditional drama, and educated horses. For the week of December 5, the Nellie Boyd Dramatic Company presented *Passion's Slave*, John A. Stevens's violent story of an impetuous youth and a villain, forgery and murder, misplaced blame and imprisonment, and the justice served upon the evildoer. Included in the program was music by the Cyclone Quartette. Engaged for the week of December 12 was tragedian George C. Miln, who, assisted by his company, performed in five plays from his repertoire—*Richard III* (Dec. 12 and 13; Dec. 18, evening), *Hamlet* (Dec. 14; Dec. 18, matinee), *Othello* (Dec. 15, matinee), *Damon and Pythias* (Dec. 15, evening; Dec. 16), and *Richelieu* (Dec. 17).

The pendulum of taste again moved to the circus on December 19, when Faranta's Theatre featured Professor T. K. Burk's "Equescurriculum," a troupe of educated ponies, donkeys, and Arabian-Mexican horses in exhibitions of their education and intellectual powers, which included the ability to distinguish colors and to tell the days of the week. Also involved was a skit in which a wise donkey officiated as judge in a trial, in addition to innumerable equine stage marches. Assisting the creatures was a group of humans who performed songs, dances, and acrobatics between the acts. Singled out for mention by the press were the Goldberg children (Rebecca, Jessie, Addie, and Sol), a musical specialty group from New Orleans.[127]

At each matinee, held daily for this engagement, the children in the audience were invited to ride Professor Burk's Shetland ponies. Faranta also issued an invitation to all newsboys in the city to attend a performance of the "Equescurriculum" on December 21, on which date, headed by "the Newsboys' Band," about 100 newsboys paraded to the theater, attended the circus, and afterwards serenaded their host, Signor Faranta.[128] The "Equescurriculum" played through Christmas and, because of its popularity, was re-engaged for the week of December 26. On the evening of December 27, several hundred neatly attired boys from the Asylum for Destitute Orphan Boys visited Faranta's Theatre as guests of the proprietor and were there treated to candy, Professor Burk's "Equescurriculum," and rides on his ponies.[129]

Shield's Great Eastern Novelty and Specialty Company was Faranta's next attraction, opening on January 2, 1888, and remaining for the first week of the new year in a variety show that offered such specialty features as bicycle and "skatorial" acts, acrobatic and gymnastic exercises, and select ballet dances. In Faranta's Theatre for the week of January 9 was Benjamin Maginley and his company in W.J. Florence's musical drama and Irish romance, *Inshavogue*, Faranta's amusement in February of the previous season. It retold the story of an exiled patriot, Brian Maguire, called "Inshavogue," the name of his village, by the covert gang he led during the Irish Rising of 1798, who returns to his home to search for his wife and child, but there must struggle with a villain who extorts his aid in marrying an Irish lord's daughter, unknowingly the daughter of Inshavogue.[130] This new production was enlivened by the music of a singing quartet, a duo performance of old Irish ballads, and jig and reel dances. This was followed on January 16 by Lizzie Kendall and the Erwood Combination in the comedy-drama *Only a Country Girl*, about a city boy who marries a country girl against his father's wishes.

At this time Faranta was also making certain California real estate available to any purchaser of a reserved ticket. Mentioned by the *Times-Democrat* on January 18, but noted officially in his theatrical advertisements only during the week of January 22, what was at stake was "A TOWN LOT (25 x 95 feet), in California, given away with every reserved ticket." The lots could be secured by filling out the order blank that accompanied each 25-cent and 50-cent theater ticket, but how much land in California was so dispensed by the showman is not known.

On Monday, January 23, the Lottie E. Church Combination presented *Unknown*, which Sargeant Aborn's Company and its star, Lottie Church, had staged in the theater in 1886. Miss Church and her new company appeared in the melodrama through Wednesday of that week, which performance was a benefit for the American Benevolent & Mutual Aid Association. They then presented a comedy-drama, *Pa-Pe-To*, about the romantic adventures of a young lady, the detective who must search for her, and their inevitable union in marriage, for the week's remainder. The Thorne and Carleton Big Specialty Company, in combination with Professor Barthold's "Celebrated Liliputian Wonders" ("Ten Funny Little Folks"), was Faranta's feature for the week of January 30. This

95

variety show was followed on February 6 by the Leonzo Brothers, their New York dramatic company, and their four acting dogs (Tiger, Lion, Panther, and Spot, a leaping dog) in four "sensational" dramas: *May's Devotion, The Dog Spy, Brother Against Brother,* and finally *Delmonte,* a Western with horse thieves, Indians, hunters, outlaws, a railroad scene, a Mexican duel, and fights with a broadsword and a Bowie knife.[131] The Leonzo Brothers were held over for a second week, beginning February 13, in three dramas—*The Planter's Child,* a play of the South and far West, another performance of *May's Devotion,* and *Back From the Dead.*

On February 20, Frank I. Frayne and his company presented *Mardo, the Hunter,* a three-act play that took its audience from California to St. Petersburg and then to Siberia, and ensured an enthusiastic audience by including in its cast a large number of animals: four dogs, a goat, two bears, two hyenas, a thoroughbred horse, and Ingersol, "The Largest Lion in Captivity." In addition to the play's many excitements, the plot requires that a group of these animals attack Mardo, who is in the Czar's imperial museum to retrieve an important state document; the hunter escapes and then slays a nihilist intent upon his destruction, after which the lion takes certain culinary liberties with the corpse and literally wipes up the stage with it.[132] Mr. Frayne and his company remained for a second week with *Si Slocum,* a five-act comedy-drama about the ups and downs of a man's life as he moves from selling cheap milk in Philadelphia to the ownership of his murdered mother's oil farm, during which there was a benefit performance, on March 2, for the Southern Rifle Club, and a visit, on March 4, by the Volunteer Fire Association of Philadelphia and their local hosts, the Irad Ferry Company No. 12.[133]

The Magic Talisman brought another series of popular performances for the week of March 5. Again under the aegis of the Miaco Brothers, the pantomime ("Like 'Humpty Dumpty,' with new names and new business," said the *Daily Picayune* of February 28) was produced with the same elaborate scenery and mechanical effects used during its successful run at the Avenue Theatre, in the week preceding its move downtown to Faranta's Theatre. Incidental to the play were a number of specialties, including vocal selections, a skating act, dancing, a rope-skipping routine, "marionette singing," and acrobatics. On March 9, one of these performances was designated another benefit for the Young Pelican Mutual Benevolent Association, with the monies derived from this source being used for the relief of the association and for aid to Charity Hospital's ambulance fund.[134]

Following *The Magic Talisman* was a theatrical excursion into labor factions by the Howe and Hummel Combination, which opened its attraction, *A Knight of Labor; or, The Master Workman's Vow,* on March 12. As it turned out, the "master workman's vow" was to kill the son of a capitalist who had run away with his daughter, and in theatrical circles Faranta's selection of talent and vehicle was the talk of the town. The *Mascot* summarized the effort in this way:

> A bum actor or ex-actor rather, named Howe, having the good fortune to lasso an "Angel" in the person of Larry Plant of the Eden Theatre, Royal Street, collected together all the unemployed talent, both dramatic and wine-room, in town and cast them in a stupid sort of dramatic carpentering called

"A Knight of Labor, or the Master Workman's Vow," expecting to draw all the knights of labor and ladies, and their uncles, aunts and cousins, to see the play. The title was catchy enough, but the show didn't catch on worth a cent, and no wonder. Probably never before was there such a gang of imbecile sticks and barnstormers gathered together on one stage; and probably never was there such a dull, listless play attempted to be put on before.[135]

The *Daily Picayune* discovered that the "play is rot and the company bad," and apparently so did Faranta's patrons.[136] After two days of scant attendance, the showman dismissed the Howe and Hummel Combination and completed the week with a hastily assembled "Vaudeville Variety Combination."

Similar variety was continued for the following two weeks with Professor Zera Semon's Novelty Combination. The Professor himself opened the show with magic and illusions, and was then followed by vaudeville, female impersonator and vocalist Harry Pierson, Hungarian juggler Karoly Ordez, ventriloquism by the Professor, and a closing performance by the Royal Marionettes, after which two hundred "Useful and Beautiful Presents" were awarded to lucky holders of selected admission tickets, a feature that was repeated every day for the two weeks of the variety show.[137]

On the day after Easter, April 2, the Dan Morris Sullivan Mirror of Ireland Comedy Company began a week of performances in Faranta's Theatre with a benefit show for the Patrick Mealy Fund, established after the shooting death, on January 1, 1888, of the labor leader and, since 1878, administrator of police and public buildings in New Orleans. The show was a romantic comedy, *Kitty's Luck; or, Sight-Seeing in the Emerald Isles*, a nostalgic play that featured special Irish dances and songs, and eighty panoramic pictures of representative scenes of Ireland.[138] Mr. Sullivan and his company gave one more benefit performance of the play on Friday, April 6, their last being for the Jackson Assembly 8444 of the Knights of Labor.

The play featuring the comical but mischievous urchin, *Peck's Bad Boy*, came to Faranta's show on April 9 with a small cast of comedians. It remained for a week in the theater, after which, according to Faranta's advertisements, the Lester and Allen "Early Birds" Combination was to begin a week's engagement in Faranta's Theatre. While *Peck's Bad Boy* played at Faranta's, the Lester and Allen troupe was putting on its show at the Avenue Theatre, and this gave the *Mascot* a chance to call it "the vilest show of the season."[139] The *Daily Picayune* described the combination's program as "a burlesque and variety performance of a low order, replete with vulgarity at times bordering on indecency."[140] The Early Birds, "eighteen Lady Artists from all parts of the world," never appeared on Faranta's stage; the showman canceled his contracts with the group and, by April 12, had dropped all references to them, hastily endeavoring to fill the resulting gap in his season's program with other attractions. Faranta announced the Grizzly Adams Combination instead, but the name of the group was dropped from his last advertisement of *Peck's Bad Boy*, on April 15, and was replaced by that of Miss Mattie Goodrich and her combination. Neither company appeared, and between April 16 and May 26 there was no theatrical activity on Faranta's stage.

On May 26, the California Minstrels and the Electric Brass Band, two groups composed chiefly of New Orleans talent, began a week's engagement in Faranta's Theatre, which was now the only theater still open in the city. With the comfort of his patrons in mind Faranta cooled his building by opening the ventilators and by dampening the floor before each performance.[141] The entire minstrel company of twenty-two performers—the seven-member band, six end men in black face, and nine vocalists and comedians dressed in English court costumes and white tie wigs—included in its program an introductory overture by the band, a schedule of eight songs, a sketch called "Sim Dimsey's Visit," topical songs, a contortion act entitled "The Bad Boy and the Frog," another contortion act, quartet dancing, and "A Dark Deed," a comic sketch.[142] The minstrel show was not continued in the following week, and this concluded Faranta's 1887-1888 season, permitting the theater to be cleaned, repaired, and otherwise renewed for its next season. The showman remained in the city for the summer, a decision no doubt resting in large part on the wishes of his new wife and the needs of their five-month-old son, Frederick William Stempel, Jr., their only child, who was born to the couple on December 14, 1887.

CHAPTER V

Faranta in 1890.
Photograph by Stevens Art Studio, Chicago, Illinois.
Courtesy Robert C. Stempel.

U naware of the devastation that would soon befall his theater, Signor Faranta inaugurated the new season with a special invitational tour of the theater for representatives of the local press and a few distinguished guests and friends.[1] This informal gathering took place on Friday, September 14, 1888, as the genial proprietor and showman greeted his guests and escorted them into the theater's barroom, where a meal had been prepared for them. After dining, the group was led into the auditorium for a performance of the Weston Brothers Combination in *The Way of the World*, which the troupe had brought to Faranta's in October of the previous season, and a view of the theater's redecorated interior. New carpet and matting were laid in the hallway. Newly placed in the parquet section were 340 opera chairs; the same number of opera chairs had been arranged in the orchestra section, where formerly were rows of cane-bottom armchairs, and new armchairs now filled the boxes situated on either side of the stage.[2] Also new were the Lungreen Regenerative Gas Lights that Faranta had installed during the summer, and it was reported that Faranta's Theatre was the first theatrical establishment to use this kind of light bulb, which was said to have the lighting power of one hundred candles.[3]

The visiting group also met members of Faranta's principal staff, which now comprised the following: Frederick H. Quick, beginning his third season as the theater's stage manager; Ed T. Adams, in his second season as treasurer; Ben Stempel, chief ticket seller for a fourth season; William H. Connelly, doorkeeper for his fourth season; Albert O. Hebrard, stage carpenter for a second season; John Loubat, chief usher, and Alex Mobery, house officer.[4] Edward Stempel, Faranta's youngest brother, had leased the large barroom (also called a café) and would operate it in conjunction with their brother Gus Stempel, who had charge of the smaller barroom, and with Jules Turnege, Willie Smith, and Ed Fox.[5]

Faranta opened the iron theater to the public on September 15, his design being to keep his reputation in New Orleans as the first to open and the last to close. With his new ten-member orchestra and band, under the fresh direction of Professor George Gauweiler,[6] the soft lights of his new gas bulbs, and Morris and Sam Weston again in multiple roles in the musical-comedy-drama *The Way of the World*, Faranta embarked on another successful season. If business continued as well as the first week, remarked the *Daily States*, the showman would be able to "live in a brownstone front next year."[7] Faranta's Theatre now exacted four entrance fees: 10 cents, the cost of general admission, and 25, 35, and 50 cents for the three separate reserved accommodations, determined primarily by their distance from the stage. The box office remained open from 9 a.m. to 4 p.m. for the purchase of reserved seats.

The theater's second presentation incorporated two amusements: the J.H. Shields Circus and the Australian Novelty Show, in a combined program that began on September 24 and continued for two weeks. This show included gymnastic feats, comedy, clown songs, a club-swinging routine, a riding dog, a song and dance, performances on the triple wire and slack wire, songs, trick ponies, a solo performance with "flying rings," a riding monkey, and a mass tumbling exhibition.[8]

On the Friday of the combination's first week, prompted by the growing number of yellow fever sufferers in Jacksonville, Fla., Shields and Faranta joined forces to present a benefit show under the auspices of the local Order of Elks, which would turn over the entire income, without any diversion of funds, to the Red Cross.[9] This benefit included many amateurs who donated their time and amateur talent to the prosperous show, portions of which were so funny, claimed the *Daily States* (on the strength of testimony by "the theatre people"), that one of the spectators "laughed so much he lost his false teeth," which were held at the theater for redemption.[10]

No one, however, was laughing at the high incidence of yellow fever in New Orleans, whose great yellow fever epidemic of 1878 killed 4,000 inhabitants, with lesser epidemics appearing in 1879, 1880, 1883, and 1897. Yellow fever in New Orleans would continue to sicken and kill residents and visitors until the great fever campaign and mosquito war of 1905. A few days after the benefit show, Faranta was given a message from the Goodyear, Cook & Dillon Refined Minstrels informing him that, because of the many shotgun quarantines in New Orleans, the group could not meet its contract with his theater. In his reply Faranta told them that there was no cause for alarm and that he nevertheless expected them to honor their commitment. Disarmed, if not reassured, the minstrels promised to appear in the city within three weeks.[11]

After two weeks of the popular circus, *The Pavements of Paris* was Faranta's show for the week of October 8. Set first in a village in Lorraine and then in Paris, *The Pavements of Paris* concerns the daughter of a wealthy aristocrat, her banishment to a peasant village during the Franco-German War, and the father's terminal illness, which prompts the remorseful man to name Marie, his daughter, the heir to his 3 million francs. She is wounded by German troops, but is rescued and cared for by a French drummer boy. Many years later, separated from her village and knowing nothing of her inheritance, Marie, now a young woman, arrives in Paris in search of a livelihood. She begins work in a questionable tavern, but flees its wicked activities and is taken in by a wealthy market stallkeeper, whose son, an officer in the municipal guard, recognizes her as the girl he rescued in Lorraine and falls in love with her. A reward for proof of Marie's death has been posted by the play's villain; she escapes an assassination attempt and the lovers find her mother, who consents to their marriage and grants Marie her inheritance. The Howard Dramatic Company, including star Lizzie Hunt, brought the talent for this production.[12]

Monday, October 15, was the initial performance of the McCabe & Young Refined Colored Operatic Minstrels, composed of thirty negro artists with their own brass band and orchestra. The group was warmly received during its week in Faranta's Theatre. On October 22, the New Orleans Juvenile Opera Company, under the direction of Professor W.T. Francis, began a series of performances in these light operas: *La Mascotte*, the Gilbert and Sullivan operetta *The Mikado*, *Giroflé-Girofla*, and the comic opera *Fatinitza*. Said the *Mascot* of opera's success in Faranta's Theatre: "The New Orleans Juvenile Opera Company filled in the week at Faranta's Theatre, and produced their repertoire of Operas to small business. Opera Companies, especially juvenile ones, are not 'the cheese' for Faranta's even when there is no disorganization or disaffection among them."[13]

Making good their word to appear in New Orleans, the Goodyear, Cook & Dillon Refined Minstrels arrived for their scheduled opening in the iron theater on October 29—without their baggage. When reminded that Edwin Booth and Joe Wheelock had once been forced to give a performance in their street clothes, the minstrels' manager said: "But we are not Edwin Booth nor Joe Wheelock. We are as strangers, with a new organization, and want to give the very best minstrel performance New Orleans has seen. We cannot do this without our baggage. We must have our tools to work with."[14] The baggage arrived on Tuesday, October 30, permitting the burnt-cork minstrels to give their initial performance on that evening.

The troupe closed its successful week on November 4, to be followed by the Grizzly Adams Combination, a group that was promised but never delivered in April of the previous season. Unfortunately, Faranta found that the group was mediocre and did not offer a "good, clean show"; the showman canceled the contract between them, remarking to the *Daily Picayune* that "a rotten show leaves a bad taste in the mouth of a theatre, and he will not have one there."[15] The theater was vacant until Saturday and Sunday, November 10 and 11, when he brought back the Juvenile Opera Company for a very brief engagement.

Majilton's Phenomenal Wonders arrived in New Orleans on November 12, and on that date began a week of performances in Faranta's Theatre. The group had been conceived and nurtured by Henry J. Majilton, who began his career as a tumbler in a one-ring circus in 1848, remaining with this circus for two years (during which time he was credited with having invented the three-pole tent), and then performed from 1850 to 1858 with the floating circus of Spalding and Rogers, becoming well known for his simian role as "Jocko, the Brazilian Ape."[16] After a tour of Europe, his career was ended when he was paralyzed in a fall during his trapeze act in London in 1861.

Majilton's latter-day organization, composed of twenty-five members, no one of whom was a Majilton, brought to Faranta's Theatre a program that included gymnastic exercises, activities on the trapeze, a routine on the Japanese swing perch, slack wire juggling, eccentric Dutch and German comedian W.S. Wheeler, songs and dances, sketch artistry, Irish character performers, pyramid artistry, aerialists George Dunbar and Joe Desmond in a flying act that terminated in a "leap for life," and a comic sketch, "The New Mayor," which closed the program.[17]

For the week of November 19 was the Foreman-Morton Combination in *The Hermit,* a four-act drama dealing marginally with the Revolutionary War and more centrally with the efforts of the commander of British forces in the Mohawk river valley to obtain the property to which his niece and ward is heir. To further his scheme, the commander procures the will and arranges his niece's demise, which is prevented by a Yankee, after which the British are defeated by colonial troops and the villainous uncle is killed by an outcast known as "The Hermit" (portrayed by Charles R. Foreman). During the course of the play were such specialty acts as a rope-skipping dance and the popular spade dance, an act done with a hard wooden prop shaped like a spade. Typically the dancer would grasp the handle with both hands, stand on the spade portion, and then hop rhythmically—as if on a pogo stick—to the accompaniment of music, often completing this ritual by hopping over various objects. The popularity of the company led to a second engagement in Faranta's Theatre, beginning November 26 with a double bill: a one-act farce entitled *The Baron's Double* and a three-act drama, *The Cuban Spy*, whose plot requires that the hero save an American girl from a shipwreck, after which they float to shore to be captured by hostile Spaniards, one of whom—the villain—has designs to marry the girl; after her repeated refusals, the villain attempts to take her life in revenge, but she is again saved from such an end.[18]

An elaborate production of Joseph Bradford's play *One of the Finest*, presented by Edward J. Hasson's New York company, moved into the iron theater on December 3. This production was said to have cost over ten thousand dollars, including the cost of the complicated scenery, mechanical devices, and "the largest surface of Real Water ever attempted on any stage," an enormous water tank (60 feet long, 12 feet wide, and 4 feet deep) that, when filled, was a reasonable facsimile of the North River at dusk, beyond which could be seen steamboats moving over the moonlit water and against the city lights of New York.[19] It is in this scene that "one of the finest," policeman John Mishler, who later captures the villain of the play, rescues a young boy in peril over his inheritance. *One of the Finest* included a cast of nineteen, not including bootblacks, sailors, newsboys, policemen, longshoremen, and inmates of a lunatic asylum. The show was enlivened by the vocal efforts of the Sacramento Quartette and the "Revels of the Wharf Rats" and a special presentation at the end of the Thursday evening performance, when House Officer Alex Mobery, who had been policing Faranta's Theatre for "a long time," was presented with a gold-headed cane by Faranta's ushers and doorkeeper, W.H. Connelly, with Treasurer Ed Adams making the presentation speech.[20]

The Hasson company left New Orleans on December 10, but the circumstances were unusual. As the company was about to depart on the Mississippi Valley Railroad, having been put on the train by Mr. Hasson, who waited on the platform for the train to leave, the manager was accosted by James Tierney, a theatrical baggage handler, who demanded nineteen dollars and insisted that Hasson had engaged him to haul the scenery and baggage from the theater to the train depot, but had not paid him. The train began to move; Hasson leaped aboard. Quickly Tierney found a policeman ("one of the finest"), who boarded the moving train, arrested Hasson, and removed him from his company until the legal issue was resolved.[21]

The Ranch King Company, under the aegis of Joseph D. Clifton, author of *The Ranch King*, opened in this border drama on December 10. Presented earlier in Faranta's tent show in August of 1884, the returning play's plot was woven from these elements: Hastings, a banker accused of forgery, flees to the mountains with his daughter Allie; in pursuit is a gambler, Wolfred Mannering, who knows the man's secret and demands Allie's hand in marriage. The Ranch King and his adopted daughter, a waif named Pug, intervene and together prevent the wedding. The gambler then claims Pug as his child, but this matter is decided by a simple card game.[22] The play included two Arabian horses and a "Semi-Human Acting Dog," and it was well received by audience and critic alike during its week in the iron theater.

In Faranta's on Monday, December 17, was *Braving the World,* a four-act melodrama. John Merriemay, a rich Australian miner, is murdered by shrewd schemer Mark Renshaw, who escapes Australia for New York and is followed by the murdered man's wife and an older daughter by a former marriage. Through the medium of forged papers, Renshaw becomes the bogus guardian of the older daughter, Sprightly, who finally brings the villain to justice—but not before the climax, in the third act, wherein Sprightly (played by Nellie Irving) escapes from a den of thieves by swinging from a second-story window on a derrick rope.[23] Nellie Irving, Harry Jackson, and their company presented *Braving the World* for the entire week, moving aside on December 24, Christmas Eve, for the McCabe & Young Operatic Minstrels, who returned to Faranta's with thirty minstrels and a brass band and orchestra, and distributed "thousands of presents" to children attending the Christmas matinee, also hosting a group of orphans during their week of minstrelsy.[24]

On December 31, Alfred F. Miaco and his company returned to Faranta's stage with a week of *The Magic Talisman*, the pantomime and loose rendition of *Humpty Dumpty*. During this production, available in the Avenue Theatre in the previous week, the Signor was the host to a delegation of children from the Protestant Orphans' Home. Said the institution's secretary, Mrs. M.L. Middlemiss, in her reply to Faranta's invitation:

> Your kind invitation for the inmates of the home to attend a performance of the 'Magic Talisman' on Jan. 3 is received and very thankfully accepted by the managers for the children and inmates of this institution, who will no doubt greatly enjoy a treat so rarely tendered to them. Please accept the thanks of the ladies for your generous thought of the orphan, to whose pleasure you are thus contributing, and which doubtless will prove a reward to you of itself.[25]

Of course, no one involved, neither Faranta nor the orphans, could have known that this was the last such event for the iron theater.

On January 7, 1889, comedian William McCready began appearing as Sim Lazarus in Henry Pettit's melodrama *The Black Flag*, which remained on Faranta's stage for a week. McCready's company portrayed the main characters in the play, which told a story of greed, murder, and false imprisonment. The hero of the story is Harry, the free and easy stepson of Owen Glyndon, a rich merchant who favors his only direct heir, Jack, a villain and schemer who is so desperate for money, and is so desirous of Naomi Blanchard, who is also the object of Harry's devotion, that he devises a plan to get both. Jack disguises himself as Harry and enters the merchant's bedroom and murders him. Naomi, who saw a figure wearing Harry's clothes enter Owen Glyndon's bedroom, testifies against Harry, who is convicted of murder and sent to prison, where he meets, among other curious characters, Hebrew schemer Sim Lazarus (whose "peezness ees svindling") and Ned, a street Arab, who helps him to escape. A black flag is hoisted to alert officials of an escape from prison, but Harry is given enough time to fix the murder on the real assassin, who is convicted and given the penalty. Naomi's sympathy for Harry becomes love, and they are married.[26] Additional features of the play included the attractive stage scenery and May DeLano's part as Naomi, whose song "Catcher in the Rye" won the actress several encores.[27]

On January 14, Aiden Benedict and his company began appearing in Dumas's *Monte Cristo*, in which Mr. Benedict portrayed Edmond Dantes, Number 17,

Abbe Busoni, Solomon Von Gripp, and the Count of Monte Cristo.[28] Harry Amlar and his company followed Benedict's group on January 21 with *A Living Lie*, the story of an innocent girl (played by Ella Moore) trapped in a mock marriage to a villain; she falls under the protection of a noble lover (played by Harry Amlar), who is forced to disguise himself as a negro at one moment and as an Irishman at another, but it delighted the audiences, as did the company's specialties. Mr. Amlar's company was kept for a second week in the theater, beginning January 28, in *Counterfeit*, a comedy and detective drama, during which, on February 1, Faranta gave a benefit performance for the Benevolent Association, Sons of Louisiana.

The theatrical company disbanded after this engagement, expecting to re-group in New York, and so moved aside, on February 4, for Theo. Hamilton's company, which had just completed *Dr. Jekyll and Mr. Hyde* in the Avenue Theatre. On Faranta's stage Mr. Hamilton and his company presented the widely known *Ten Nights in a Barroom*, a lachrymose temperance tale in which Hamilton gave a realistic performance as the drunken father and Little Minerva Adams (of the New Orleans Juvenile Opera Company) gave an effectively pathetic performance as the young daughter, whose song "Father, dear Father, come home" brought her repeated encores, before a thrown bottle kills her, sobers her father, and changes his life completely.[29] On the last night of the company's engagement a single presentation of *Dr. Jekyll and Mr. Hyde* was given instead.

During the week of February 11, soubrette Addie Phillips and the two "Eccentric Comedians" Frank Burt and Harry Hamilton appeared in a series of performances of a comedy-drama entitled *Just in Time*. Frank Burt was given two characters, and the rest of the ten-member cast each appeared as a character in the play, noted for its scenery and mechanical effects, including a leap for life into a whirlpool (a tank of water) beside a spectacular drawbridge scene. For this attraction the Southern Rifle Club was given another benefit performance, on February 5.

On February 18, Elliot's Jolly Voyagers opened a week of vehicular variety in Faranta's Theatre. Joined by their double band and orchestra, the Elliots, a family of unicyclists and bicyclists, presented their 25-member combination in such diverse amusements as: performances by Maud and Hazel Earl, who exercised difficult feats on the trapeze; unicycling; the Elliots (Kitty, Tom, Jim, and Little Dot) in their bicycle tournament on wheels, during which Tom rode on a table revolving at 500 revolutions per minute; Kate Elliot in rapid costume changes for her dances of various nations; and Toney Grice and Luie Conrad as jugglers, hat spinners, hat throwers, and finally as clowns.[30]

The entertainment for the week of February 25 was *Uncle Tom's Cabin*, presented by the Boston Ideal Company, which enlivened the play with the jubilee songs of a quartet and included two bloodhounds and a donkey in the cast. On February 28, Faranta rendered one of these performances a benefit for Algiers's Crescent Lodge No. 3, Knights of Pythias, and, on March 4, the entertainment was moved aside for a carnival attraction by another combination of shows: the McBride and Bryant Great Eastern Specialty Show and the Muldoon Picnic Company in songs, dances, specialty acts, and a play that gained notoriety for its daring humor and its approach to religion as theatrical material—the popular comedy *Muldoon's Picnic*, in which Muldoon and another character, both drunk at the time, beat up a Presbyterian minister, a foolish deed that angers the local Presbyterian ministers into arranging Muldoon's "picnic," where the outrage is avenged in a free-for-all and slug-fest that concludes the comedy. Minerva Adams, the juvenile opera singer, and a donkey were also featured in the play. Although the songs, dances, and play were well received, neither of the combined companies was able to draw a large audience, but it was suggested that this was the result of the many counterattractions available in the uptown district of the city.[31] Because attendance continued to be poor, Faranta set aside March 8 as another benefit performance, again for the Benevolent Association, Sons of Louisiana. It would never take place.

Shortly before midnight on the evening of Ash Wednesday, March 6, the showman retired to his new residence at No. 92 (now 822) St. Peter Street. Early in the next morning he was awakened by "calls of the members of his household, crying out to rise speedily and prepare for the dire news, the theatre was burning."[32] Faranta put on clothes and rushed to his theater, but on reaching the corner of St. Peter and Bourbon he saw immediately the extent of his misfortune—within a few yards from him was a sheet of flame devouring his ironclad theater. According to a report to the press, he "felt deathly sick; a choking sensation gripped him at the throat; a nauseating feeling pervaded his whole system, and his eyes welled up with bitter tears, drawn from his very heart, at the realization of the calamity that had befallen him."[33]

It was 4:30 in the morning when private watchman Charles Fenar first discovered the flames in the theater's dressing rooms on St. Ann Street. He hurried to the barroom on Bourbon to alert William H. Connelly, who slept on a cot there every night. Connelly rushed to the Third Precinct Station to give a verbal alarm while Fenar tried to manipulate one of the Babcock chemical fire extinguishers located in the main barroom. Before Fenar could operate the machine, which effectively required more than two hands, the flames had advanced upon him and he was compelled to abandon his impromptu post. By this time two alarms had been sent simultaneously from different fireboxes, from Jackson Square and from the corner of Toulouse and Burgundy, confusing the operator and delaying the dispatch of the fire department to the correct address. When the firemen did arrive, the entire theater was aflame and the facades of several structures facing the theater were on fire. Judging that the theater could not be saved, Chief Thomas O'Connor directed his men to attend to the nearby buildings. The roof of the motherhouse and novitiate of the Sisters of the Holy Family Convent, separated from Faranta's Theatre by a narrow alley, was burning, but that fire was speedily extinguished. By 5:30 all the fires were under control, the structures adjoining the theater were saved, but Faranta's iron theater was destroyed.[34]

Faranta pushed his way through the crowd to gaze at the ruins of his theater. The protective sheets of corrugated iron had bent under the high heat, and had fallen from their wooden supports and melted; the whole edifice had been consumed within the span of an hour. This catastrophe was the result, it was guessed, of a carelessly discarded cigarette.

Because he had so little insurance, Faranta's loss was heavy.[35] Everything was gone. The nine thousand dollars he had invested in insuring the building itself could not cover its rebuilding, and it could not, of course, cover the loss of furniture, scenery, mechanical devices, costumes, theatrical properties, music, the orchestra's musical instruments, valued at $250, the band's uniforms, a policeman's uniform, Faranta's popular red advertising bandwagon, a tent with furnishings and accessories, two extra wagons, ten sets of fine harness, circus-riding equipment valued at $350, over $1,500 in magic apparatus, fine furniture valued at $2,000, and the ornate bar counter and shelving in the main barroom.[36]

The performers of the Muldoon Picnic Company lost every particle of their baggage, which contained their costumes and property, and Faranta's brothers lost the soda water stand, the cake and fruit booths, and all of the stock in the two barrooms; gone also were the three Babcock fire extinguishers (a loss of $950) and twenty-seven fire buckets—equipment in which Faranta regretted having put his confidence.[37] Faranta had just recently renewed his lease with Mary Roberts for an additional five years, and had paid $462.25 to the State of Louisiana for his annual theatrical license, planning to pay (on the day of the disaster) $500 for his city license.[38]

"You can tell the people," Faranta told a *Daily States* reporter, "that they will soon see Faranta's show again. Whether I'll clear the site of the debris and rig up tents provisionally, or whether I'll pitch my canvas in some other locality, I do not know, but one thing is sure, Faranta will remain with the good people of this city among whom he has cast his lot, and who have helped him so substantially and generously in his venture—I am not prepared to say, yet if I will rebuild. I have not quite made up my mind to erect another theatre on the same spot, or seek another locality. You will hear from me ere long, when I will be more composed."[39]

Faranta's reconstruction began immediately. Within eleven days after the fire the debris had been removed from the site, and a large pavilion fitted with a bright electric light had been erected to cover his planned attractions.[40] His reopening on March 18 drew a large audience for the following performances (available for an admission fee of 10 cents) by the Shields Circus: tumbling, comic songs by clown Charles Sherman, Professor White with his performing monkeys, riding goats, trained dogs, and trick pony; Cappola, "the boneless wonder," activities on Spanish rings and the horizontal bars, a Mexican ladder act, an educated donkey, a Zouave drill, a monkey on a tightrope, see-saw ponies, hurdling, balancing, acrobatics, and Molestomo "in his wonderful act, walking and performing on a ladder of swords, edge upward, barefooted."[41]

By March 29, because of the continued success of the circus, Faranta's show had regained its former popularity, and we find that he was contemplating an uptown theater.[42] On the first of April he did move uptown, putting his tent on a vacant lot at the corner of Napoleon and Magazine streets, drawing good attendance at every performance.[43] Later he moved to Carrollton, still drawing enthusiastic crowds, and then from Carrollton he moved his tent to Keller's Market for the week of April 14.[44] By the 23rd of April his tent and show were located at the corner of Triton Walk (now Howard Avenue) and Franklin Street, where he was again reported to be doing an excellent business.[45] This was apparently his last engagement for the season.

Faranta's Automobile Parade. January 2, 1905.
This street parade inaugurated the engagement of Gorton's Mastodon Minstrels
in Faranta's Theatre on Elysian Fields Avenue and Burgundy Street.
Photograph by Ernest J. Bellocq.
Courtesy Robert C. Stempel.

Signor Faranta and Family.
Left to Right: Frederick W. Stempel, Jr., Signor Faranta,
Rose Marie Stempel, Edward William Stempel, Robert Clifford Stempel,
and Isabelle Marie Lagarosse Stempel.
Photograph by Charles Franck, ca. 1920.
Courtesy Robert C. Stempel.

Six weeks later, the *New York Clipper* reported that the Signor and his "young wife" were en route to New York via Chicago, and intended to sail for Europe on about June 29, after which, upon his return, he proposed to pitch his tent again, but would not rebuild his theater for the 1889-1890 season.[46]

Faranta returned to New Orleans on October 18, 1889, after a lengthy European tour that took him to Paris for that city's 1889 exposition. He was said to be "full of life and hope" and firmly convinced that he wished to make his home in New Orleans only.[47] He put his tent show back onto the lot at the corner of Bourbon and Orleans, and advertised his seasonal opening for Sunday, November 24, 1889, with a carnival and spectacular act by Professor Baptiste Peynaud, a French athlete famous for his daring dives from high altitudes, his highest leap having been from a height of 250 feet. It was during the 1889 exposition in Paris that the 37-year-old athlete announced that he would leap from the summit of the Eiffel Tower, if he were given a purse that would suitably repay him for his life-threatening trouble. The French government, however, refused to permit the dive and Peynaud was forced to abandon the plan. His most thrilling dives were made in Rome and Rio de Janeiro, and his American debut was made in New Jersey on August 5, 1889, from the top of a tower 150 feet high. He later executed his specialty in Toronto, Montreal, and Ottawa before arriving in New Orleans.[48] The great event in Faranta's new pavilion, Prof. Peynaud's debut in the city, was expected to be the athlete's dive into a waiting net from a tower standing 150 feet high. The cost of Faranta's new show was 10 cents, or 20 cents for reserved seating.

Faranta's theatrical arena was fenced in and a wooden tower was constructed. In front of the tower was stretched a net five yards wide by sixteen yards long; placed ten feet from the ground, the net was fastened at the corners to several ground supports and covered in the center by a canvas cloth.[49] The contractors failed to complete the tower in time for Peynaud's first exhibition, however, and left the structure thirty-eight feet short of its required height. Carpenters continued to work on the tower right up to a few minutes before the hour of his jump, and then in haste had to erect a temporary platform for the Professor to leap from, thus making his takeoff more difficult than usual.[50]

It was shortly before 1 p.m. on November 24 when Prof. Peynaud made his first flight. Mounting the ladder was a black-haired and mustachioed athlete in a fancy costume consisting of blue tights, black trunks, and a shirt with red, white, and blue trimmings. After reaching the makeshift platform, Peynaud clasped his hands together and then sprang forward, fell, and landed on his shoulders on the net below.[51] By the next day the carpenters had finished the tower, bringing it to its planned limit of 150 feet, and Peynaud gave his third and fourth performances for Faranta's patrons.[52] The athlete's plan was to jump twice a day—at 1 p.m. and at 8 p.m.—for the two weeks of his engagement, from November 24 to December 8. Until his last performance, which killed him, his act was a frightening delight of New Orleans, drawing curiosity seekers from all parts of the city.

On the evening of Friday, November 29, on the fifth day of Faranta's new season, the fenced enclosure held an expectant crowd of onlookers for Peynaud's second jump of the day. The weather was cold and misty. Peynaud sprang from his perch, landed on his back, and bounced unconscious on the net. He was attended by a physician who diagnosed his condition as a concussion of the spine.[53] When he was again conscious, he attributed the accident to the fog and to his insistence that the net be tightened before his jump.[54] He was paralyzed in his lower extremities. By Sunday, attended by Mrs. Faranta and his wife and his doctor, he seemed to have improved, but he was suffering from "spinal fever" and in the course of the night he called for his wife, told her goodbye in their language, and then turned to Mrs. Faranta with these words: "God will reward you for all your kindness."[55] About 2 a.m. on Monday he died. He was later interred in St. Louis Cemetery, the cost of which was borne by Faranta and charitable donations, after a ceremonial procession highlighted by street peddlers hawking photographs of Peynaud's last, tragic leap through the air.[56]

A money box with a placard seeking alms for the widow was placed in every theater vestibule in the city, and at noon on Friday, December 6, there was held a Peynaud benefit at the St. Charles Theatre. Under the complete management of Signor Faranta, the event brought together the first act of *The Little Sinner* by the Cora Van Tassel Company, from the Academy of Music; variety and specialty acts; Maude Atkinson and her company in the third act of *Forget Me Not*, then the current attraction at the Avenue Theatre; the third act of *The Little Coquette* by the Hettie Bernard Chase Company of the St. Charles Theatre; and several acts by artists from Robinson's Dime Museum. It was advertised as the "biggest bill ever offered in this city," but, despite the competence of its talent and management, the benefit show was only "fairly well attended," said the *Daily Picayune* of December 7.

Faranta's last effort to stem the tide of his bad theatrical luck was an abortive one. He advertised that he would reopen his tent show on Sunday, December 15, with Diefenbach's Great Transatlantic Shows, but the event did not take place. During this week, on December 18, Faranta's mentor, David Bidwell, died. Faranta was a pallbearer at Bidwell's funeral, held on December 19, which saw the famed theater manager and showman buried in Greenwood Cemetery.[57] On July 6, 1889, after six months of unannounced activities, Faranta left New Orleans with his wife and son for Chicago, where, at the age of forty-three, he would begin a new career.[58]

Fifteen years later, when speaking to the *Daily Picayune* about the changes in his life, his failed attempt to rebuild his fortune in New Orleans after the burning of his iron theater was prominently absent from the conversation: "I again moved. I went to England, France and Germany for pleasure, and came back in 1890 and landed in Chicago, where I immediately became the manager of the old Park Theatre on State Street. This for a year or so was successful. Then I drifted from real estate to the proprietorship of a hotel, and a livery stable on Michigan Avenue. From that I continued to roll around like the proverbial stone, gathering moss here and there. During a small part of this time I was agent for an insect exterminator . . . And now I have come back, when on the shady side of life, to my first love."[59]

It was in 1903, a year before Faranta's return to New Orleans and his "first love," that the "Third District Theatre Company, Limited" was formed to construct a theater and present plays for the large body of theater-going citizens residing below Canal Street, in the city's third district. This new organization, which received its governing charter on July 20, 1903, was begun with a fixed capital stock of fifty thousand dollars, under the control of a board of directors that comprised the following twelve stockholders, all of whom were to remain in this position until June 30 of the next year: Pierre A. Capdau, Dr. Lucien L. Rabouin, William R. Wilson, Dr. J. Ernest Capdau, Adolphe Dumser, W.J. Hannon, Dr. Joseph M. Suarez, W.E. Arms, Theodore T. Reboul, Manuel Villa, William M. Garic, and the notary who passed the act of incorporation, Robert Legier.[60]

By the direction of the group's new president, Adolphe Dumser, the Third District Theatre Company purchased from stockholder Pierre Capdau two unattended lots on the uptown lake corner of Elysian Fields Avenue and Burgundy Street.[61] Together the two lots presented a front on Elysian Fields of 64 feet and a depth and front on Burgundy of 120 feet. It was decided that the firm of Favrot & Livaudais should design the building, whose construction was subsequently placed in the hands of builder Henry P. Burns.[62] The land was stripped of two antebellum structures—a two-story building on the corner, formerly used as the Third District High School, and, beside it, a Creole home—and the new playhouse was completed in time for its grand opening in November of the same year.

Capable of seating 1,800 persons, the theater, though small, was reminiscent of Faranta's Iron Theatre: a wood frame sheathed with sheets of corrugated iron.[63] Extending to the banquette were the theater's two wings, in which were situated a box office, a manager's office, dressing rooms, and stairways to the upper two floors; between the wings was the main entrance, set inside a small foyer; three exits, not including those from the stage area, opened to the outside. The ceiling of the playhouse was finished in white and from its center hung a cluster of electric lights. Hard-bottom chairs filled the theater's three floors, which included a balcony.

Outside was a sign of electric lights that spelled out the name of the new amusement—"Elysium"—a name selected in a popular contest. Begun on August 10 and lasting two weeks, the contest drew 1,742 letters; of these entries 104 suggested "Elysian," after the avenue the building faced, and 105 recommended "Elysium."[64] Winning a season's ticket was Helen E. Vanney, a teacher in the Jefferson Davis public school, who was the first to suggest "Elysium," the appellation unanimously accepted by the stockholders for the new playhouse.[65]

Under the theatrical management of stockholder William R. Wilson, and with the assistance of orchestra leader William Specht, stage manager Lewis Mitchell, and the Elysium Stock Company, the playhouse's first production, *Duchesse du Barry*, was begun on November 21, 1903.[66] Tickets to the shows were available at Pierre Capdau's drugstore on Canal Street, where they were sold for ten, twenty, and thirty cents, with the exception of a few choice seats at fifty cents each. The management's plan was to present ten complete shows each week, that is, one show each night and one at each Wednesday, Saturday, and Sunday matinee. This plan was adhered to, with few exceptions, during the first season, which brought to its stage a total of twenty-eight plays (all enacted by the Elysium Stock Company) from November 21 to the last week of May, 1904, when the theater was suddenly closed, and the stock company was dismissed. The only activity in the playhouse during the summer of 1904 was a group of benefit performances on June 15, June 24, July 20, July 21, and four days in August.

The Elysium was reopened on October 2 with a domestic drama, *Woman Against Woman*, presented by J.H. Huntley's Savoy Theater Company from Atlantic City. This same company presented *The Lost Paradise* for the week of October 9 and *Roanoke* for the week of November 13, after the theater was closed during the U.S. presidential election. It was during the run of *Roanoke*, on November 15, 1904, that Signor Faranta arrived in New Orleans to discuss with the theater's directors his management of the Elysium Theatre. "It is rather premature to discuss my plans before the meeting of the directors," Faranta told the *Daily Picayune*: "Yet I will say that I believe a popular priced theatre in the downtown district will pay. I mean to give the theatre-goers lively but clean amusement, and the man who cannot afford to take his family to a higher priced house may there enjoy the evening without going too far out of the way. The man who would like to find amusement, but cannot afford it when there is not such a theatre, often winds up at the corner saloon. If my proposition is accepted I expect to meet with unqualified success."[67]

On the day of his arrival Faranta met formally with the Elysium's stock-holders. After some discussion, the necessary papers were signed and Faranta was given control over the activities of the year-old playhouse. The showman promptly changed its name to "Faranta's Theatre" and then, repeating a familiar move, reduced the prices of evening admission to ten and twenty cents and reduced the cost of the weekday matinees to ten cents. His plan was to present high quality road shows and to augment each presentation in his theater with variety performances, or vaudeville, between each act of every daily matinee and evening show. The addition of vaudeville to the playhouse's programs was "an innovation which won instant popularity," said the *Daily Picayune*.[68]

The first production in Faranta's Theatre, for the week of November 27, was the comedy-drama *Beyond the Law*, concerned with the departure of soldiers to Cuba, the theft of an important military dispatch, and the capture of the villain. Presenting this play, and remaining with Faranta's Theatre for two weeks, was the Hoyt Comedy Company. The new theater's second presentation was *Deadwood Dick*, a melodrama, which opened on Thursday, December 1, and played until December 4, after which a new company, under the direction of George Samuels, began an indefinite engagement on Monday, December 5, with *The Convict's Daughter*. For the week of December 12 a new group, assembled by George Samuels and headed by John J. Villansana and, from the Elysium's old stock company, June Adams, appeared in a comedy-drama, *The Scout's Revenge*, a western tale about a society leader and renegade whose double life is ended by a government scout. On December 19, the group presented *A Desert Bride*, which continued to play through Christmas and during which "High-Class Vaudeville" continued to appear between the acts.

On Monday, December 26, Alfred Miaco's Humpty Dumpty Pantomime and Vaudeville Company, a favorite of the old iron theater, was engaged for a week, bringing pantomime and Mother Goose characters together in *Humpty Dumpty*, along with the six-member Eddy Family of acrobats, contortionism, songs, and other entertainments. This was the type of spectacle the showman took

114

delight in presenting, but it was a departure from the usual attractions of the Elysium and of Faranta's early features in his new theater. It was just such an attraction, though, that turned the playhouse into a variety theater, which it would be for the remainder of the season. Miaco's troupe gathered full houses to each performance, and by doing so broke all previous attendance records in the small theater.[69]

A company equally fitting of the showman's well-known style followed Miaco's group—Gorton's Mastodon Minstrels—in a week of burnt-cork minstrelsy, beginning January 2, 1905. The first part of the show opened onto a tropical garden scene, complete with a lush stage set, where the minstrels were to entertain guests in a St. Augustine, Florida, hotel; following this was a one-act sketch depicting the Southern negro; further vaudeville rounded out the program, which included acrobatics and gymnastics, vocal and instrumental artists, a burlesque on the behavior of shop girls and their customers, and a trio of acrobatic comedians.[70] The special feature of the minstrels' week was the automobile parade that Faranta organized for the day of the group's opening performance—an assembly of cars bearing the thirty-five minstrels and a full brass band, led, of course, by Faranta himself, through the principal streets of the city.[71]

On Monday, January 9, the Payton Sisters Company, headed by Iola and Cornelia Payton, began a two-week engagement in Faranta's Theatre, starting this with a comedy-drama, *Utah*, from their repertoire. On Friday of that week *Utah* was replaced by *A Soldier's Honor*, a war and romance drama. On January 16, 17, and 18, the group presented *A Husband on Salary*, a comedy in three acts, and then *The Lighthouse Robbery* on January 19 and 20 and *The Miner's Oath* on January 21. Between the acts of each play was the vaudeville that Faranta offered his patrons during the season. Greater variety arrived with Albert Taylor and his Peerless Stock Company. First was *Peaceful Valley*, a drama, beginning January 23, that the group replaced on Wednesday with *A Royal Rival;* on Thursday and Friday was *The Man From Mexico* and on Saturday was both *The Siege of the Alamo* and *The Man From Mexico;* the week was concluded on Sunday with two performances of *A Hot Time*. Vaudeville acts accompanied each performance by Taylor's Peerless Stock Company, and between the acts of *Peaceful Valley* and the Thursday evening presentation of *The Man From Mexico* Faranta also offered his patrons motion pictures.

The DePew-Burdette Company also shared the stage with the cinema, as did many others during the season. Between the acts of their first stage presentation, a railroad drama entitled *The Midnight Special*, were moving pictures of the Russian-Japanese War. On Thursday, February 2, when he offered the theater's second feature, a four-act comedy-drama entitled *The Country Boy*, Faranta showed a cinematic rendition of the Metropolitan Opera Company's performance of Wagner's opera *Parsifal*, in addition to the variety acts between breaks in the play. On the following Sunday, at ten o'clock in the morning, Faranta gave a special showing of Wagner's "sacred opera," the complete film extending to 2,000 feet in length, but on the same day, at the matinee and evening performance, was the DePew-Burdette group's version of *Rip Van Winkle*, accompanied by seven new vaudeville skits. During the week of February 6, the troupe's second week in Faranta's Theatre, *The Lights of Gotham*, a drama of life in New York

City, was produced from Monday to Wednesday, moving aside on Thursday for *Diamond Dick*, a tale of California mining life. From Thursday to Sunday Faranta showed *Parsifal* again every morning. *Little Red Riding Hood* was the play for the Saturday matinee, and the DePew-Burdette Company closed its engagement on Sunday with a satirical comedy, *The Senator From Kentucky*.

The fifty Georgia Minstrels opened their engagement in the theater on February 13, bringing such a popular three-hour show that Faranta was compelled to arrange three performances on their last day, February 19, at ten, two, and eight o'clock. During the minstrels' week of entertainment, introduced daily by automobile parades at eleven in the morning, Faranta was joined by his wife and son, who remained in the city with him until the end of the season.[72]

No motion pictures attended the Georgia Minstrels' ten-act show, but these did return to Faranta's stage during the week of February 20, when Miaco's troupe incorporated motion pictures and vaudeville into their elaborate production of *Mother Goose and the Golden Egg*. Miaco's engagement apparently brought the last of the cinema for the season in Faranta's Theatre, but the diversity of entertainments on his stage seemed not to require movies to draw a large audience to the variety theater.

For the last two days of February and the first two weeks of March, the Spooner Dramatic Company presented *Nature's Nobleman*, a comedy-drama (February 27-March 1), *The Pearl of Savoy; or, A Mother's Blessing*, a domestic drama (March 2-4), *Dr. Jekyll and Mr. Hyde* (March 5), *Ben Bolt* (March 6-7), Tolstoy's *Resurrection* (March 8-9), and *Nell Gwynne* (March 10-11), completing the engagement with *Yankee in Cuba* on March 12. Greater variety was offered by the Arnold Stock Company, which brought a different stage presentation each day, from March 13 to March 26, with the following plays from the group's repertoire: *A Daughter of Satan*, *Midnight in Chinatown*, *The Little Mother*, *In the Rockies*, *East Lynne*, *The Sleeping City*, *The James Boys in Missouri*, *The Child Stealer*, *The Price of Silence*, *Resurrection*, *The Lighthouse Robbery*, *Ten Nights in a Barroom*, *Peck's Bad Boy*, *Midnight in Chinatown* again, and concluding with *In His Power*.

Three companies presented all of the plays and variety acts for the remainder of Faranta's returning season as a showman. The first was Albert Taylor's Company, which dropped "Peerless" from its title before its re-engagement with Faranta, opening on Monday, March 27, with a comedy entitled *A Fool and His Money* and remaining for two weeks in the following plays: *A Southern Romance* (March 30-April 1), *My Old Kentucky Home* (April 2), *Peaceful Valley* (April 3-5), *Because He Loved Her So* (April 6), *Texas, or the Siege of the Alamo* (April 7), *Lost in Boston* (April 8), and a musical comedy, *The Circus Girl*, which concluded the group's engagement on April 9.

The Frank Dudley Company brought less diversity with *Ben Bolt* (April 10-12), *Dr. Jekyll and Mr. Hyde* (April 13-15), *Camille* (April 16), *A Gigantic Liar* (April 17-19), *Man and Master* (April 22), and *The Tradesman* (April 23). The longest stay of any company of the season was the Harris-Parkinson Stock Company, which closed the season after a four-week engagement in Faranta's Theatre and the following plays: *Slaves of the Orient* (April 24-26), *Monte Cristo* (April 27-29), *In Darkest Russia* (April 30), *Hearts of the Blue Ridge* (May 1-

4), *Rip Van Winkle* (May 5-6), *Brother Against Brother* (May 7), *Capital Against Labor* (May 8-10), *Among the Moonshiners* (May 11-13), *The World Against Him* (May 14), *The Opium Fiend* (May 15-17), *A Southern Romance* (May 18-20), and *The James Boys in Kentucky* (May 21). A special feature of the group's engagement was "Amateur Night," during which anyone believing himself possessed of talent worth exhibiting before the public could do so on Faranta's stage. Faranta inaugurated this on Friday, April 28, and it was an event, held only on Fridays, that the showman retained for the final three weeks of the season.

By the last night of the Harris-Parkinson Stock Company, Faranta had revealed his general plans for the future of the theater, letting it be known that the necessary contracts were made and that the refurbished theater would be ready for its 1905-1906 season in September.[73] With the closing of the theater for the summer, Faranta returned to Chicago and there helped to care for his ailing wife, who was confined to bed with an illness that would bring her death, announced in New Orleans on August 28, 1905.[74] Faranta remained in Chicago after her death, and thus did not renew his contract with the stockholders of the theater. This marked the end of Signor Faranta's professional management career with any theater.

William A. Miller, Faranta's manager for two years in the five-year life of the old iron theater, was appointed the new manager of the Elysium Theatre, opening the refurbished playhouse on October 1, 1905, and retaining the style and kind of entertainment his protégé had introduced in the previous year, including the popular Amateur Night, held again on the Friday of each week. On January 14, 1906, the Elysium was again given a stock company of actors—a group that took the name "New Elysium Stock Company"—which remained with the theater, as did Manager Miller, until April, when the theater was closed.[75]

The Third District Theatre Company had applied for receivership of the playhouse on March 30, 1906, finding itself then unable to meet its obligations to its many creditors;[76] the Elysium was auctioned on May 16, but was not sold until September 5, and then for $12,500 to Henry Greenwall, the manager of the Greenwall Theatre on Dauphine Street,[77] who two weeks later sold an undivided one-half interest in the building to Steve Ciolina,[78] who acquired full interest in the theater in 1915.[79] The Elysium remained a playhouse for many years, later being converted to a cinema, which it still is today.

Faranta did visit the Crescent City in January of 1906, but said nothing definite about his future plans and promptly returned to Chicago, where his son was attending automobile school.[80] He came back to New Orleans with his son in 1907, at the age of sixty-one. He was offered the chance to direct the distribution of motion pictures throughout the South, but he declined the offer, according to later family testimony, because he found himself unable to make the transition from management of vaudeville and stage to motion pictures. Instead he lived in semi-retirement in the Elks Home on Basin Street, between Canal and Tulane Avenue, and formed a theatrical company, in which his son acted and for which he became a business manager, and brought this group to small playhouses throughout Louisiana.

Faranta's son, Fred Stempel, showed promise as an actor, but returned to New Orleans in 1912[?] to work as a chauffeur and taxi driver. After marrying

Isabel Marie Lagarosse, who bore him three children, he took up his final career as a public health inspector. By this time Faranta had retired from show business entirely, although, while living in the Elks Home, he helped to direct and organize the club's social functions, including many circus attractions and parades. He later lived with his son and family on St. Claude Street, becoming a respected grandfather to his three grandchildren, who were told many stories of his life and adventures. He had an abundance of such stories. With the showman's gift for hyperbole he would often say that he had seen everything and had done everything, and that he was satisfied with his life—the world owed him nothing. Faranta died in Touro Infirmary on January 10, 1924, and was interred in the Elks tomb in Metairie Cemetery.

NOTES

PROLOGUE

1. David Bidwell was manager of the Academy of Music and a silent partner with Dr. Gilbert R. Spalding and Charles J. Rogers, the theater's other proprietors, who were absent from the city at the time. Bidwell was sole owner of the Academy of Music by 1872.

2. *Daily True Delta*, October 16, 1863.

3. *Era*, October 13, 1863.

4. The Varieties Theatre on Gravier Street, between Carondelet and Baronne, first opened on December 8, 1849. It was rebuilt on the same site, reopening on December 6, 1855, as the Gaiety, and again in 1858 as the (second) Varieties Theatre. This burned down on December 2, 1870. A new Varieties was erected in 1871 in the square bounded by Canal, Dauphine, Iberville, and Burgundy streets, and was renamed Grand Opera House in 1882. This held its last performance on April 30, 1906, and shortly thereafter was destroyed to make room for an office building. For an extended account of the three Varieties Theatres, see Charles Bernard Melebeck, Jr., "A History of the First and Second Varieties Theatres of New Orleans, Louisiana, 1849-1870" (Ph.D. dissertation, Louisiana State University, 1973) and Shirley Madeline Harrison, "The Grand Opera House (Third Varieties Theatre) of New Orleans, Louisiana, 1871 to 1906: A History and Analysis" (Ph.D. dissertation, Louisiana State University, 1965). See also John S. Kendall, *The Golden Age of the New Orleans Theater* (Baton Rouge: Louisiana State University Press, 1952).

5. The illusion was conducted with mirrors and apparatus contrived by Henry Dircks, a civil engineer, and John Henry Pepper, a professor in London's Royal Polytechnic Institution. See Milbourne Christopher, *Panorama of Magic* (New York: Dover Publications, 1962), p. 137. See also Richard D. Altick, *The Shows of London* (Cambridge, Mass.: Harvard University Press, 1978), pp. 504-505.

6. *New Orleans Bee (L'Abeille de la Nouvelle Orleans)*, November 26, 1863, and *Daily Picayune*, November 26, 1863.

7. *Daily True Delta*, December 2, 1863. The Academy of Music was originally built for this manner of entertainment. In 1853 George C. Lawrason, who then owned the site on St. Charles, between Commercial Alley and Poydras Street, planned and (with David Bidwell) financed the building's construction for Dan Rice, the circus king. It was first known as Dan Rice's Amphitheatre when it opened on December 3, 1853. In addition to a regulation circus ring, which was flanked by seats arranged on an ascending floor, a "portable" stage would be erected on the unfloored section of the ring whenever dramatic offerings required its use. A permanent stage above the dressing room doors made it possible for stage and circus ring performances to be held simultaneously. Rice's Amphitheatre could seat 2,500 persons, although this number was considerably less when the portable stage was in place, for the parquet circle had to be removed each time to accommodate its use. After the old Varieties Theatre was destroyed by fire on November 21, 1854, a party of interested citizens, in quest of a new theater in which to hold serious drama, approached Dan Rice and convinced him to relinquish his lease on the amphitheater. On January 5, 1855, the amphitheater was opened as the Pelican Theatre. This was a successful venture, but it lasted no longer than June 8, 1856, when the last company to appear there disbanded.

The theater's new proprietors, Dr. Gilbert R. Spalding and Charles J. Rogers, reopened it as an amphitheater. Spalding and Rogers had arrived in New Orleans in January of 1856, bringing with them on the steamboat *Floating Palace* their circus, museum, and menagerie. Within a short time they had arranged a lease for the Pelican with Lawrason, who welcomed their plan to open a permanent museum and amphitheater. The chief astonishments from the *Floating Palace* were moved to the front of the theater, and the new lessees spent an estimated ten thousand dollars rearranging, altering, and redecorating the interior. The theater, which would be turned into a circus arena from time to time, was opened to the public on November 5, 1856. Four years later, at the opening of the 1860-1861 season, Spalding and Rogers' Museum and Amphitheatre was renamed the Academy of Music, and by this name it is remembered today.

On April 15, 1861, the Civil War closed the Academy. When it opened again, on September 6, David Bidwell had joined Spalding and Rogers as an owner. It was Bidwell who managed the theater's affairs during the 1861-1862 seasons, when federal troops occupied New Orleans and the Academy was open only at scattered intervals, and there is no evidence· that either Spalding or

Rogers was in the city during this time. Bidwell oversaw the visit of Sanford's Opera Troupe, and under his supervision the circus returned to the Academy of Music. See Kendall, *Golden Age*, for a full account of the Academy of Music. See also John C. Kunzog, *The One-Horse Show* (Jamestown, N.Y.: John C. Kunzog, 1962), pp. 102-103, for pertinent information on Dan Rice.

    8. *Era*, December 5, 1863.

    9. Ibid., December 10, 1863.

    10. *Daily True Delta*, December 11, 1863.

    11. Ibid., December 23, 1863.

    12. *Era*, December 27, 1863.

    13. The facts concerning Mr. Stempel's early years have been assembled from his family's remembrances, scrapbook, and photographs, and from two articles based on interviews with him: See *Times-Picayune*, November 27, 1904, and *Bulletin of New Orleans Lodge of Elks*, February 7, 1921. These have been compared with his obituaries in the *Times-Picayune*, January 13, 1924, and the *Bulletin of New Orleans Lodge of Elks*, January 21, 1924, both of which contain inaccurate information that has unfortunately been perpetuated by John Kendall in *The Golden Age of the New Orleans Theater*, pp. 602-604.

    14. According to his own account, made public much later in his life, he joined the "Irish Brigade" (the 23rd Illinois Volunteers), under the command of Colonel James A. Mulligan. All were captured by Confederate troops in Lexington, Missouri, on September 20, 1861, but were quickly paroled and set free. Colonel Mulligan, the last to be paroled, was released on October 30.

    15. *Daily Picayune*, December 27, 1863.

    16. Ibid., February 5, 1864.

    17. Ibid., February 10, 1864.

    18. Ibid., February 13, 1864.

    19. Cf. Kunzog, p. 350.

CHAPTER ONE

    1. *Times-Democrat*, March 19, 1883.

    2. *Daily States*, March 8, 1889.

    3. Ibid., February 24, 1883.

    4. It was first entered on February 23, 1883.

    5. *New York Clipper*, January 28, 1882.

    6. Ibid., April 1, 1882.

    7. Ibid., July 15, July 22, August 19, and August 26, 1882.

    8. Ibid., September 30, 1882.

    9. Ibid., December 9, 1882.

    10. Ibid., December 2, 1882.

    11. *Passenger Lists of Vessels Arriving at New Orleans, 1820-1902* (National Archives Microfilm), New Orleans Public Library.

    12. Ibid. Curiously, "S.G.S. Faranta" was noted on the passenger list as forty-two years old. His wife, Alva Lowe, was listed as twenty-three-year-old "Miss S.G.S. Faranta."

    13. *New York Clipper*, March 10, 1883: Harry Rollande, treasurer, August Ault, orchestra leader, and Johnny Patterson, stage manager.

    14. See "John H. Scott vs. Frederick W. Stemple," Civil District Court # 8505, June 5, 1883, New Orleans Public Library.

    15. *Mascot*, March 3, 1883.

    16. See *Daily Picayune*, February 22, 1883.

    17. *Mascot*, March 3, 1883.

    18. On March 19, 1883, the *Daily States* reported an attendance of two thousand, the *Daily Picayune* reported three thousand, and the *Times-Democrat* estimated a crowd of five thousand. The *Daily Picayune* of March 20 corrected this, after Mrs. Faranta produced the appropriate records, to 1,752 persons admitted with purchased tickets and 20 persons admitted with complimentary passes. The seating capacity was set by Mrs. Faranta at 2,500.

    19. See *Daily Picayune*, *Daily States*, and *Times-Democrat*, March 19 and March 20, 1883.

    20. *Daily Picayune*, March 21, 1883.

    21. See *Mascot*, March 8, 1884. Livesey died on March 3, 1884, at the age of 33.

    22. *Mascot*, March 24, 1883.

    23. *Daily Picayune*, March 21, 1883.

24. *Daily Picayune*, March 20, 1883.
25. *New York Clipper*, March 31, 1883.
26. *Times-Democrat*, March 20, 1883.
27. Ibid., March 22, 1883.
28. *Daily States*, March 18, 1883.
29. Ibid., March 23, 1883.
30. *Daily Picayune*, March 25, 1883.
31. *Daily States*, March 15, 1883.
32. Ibid., March 24, 1883.
33. *New York Clipper*, April 7, 1883. Born in 1850 in Hanover, Germany, Harry Dressel received art instruction from his uncle, a scenic artist for the Royal Opera House in Hanover. Coming to the United States, he found work as a scenic artist in Chicago, and then in Toronto, Canada, where he joined Mrs. Frank S. Chanfrau's theatrical troupe for an extended tour, which brought him to New Orleans. He remained in this city for one season, but went back to Chicago before David Bidwell persuaded him to return to New Orleans. He did scenic painting for nearly every important theater in the city, as well as for the theater at Spanish Fort and other summer resorts on Lake Pontchartrain. He also redesigned Brown's Hotel at West End, of which he was proprietor from 1883 to 1885. Dressel died in New Orleans on May 29, 1905.
34. *Mascot*, March 31, 1883.
35. *Daily States*, April 10, 1883.
36. Ibid., April 8, 1883.
37. Ibid., April 9, 1883.
38. Ibid., April 8, 1883.
39. *Times-Democrat*, April 21, 1883.
40. *Daily States*, May 4, 1883.
41. Ibid., April 22, 1883.
42. Ibid., April 6, 1883.
43. "John H. Scott vs. Frederick W. Stemple," Civil District Court # 8505.
44. Ibid. The list of purchases comprised: 2 pieces of oil cloth on stage ($3.75), 6 buckets ($1.80), 1 flag on center pole ($1.50), 1 bill ($.50); 1 rake, 1 pair of pliers, 1 tape line, and 1 brass cock ($5.10); 12 flags ($5.90), 1 ticket box and 1 cash box ($6.25); 1 table, 1 pistol, 1 lot of iron pipes, and 1 watch ($9.85); 1 brass drum, 1 kettle drum, and 3 cymbals ($17.00); 1 piece of felt ($9.00), ticking for felt ($7.30); 1 fountain, posts, and gas fixtures ($10.00); 1 suspension frame and 2 trick bottles ($15.00), 1 lot of advertising banners ($9.00), 1 marble top pedestal and 35 dozen chairs ($188.75); 1 lot of stage scenery, 1 stage curtain, and fixtures ($127.00); 1 lot of carpeting ($25.00), and 1 row of center lights and 7 caps ($15.25).
45. *Daily Picayune*, June 15, 1883.
46. Ibid., July 5, 1883.
47. Ibid.
48. *Daily States*, July 1, 1883.
49. *Daily Picayune*, July 5, 1883.
50. *Times-Democrat*, July 15, 1883.
51. Ibid. See also *Chicago Tribune*, April 25, 1883.
52. *Daily Picayune*, July 21, 1883.
53. *Daily Picayune*, July 8, 1883.
54. Ibid.
55. *Mascot*, May 10, 1883.
56. *Daily Picayune*, July 31, 1883.
57. *Daily States*, August 2, 1883.
58. *Daily Picayune*, August 14, 1883.
59. Ibid., October 14, 1883.
60. *Daily States*, October 20, 1883.
61. Ibid., October 23, 1883.
62. *Daily States*, November 12, 1883.
63. *New York Clipper*, November 3, 1883.
64. *Daily Picayune*, November 13, 1883.
65. *Daily States*, November 14, 1883.
66. Often preceded by a lofty proclamation containing rich phrases inspired by some local topic, Sambola's ritual was a much anticipated event, despite early attempts to stop it. In 1883 he was

issued an injunction that failed to keep him from firing his "pet gun" (a cannon) to communicate a "warning to cast aside straw hats and get winter derbys" (*Daily States*, August 15, 1883). He was again threatened with an injunction in 1884, the year in which he was elected Judge of the Third Recorder's Court, but he was nevertheless able to "shoot the signal," as thirteen guns were fired to salute "the downfall of the straw hat gear."

In the succeeding years, during which time Judge Sambola was elected to the state senate, additions and refinements were made to the ceremony. Parades were included, changes were made to the number and kind of explosive devises used to "shoot the hats," and even the aim of the salutes was broadened. On Sunday, October 15, 1899, instead of the usual location on the Canal Street levee, a salute of one hundred guns was to be given at Elk Place, between Canal and Tulane Avenue (*Daily States*, October 9, 1899). This was announced by "Edict Number 99," issued by Sambola from "Headquarters War Department, New Orleans," and it signaled the downfall of not only straw hats but also white linen suits and alpaca coats (*Daily Picayune*, October 12, 1899). Featured in this grand event were 100 imported aerial bombs of Chinese manufacture. Enclosed in each bomb was a large tissue hat, folded to fit inside; when ignited, each bomb ascended and exploded, releasing its hat, which then unfolded and descended (*Daily Picayune*, October 16, 1899). Assisting the affair was a parade of decorated wagons that disbanded only after traversing Claiborne, Esplanade, Rampart, Canal, Camp, Calliope, Tchoupitoulas, Washington, and St. Charles, returning to Canal Street and the Clay Statue, where the parade stopped.

Sambola died on the morning of June 12, 1903, having eight months earlier fired his last straw hat salute. There were later echoes of the occasion, but none has matched the fervor of Sambola's ritual since that time—not even in 1934, when, on April 5, the *Times-Picayune* announced this queer reversal of a short tradition: "Today is Straw Hat Day, when fashion decrees that winter and spring felts be discarded to be replaced by new straws. . . . Designated as Straw Hat day, today means the official death of felt hats." See Sambola's obituaries in the *Daily Picayune*, June 13, 1903, and the *New Orleans Item*, June 12, 1903.

CHAPTER TWO

1. *Daily States*, December 10, 1883.
2. See *Daily Picayune*, April 25, 1883.
3. *New York Clipper*, December 15, 1883. See Ira W. Ford, *Traditional Music of America* (New York: Da Capo Press, 1978), p. 277, for the first verse of Patterson's song "Bridget Donohue."
4. *Daily Picayune*, December 3, 1883.
5. Ibid., December 6, 1883.
6. Ibid., December 9, 1883.
7. *New York Clipper*, December 15, 1883.
8. *Times-Democrat*, December 26, 1883.
9. Ibid., December 20, 1883.
10. *Daily States*, January 11, 1884.
11. *Times-Democrat*, February 11, 1884. Judge Sambola, who helped to contrive these tournaments, presided (*sans* straw hat) over all three.
12. *Daily Picayune*, December 30, 1883.
13. Ibid., January 6, 1884.
14. Ibid., January 9, 1884.
15. Ibid., January 27, 1884.
16. Theatre program of the Pickwick Theater, St. Louis, Missouri, dated September 29 and October 1 [1883], Missouri Historical Society.
17. *Daily States*, October 7, 1883. See *New York Clipper*, September-October, 1883, for exact dates of the play's engagements.
18. *Daily States*, June 14, 1884.
19. *New York Clipper*, March 1, 1884.
20. *Daily Picayune*, October 30, 1882.
21. *Daily States*, March 29, 1884; *Daily Picayune*, July 26, 1884.
22. *Daily States*, May 24, 1883; *Times-Democrat*, May 26, 1883.
23. The Kehoe club, named after its inventor, was a special club for club-swinging activities.
24. *Daily Picayune*, April 8, 1884.
25. See the Theater Collection, New York Public Library, for several different programs of this play.

26. *Times-Democrat,* April 20, 1884.

27. *New York Clipper,* April 19, 1884.

28. *Daily Picayune,* May 2, 1884.

29. *New York Clipper,* May 10, 1884.

30. Ibid., May 17, 1884.

31. H. Chance Newton, *Crime and Drama or Dark Deeds Dramatized* (London: Stanley Paul & Co., 1927), pp. 67-68. "Jack Sheppard" was serialized by William Harrison Ainsworth in vols. 5-7 (1839-1840) of *Bentley's Miscellany.*

32. *Daily Picayune,* June 7, 1884.

33. Ibid., June 10, 1884.

34. Ibid.

35. Acts of William O. Hart, N.P., 4/838, June 11, 1884, Orleans Parish Archives.

36. *Daily States,* July 9, 1884.

37. *Daily Picayune,* July 10 and 11, 1884; *New York Clipper,* July 19, 1884.

38. The club's elected officers were William Graff, president; Aug. Beechler, vice-president; P. Petemonde, treasurer; William H. McMurray, secretary; E.A. Rod, captain; and Charles A. Aron, manager. See *Daily Picayune,* June 8, 1884. Modern Baseball, a game with a medieval ancestry, was then over forty years old, the first baseball club, according to tradition, having been formed in New York in 1842. In the fall of 1845 this club, the Knickerbocker, devised and had printed the first formal rules for a national game, prescribing, among other things, nine men to a side and three outs per team in each inning. By 1884 a national enthusiasm for the sport had spawned in New Orleans an inestimable number of clubs known for their remarkable names, if for nothing else, and it was odd to find in this city a baseball club without a picturesque name, a splendid uniform, or a distinguished sponsor. The clubs were generally formed by men or boys from the same economic, social, or occupational background, and the lifespan of a club was usually very short.

Between May and October of 1884 we find among these clubs such names as the Rosebuds, the Ice Waters, the Car Washers, the Sunflowers, the Windbusters, the Bonepickers, the Birth Cases, the Model Midnight Dudes, the Strawberry Blonds, the Cradle of Innocence, the Doughnut Snatchers, the Southern Bells, the Hoisting Horse Drivers, the Fruit of the Loom (as the clerks from John P. Richardson's dry goods store called themselves), and the Sick, Lame, and Lazy, whose principal feature was that its members tipped the scales at the two hundred mark. Notable among later clubs was the Daddies, which in 1885 sported red Mother Hubbard gowns, blue sunbonnets, and gingham umbrellas for a game with the Red Warriors (see *Evening Chronicle,* August 19, 1885). The uniforms worn by the New Orleans Elks in the summer of 1888 were equally colorful. Billed as the Lilies and the Pinks, the two teams appeared on the diamond costumed as ballet dancers in white tarlatan. On September 1, 1888, the *Mascot,* which published a lithographic view of the action, noted that the players on the grassy field "got their skirts and panties all green and brown" during the game, but remarked that the entire situation had great possibilities, especially if put "in the hands of Brother Faranta, acting as manager." See Dale A. Somers, *The Rise of Sports in New Orleans, 1850-1900* (Baton Rouge: Louisiana State University Press, 1972), esp. pp. 115-139, for more information on baseball in New Orleans.

39. *Daily Picayune,* August 3, 1884.

40. *Evening Chronicle,* August 28, 1884. The new officers were T. Favetto, president; J. Roth, secretary; and J. Berkery, captain. Both Charles Aron and the Signor retained their titles.

41. *New York Clipper,* August 30, 1884.

42. See *Evening Chronicle,* October 9 and October 24, 1884.

43. Joseph T. Shipley, *Guide to Great Plays* (Washington, D.C.: Public Affairs Press, 1956), p. 182.

44. *Daily Picayune,* July 16, 1884.

45. Ibid., July 26, 1884.

46. *Daily Picayune,* July 30, 1884.

47. *Daily Picayune,* August 5, 1884.

48. Ibid.

49. *Evening Chronicle,* August 13, 1884.

50. Ibid.

51. *Times-Democrat,* August 4, 1884.

52. *Daily Picayune,* August 5, 1884.

53. Ibid., July 6, 1884.

54. Acts of William O. Hart, N.P., 4/890, August 14, 1884.

55. *Proceedings of the City Council*, August 26, 1884.

56. Ibid., September 2, 1884. Faranta was not issued a building permit until September 15. See *Daily States*, September 16, 1884.

57. *Evening Chronicle*, September 24, 1884.

58. Acts of William O. Hart, N.P., 4/929, September 19, 1884.

CHAPTER THREE

1. For historical treatments of this theater see *Historical Sketch Book and Guide to New Orleans and Environs* (New York: Will H. Coleman, 1885), pp. 134-141; "New Orleans Stage," in *Times-Democrat*, August 31, September 16, and September 23, 1894; and J.G. de Baroncelli, *Le Théâtre-Francais, à la Nlle Orleans* (New Orleans: George Muller, 1906), esp. pp. 26-30. By far the best account is to be found in Henry A. Kmen's *Music in New Orleans: The Formative Years, 1791-1841* (Baton Rouge: Louisiana State University Press, 1966) and "The Music of New Orleans," in Hodding Carter, ed., *The Past as Prelude: New Orleans, 1718-1968* (New Orleans: Tulane University Press, 1968), pp. 210-232.

2. See Rene J. Le Gardeur, Jr., *The First New Orleans Theatre, 1792-1803* (New Orleans: Leeward Books, 1963) for the standard work on Tabary's connection with the theater in New Orleans.

3. *Moniteur de la Louisiane*, October 11, 1806.

4. Acts of Marc Lafitte, N.P., 2/193, October 9, 1812.

5. Ibid., 8/72, February 23, 1816, and Acts of Philippe Pedesclaux, N.P., 73/585, October 8, 1816.

6. *Louisiana Courier*, September 30, 1816.

7. Ibid., November 13, 1816.

8. *Proceedings of the City Council*, October 24, 1818, New Orleans Public Library.

9. *Daily True Delta*, February 2, February 3, and February 15, 1861.

10. *New Orleans Times*, November 26, 1867.

11. The *Historical Sketch Book and Guide to New Orleans and Environs*, written for visitors to the World's Industrial and Cotton Centennial Exposition but compiled before Faranta's Iron Theatre was completed, describes the site as "a vacant space." See p. 134.

12. Ownership of the site was passed on to Henry Parlange in 1859, and then to John H. O'Connor in 1873, the Roman Catholic Church in 1873, and Mary A. Roberts in 1881. See the *Vieux Carré Survey*, Square 59, The Historic New Orleans Collection, for the list of transactions involving this site.

13. Thomas O'Connor, ed., *The New Orleans Fire Department* (New Orleans, 1895), p. 263.

14. Ibid. See J.Q. Flynn, *Flynn's Digest of the City Ordinances ... of New Orleans* (New Orleans, 1896), art. 314, p. 174, and art. 317, pp. 183-184, for restrictions on the use of iron shutters; see also art. 736, pp. 351-352, for the city's fire limits and a ruling against any building constructed of combustible material.

15. Herbert S. Fairall, *The World's Industrial and Cotton Centennial Exposition* (Iowa City: Republican Publishing Co., 1885), p. 428. See also *Historical Sketch Book*, p. 321, and *Visitor's Guide to the World's Industrial and Cotton Centennial Exposition and New Orleans* (Louisville, Ky.: Courier-Journal Job Printing Co., 1884), p. 16.

16. Fairall, p. 429, and *Historical Sketch Book*, p. 321. Cf. *Visitor's Guide*, pp. 16-17.

17. Fairall, p. 430, and *Historical Sketch Book*, p. 322.

18. *Daily Picayune*, December 22, 1884; see also *Daily Picayune*, September 1, 1885.

19. *Evening Chronicle*, January 2, 1885.

20. *Daily States*, August 19, 1884; *Times-Democrat*, November 5, 1885.

21. *Daily Picayune*, September 1, 1885.

22. *Times-Democrat*, November 6, 1885. For a description of this theater see *Evening Chronicle*, November 7, 1885. The ironclad Avenue Theatre was destroyed by fire in 1891.

23. *Daily States*, September 26 and September 28, 1884.

24. Ibid., October 5, 1884.

25. *Evening Chronicle*, October 5, 1884.

26. *New Orleans Bee*, October 7, 1884.

27. *Evening Chronicle*, October 4 and October 7, 1884.

28. Ibid., October 15, 1884.

29. Ibid., October 11, 1884. D. A. Sanborn's *Insurance Maps of New Orleans, 1885*, in the School of Geoscience Map Library, Louisiana State University, Baton Rouge, includes a map (dated 1884) of square no. 59 (bounded by Orleans, Bourbon, St. Ann, and Royal), giving the iron theater's position on the square, its exact structural dimensions, and the locations of its internal facilities. This is the only known architectural record of Faranta's Iron Theatre.

30. *Evening Chronicle*, October 11, 1884; *New York Clipper*, November 22, 1884.

31. *Evening Chronicle*, October 11, 1884.

32. Ibid.

33. *Daily States*, March 8, 1889; *New York Clipper*, March 16, 1889.

34. Ibid.

35. See *Soards' New Orleans City Directory, for 1887*, p. 801b.

36. *Mascot*, October 18, 1884.

37. *Daily Picayune*, October 29, 1884.

38. Ibid., November 27, 1884; George C.D. Odell, *Annals of the New York Stage* (New York: Columbia University Press, 1927-49), XI, p. 331.

39. *Mascot*, November 29, 1884.

40. *Daily Picayune*, November 4, 1884.

41. Adah Isaacs Menken was not the first woman to play the lead in *Mazeppa*, but she was the first to create a stir with the role. She was an actress without much talent, according to her contemporaries, and she was urged to render her new role as Mazeppa a sensational one. This she did. She cut her hair to a point above her shoulders, since she was cast as a man and wanted to look the part, but she possessed a voluptuous physique and used it to her advantage by wearing, instead of the modest covering chosen by other actresses in the part, a flesh-colored body stocking, which was revealed when, as Mazeppa, she was stripped, bound to a horse, and carried through the scenery, consequently giving the audience the unforgettable impression that riding on the wild steed was a nude and beautifully proportioned young woman. That this was supposed to be the male Tartar seemed not to make the play at all incongruous with its main character. Following her innovative appearance in Albany, N.Y., and amid other stage performances, Miss Menken played Mazeppa in New York City and throughout England. In 1868, after four marriages, a successful acting career in Europe, and romantic encounters with the elder Alexandre Dumas and the poet Swinburne, she died in Paris at the age of thirty-three. See Bernard Falk, *The Naked Lady: A Biography of Adah Isaacs Menken* (London: Hutchinson, 1934); John S. Kendall, "'The World's Delight': The Story of Adah Isaacs Menken," *Louisiana Historical Quarterly*, 21 (1938), pp. 846-868; Paul Lewis, *Queen of the Plaza: A Biography of Adah Isaacs Menken* (New York: Funk & Wagnalls, 1964); Leo Shpall, "Adah Isaacs Menken," *Louisiana Historical Quarterly*, 26 (1943), pp. 162-168.

42. Kendall, *Golden Age*, p. 62.

43. *Daily Picayune*, November 4, 1884.

44. *Times-Democrat*, November 13, 1884.

45. *Mascot*, November 15, 1884.

46. *Louisiana Courier*, February 16, 1818; see Kendall, *Golden Age*, for other dates.

47. *New York Clipper*, November 29, 1884.

48. *Mascot*, November 22, 1884.

49. Ibid., November 29, 1884.

50. Ibid.

51. *Daily States*, November 28, 1884.

52. Ibid.

53. Ibid.

54. Ibid.

55. *New York Dramatic Mirror*, February 15, 1879.

56. *Times-Democrat*, November 8, 1884.

57. Ibid., November 16, 1884.

58. Ibid., November 30, 1884.

59. *Daily Picayune*, *Evening Chronicle*, and *Times-Democrat*, December 8, 1884.

60. Ibid.

61. *Mascot*, December 13, 1884.

62. *New York Clipper*, December 20, 1884.

63. Ibid.

64. Several of these so-called white elephants toured the United States with various circuses and menageries, and not one of them was given a white skin by nature. Eight months before Faranta's

elephant visited New Orleans, circus king Adam Forepaugh was involved in competition with P.T. Barnum over just such an elephant, and was subsequently accused of fraud. On March 28, 1884, Barnum's "sacred white elephant," Toung Taloung, purchased from an oriental potentate at an estimated expense of $250,000, arrived in New York from Burma. Barnum had already advertised the elephant as white in color, but, upon inspecting it, he found that it was grey with pink spots and pink eyes, and then went to great lengths to have Siamese experts authenticate it. By this time, though, Adam Forepaugh was advertising his own "White Elephant" and making public the disparity between what Barnum advertised and what he in fact owned. Forepaugh's own elephant, Light of Asia, was indeed white, but before the end of April two animal trainers from Liverpool publicly attested to Forepaugh's gross humbuggery: the Light of Asia, they maintained, was just an ordinary elephant painted with kalsomine (a whitewash) in a Liverpool stable, and both men admitted their part in the deception (*Daily States*, April 20, 1884). See Irving Wallace, *The Fabulous Showman* (New York: Alfred A. Knopf, 1959), pp. 296-297; Morris R. Werner, *Barnum* (New York: Harcourt, Brace and Company, 1923), pp. 348-354; Neil Harris, *Humbug: The Art of P.T. Barnum* (Boston: Little, Brown and Co., 1973), pp. 266-271.

65. *Daily Picayune*, January 16, 1876.

66. *New York Clipper*, September 20, 1873; cf. *Daily Picayune*, January 16, 1876.

67. Acts of William O. Hart, N.P., 4/1024, December 15, 1884.

68. Ibid.

69. *Evening Chronicle*, December 15, 1884.

70. *New York Clipper*, December 27, 1884.

71. *Daily Picayune*, December 23, 1884.

72. Ibid.

73. *Evening Chronicle*, December 26, 1884.

74. Ibid.; *Daily States*, December 26, 1884.

75. *Times-Democrat*, December 27, 1884.

76. *Evening Chronicle*, January 8, 1885.

77. *Daily States*, January 15, 1885.

78. *Evening Chronicle*, January 12, 1885. See also *New York Clipper*, January 17, 1885.

79. *Mascot*, January 31, 1885. At least one of these performers had outside interests. On February 8, Thomas G. Scott, a New Zealand athlete then appearing in Faranta's circus, wrestled Charles Bixamos, formerly the "Iron Man" in Faranta's pavilion (*Evening Chronicle*, February 9, 1885). Bixamos won this match, and then bested Scott in three pugilistic competitions later in February and early in March. (On March 19, however, the 153-pound Bixamos was knocked senseless in the fifth round of his bout with a boxer named Jack Dempsey: see *Daily Picayune* and *Evening Chronicle*, March 20, 1885).

80. *Daily Picayune*, February 1, 1885; *Mascot*, February 14, 1885.

81. *Daily Picayune*, February 3, 1885.

82. February 14, 1885.

83. See *Evening Chronicle*, February 18 and March 9, 1885.

84. Acts of William O. Hart, N.P., 4/1057, January 21, 1885. See also 4/1083, February 23, 1885, which certifies that Faranta paid all monies required by his promissory notes to John A. Sicard & Son.

85. *Mascot*, February 28, 1885.

86. *Daily Picayune*, March 6, 1885.

87. See *Daily States*, March 19 and 25, 1885.

88. Ibid., March 17, 1885.

89. See *Daily Picayune*, June 29, 1885.

90. *Mascot*, March 28, 1885.

91. *Daily States*, April 6, 1885.

92. *Mascot*, April 4, 1885.

93. Ibid., April 18, 1885.

94. *Daily Picayune*, May 2, 1885.

95. *Evening Chronicle*, May 1, 1885.

96. *Mascot*, May 9, 1885.

97. Cf. Shipley, *Guide to Great Plays*, pp. 111-112.

98. *Evening Chronicle*, May 13, 1885; *Daily Picayune*, May 19, 1885; *Daily States*, May 19-21, 1885.

99. *Mascot*, May 16, 1885.

100. *Daily States,* June 3, 1885.
101. *Mascot,* June 6, 1885.
102. See *New York Clipper,* June 27, 1885.
103. Ibid., July 4, 1885.
104. *Daily Picayune,* June 30, 1885.
105. Ibid.; *New York Clipper,* July 11, 1885.
106. *Mascot,* July 18, 1885.
107. *Daily Picayune,* July 17, 1885; *Evening Chronicle,* July 25, 1885.
108. *Mascot,* July 25, 1885.

CHAPTER FOUR

1. *Daily Picayune,* September 6 and 20, 1885.
2. *Evening Chronicle,* September 19, 1885.
3. *Daily Picayune,* September 20, 1885.
4. *Mascot,* September 19, 1885.
5. Ibid.
6. Ibid.
7. *Daily Picayune,* September 20, 1885.
8. *Daily States,* September 13, 1885.
9. *Evening Chronicle,* August 30, 1885; *Mascot,* September 5, 1885; *Daily Picayune,* September 20, 1885. See also *Times-Democrat,* September 15, 1888, and *Mascot,* September 22, 1888.
10. *Daily Picayune,* September 20, 1885; see also *Daily States,* September 21, 1885.
11. *Mascot,* September 26, 1885.
12. *Times-Democrat,* September 20, 1885; see also *Daily Picayune,* September 20, 1885.
13. *Daily States* and *Daily Picayune,* September 21, 1885.
14. *Times-Democrat,* September 27, 1885; cf. *Daily States,* September 27, 1885.
15. *Daily States,* September 27 and 28, 1885.
16. Ibid., October 5, 1885.
17. See *Mascot,* October 3, 1885, and *Evening Chronicle,* October 5, 1885.
18. See *Mascot,* October 17, 1885.
19. *Daily Picayune,* October 13, 1885.
20. See *Daily Picayune,* October 13, 1885.
21. *Evening Chronicle,* October 31, 1885.
22. *Daily Picayune,* October 20, 1885.
23. *New York Clipper,* November 7, 1885.
24. See *Evening Chronicle,* July 28, 1885.
25. *Daily Picayune,* October 25, 1885.
26. Ibid., October 31, 1885.
27. Faranta also purchased a pair of horses from the departing circus. See *New York Clipper,* November 7, 1885.
28. *Daily Picayune,* November 3, 1885.
29. Ibid., November 20, 1885; see also *Evening Chronicle,* November 27, 1885, and *Times-Democrat,* November 22, 1885.
30. *Daily Picayune,* November 20, 1885.
31. Cf. *Daily Picayune,* November 17, 1885.
32. *Mascot,* November 21, 1885.
33. *Daily Picayune,* November 20, 1885.
34. *Mascot,* November 28, 1885.
35. *Evening Chronicle,* December 3, 1885.
36. *Mascot,* December 5, 1885.
37. See *New York Clipper,* December 12, 1885. Davis committed suicide in the Southern Hotel on November 24, a few minutes after the gun he was examining accidentally went off, killing his wife (*Evening Chronicle,* November 26, 1885). Strangely enough, within forty days the Southern Hotel, at the corner of Julia and Carondelet streets, was destroyed by fire (*Daily States,* January 8, 1886). What became of Faranta's new circus is not known, but then see *New York Clipper,* March 6 and April 24, 1886, for some likely clues.
38. *Daily States,* December 13, 1885.

39. It was well known that Kersands and his minstrels usually appeared on stage in black face, whether or not it was needed. See Dailey Paskman, *"Gentlemen, Be Seated!": A Parade of the American Minstrels*, rev. ed. (New York: Clarkson N. Potter, Inc., 1976), p. 173.

40. *Times-Democrat*, December 20, 1885.

41. *Evening Chronicle*, December 19, 1885.

42. *Mascot*, December 25, 1885.

43. *Times-Democrat*, December 26, 1885. Winning the goat and appurtenances was Benjamin Martico, the holder of ticket number 774.

44. *Evening Chronicle* and *Daily States*, December 26, 1885.

45. Ibid.

46. *Times-Democrat*, December 24, 1885. The group continued to meet every Wednesday evening, and enjoyed social meetings on the second and fourth Wednesday of each month.

47. *Daily Picayune*, January 10, 1886.

48. Ibid., January 12, 1886; *Evening Chronicle*, January 12, 1886.

49. *Daily States*, February 20, 1886.

50. See *New York Clipper*, February 27, 1886.

51. Ibid., March 20, 1886.

52. *Mascot*, March 27, 1886.

53. Ibid., April 3, 1886.

54. Ibid.

55. Ibid., April 10, 1886.

56. *Times-Democrat*, April 13, 1886.

57. *Daily States*, April 20, 1886.

58. *Mascot*, May 1, 1886.

59. Ibid., April 17, 1886.

60. Ibid., September 11, 1886. See the gossip column "Mrs. Mulcahey's Contribution."

61. See *New York Clipper*, April 24, 1886.

62. *Times-Democrat*, May 19, 1886.

63. Ibid., June 6, 1886.

64. *New York Clipper*, May 22, 1886.

65. Ibid., June 12, 1886.

66. Ibid., May 15, 1886.

67. Acts of Charles E. Sel, N.P., 1/1473, May 12, 1886.

68. *Daily States*, June 18, 1886; *Times-Democrat*, June 19, 1886.

69. See *Daily Picayune*, June 14, 1886, and *Times-Democrat*, June 30, 1886.

70. See *New York Clipper*, August 14, 1886, and *Daily States*, August 5, 1886.

71. Ibid.

72. *Daily States*, September 2, 1886.

73. Ibid., September 5 and 6, 1886.

74. Ibid., September 6, 1886.

75. See *Daily Picayune*, September 18, 1886; cf. *Daily States*, September 18, 1886.

76. *Daily Picayune*, September 18, 1886; *Times-Democrat*, October 3, 1886.

77. *Daily States*, September 18, 1886; see also *Times-Democrat* and *Daily Picayune*, September 18, 1886.

78. *Mascot*, September 18, 1886.

79. *Times-Democrat*, September 19, 1886.

80. Ibid.

81. *Daily Picayune* and *Daily States*, September 19, 1886.

82. *Daily States*, September 19, 1886.

83. Ibid.

84. *Daily Picayune*, September 28, 1886; *Lantern*, October 6, 1886.

85. *Daily Picayune*, October 12, 1886.

86. Ibid., October 19, 1886.

87. Ibid., November 2, 1886; *Times-Democrat*, November 2, 1886.

88. Cole had just recently purchased an interest in P.T. Barnum's circus. See George L. Chindahl, *A History of the Circus in America* (Caldwell, Idaho: The Caxton Printers, Ltd., 1959), p. 102.

89. *Daily Picayune*, November 24, 1886.

90. Ibid. See also *New York Clipper*, December 4, 1886.

91. *Daily Picayune* and *Daily States*, December 13, 1886.

92. See *Daily Picayune*, December 28, 1886.

93. Ibid., December 29, 1886.

94. *Times-Democrat*, January 14, 1887.

95. Ibid., January 17, 1887.

96. *Daily Picayune* and *Times-Democrat*, January 25, 1887.

97. *Daily Picayune*, March 9, 1887: "Signor Faranta, the live manager of Faranta's Theatre, knows a good show when he sees it, and he also knows a bad one. When he has a bad show he has the nerve to bounce it before it wears out his public."

98. Ibid., March 12, 1887.

99. Ibid., March 15, 1887.

100. Ibid., March 29, 1887.

101. Ibid., April 11, 1887.

102. *Times-Democrat*, May 13 and 14, 1887.

103. *New York Clipper*, June 4, 1887; *Daily Picayune*, July 31, 1887.

104. *Daily States*, September 18, 1887.

105. *Mascot*, September 17, 1887.

106. *Daily States*, September 18, 1887.

107. *Times-Democrat*, July 25, 1887.

108. Ibid., September 14, 1887; see also *New York Clipper*, September 17, 1887.

109. *Times-Democrat*, September 14, 1887; *Daily Picayune*, September 17, 1887. It should be mentioned that the theater's new stage carpenter was Albert O. Hebrard. See *Times-Democrat*, September 15, 1888; cf. *Mascot*, September 22, 1888.

110. *Times-Democrat* and *Daily States*, September 18, 1887.

111. See, e.g., *Times-Democrat*, September 20, 1887.

112. *Daily States*, September 27, 1887.

113. See *Daily Picayune*, September 19, 1887. This play is not to be confused with William Congreve's five-act comedy.

114. See *Daily Picayune*, October 4, 1887.

115. Ibid., October 14, 1887.

116. Ibid., October 18, 1887; *Times-Democrat*, October 18, 1887.

117. *Daily Picayune*, October 25, 1887; *Times-Democrat*, October 25, 1887; *Daily States*, April 17, 1887.

118. *Daily Picayune*, February 6, 1899; *Times-Democrat*, November 1, 1887.

119. *Times-Democrat*, November 1, 1887.

120. *Lantern*, November 5, 1887.

121. *Daily Picayune*, November 8, 1887.

122. Ibid., November 15, 1887.

123. See Joe Laurie, Jr., *Vaudeville: From the Honky-tonks to the Palace* (New York: Henry Holt & Co., 1953), p. 203.

124. *Times-Democrat*, November 22, 1887.

125. *Daily Picayune*, November 22, 1887.

126. *Times-Democrat*, November 22, 1887.

127. See *Daily Picayune* and *Times-Democrat*, December 20, 1887.

128. *Times-Democrat*, December 22, 1887.

129. Ibid., December 28, 1887.

130. See *Daily Picayune*, January 3, 1888.

131. See *Daily Picayune* and *Times-Democrat*, February 7, 1888.

132. *Daily Picayune*, February 21, 1888.

133. Ibid., March 4 and 5, 1888.

134. *Times-Democrat*, March 10, 1888.

135. *Mascot*, March 17, 1888.

136. See *Daily Picayune*, March 13, 1888.

137. See *Times-Democrat*, March 20, 1888.

138. *Daily Picayune*, April 3, 1888.

139. *Mascot*, April 14, 1888.

140. *Daily Picayune*, April 10, 1888.

141. *Times-Democrat*, May 28, 1888.

142. *Daily Picayune*, May 27, 1888.

CHAPTER FIVE

1. See *Daily States*, September 14, 1888.
2. *Mascot*, September 22, 1888.
3. Ibid.
4. *Times-Democrat*, September 15, 1888; *Mascot*, September 22, 1888.
5. *Mascot*, September 22, 1888. The large barroom was stocked with a soda water stand owned by Ben Stempel and such concessions as cake and fruit booths. See *Daily States*, March 7, 1889.
6. See *Daily States*, September 9, 1888; *Times-Democrat*, September 15, 1888; cf. *Soards' New Orleans City Directory, for 1889*, p. 387b, and *Daily States*, March 7, 1889.
7. *Daily States*, September 18, 1888.
8. Ibid., September 25, 1888.
9. See *Daily States*, September 25 and 28, 1888; *Times-Democrat*, September 27 and 29, 1888.
10. See *Daily States*, September 28, 1888.
11. *Times-Democrat*, September 29, 1888.
12. See *Mascot*, October 13, 1888.
13. Ibid., October 27, 1888.
14. *Daily Picayune*, October 30, 1888.
15. Ibid., November 5, 1888.
16. *Daily States*, April 12, 1887.
17. Ibid., November 13, 1888; *Times-Democrat*, November 13, 1888.
18. See *Daily Picayune*, November 27, 1888.
19. See *Daily Picayune*, December 4, 1888.
20. *Daily States*, December 8, 1888. The ushers were Jessie Mesmer, John Lubat, Charles Baker, and Eddie Smith.
21. *Daily Picayune*, December 11, 1888.
22. Ibid.
23. See *Daily States*, January 8, 1893.
24. *Daily Picayune*, December 30, 1888.
25. Ibid.
26. *Daily States*, March 12, 1905; *Daily Picayune*, January 23, 1899.
27. *Daily States*, January 6, 1889.
28. *Daily Picayune* and *Times-Democrat*, January 15, 1889.
29. See *Daily Picayune*, February 5, 1889.
30. See *Times-Democrat*, February 19, 1889; *Daily States*, February 19, 1889; cf. *Daily Picayune*, February 19, 1889.
31. *Times-Democrat*, March 5, 1889.
32. *Daily States*, March 7, 1889.
33. Ibid.
34. Ibid.; *Daily Picayune*, March 8, 1889; *Times-Democrat*, March 8, 1889.
35. See *Daily States*, March 7, 1889. Valued at $35,000, but built at an original cost of $12,000, Faranta's Theatre possessed only $9,000 of insurance. He was insured with Germania American Insurance Company of New York ($2,000), Germania of New Orleans ($2,000), Southern of New Orleans ($1,000), London & Liverpool & Globe Company ($1,000), Security of New Haven ($1,000), St. Paul of Minnesota ($1,000), and American of Philadelphia ($1,000).
36. *Daily Picayune*, March 8, 1889; cf. *Daily States*, March 7, 1889.
37. *Daily States*, March 7, 1889; cf. *Daily Picayune*, March 8, 1889.
38. *Times-Democrat*, March 8, 1889.
39. *Daily States*, March 7, 1889.
40. Ibid., March 19, 1889.
41. Ibid.; *Daily Picayune*, March 19, 1889.
42. *Times-Democrat*, March 29, 1889.
43. *Daily States*, April 2 and 7, 1889.
44. See *Daily States*, April 14, 1889.
45. *Daily States*, April 23 and 28, 1889.
46. See *New York Clipper*, June 15, 1889.
47. *Daily Picayune*, October 19, 1889.

48. See *Daily Picayune*, November 24 and December 3, 1889.
49. *Daily Picayune*, November 25, 1889.
50. Ibid.
51. Ibid.
52. See *Daily States*, November 25, 1889.
53. *Daily Picayune*, November 30, 1889.
54. Ibid., December 5, 1889.
55. Ibid., December 3, 1889.
56. Ibid., December 4, 1889.
57. Ibid., December 20, 1889.
58. Ibid., July 4, 1890.
59. Ibid., November 20, 1904.
60. Acts of Robert Legier, N.P., 12/157, July 20, 1903.
61. Ibid., 12/172, August 3, 1903.
62. *Daily States*, November 22, 1903; *Times-Democrat*, August 8, 1903.
63. See *Daily States* and *Daily Picayune*, November 22, 1903, for short descriptions of this theater.
64. See *Daily States*, August 26, 1903; cf. *Times-Democrat*, August 26, 1903.
65. *Times-Democrat*, August 26 and August 30, 1903.
66. See *New Orleans Item*, November 8, 1903.
67. *Daily Picayune*, November 16, 1904.
68. Ibid., November 28, 1904.
69. See *Daily Picayune*, December 28, 1904; see also *Daily States*, December 27, 1904.
70. *Daily Picayune*, January 3, 1905.
71. See *Daily States*, January 3, 1905.
72. *Daily Picayune*, February 19, 1905.
73. *Times-Democrat*, May 21, 1905.
74. *Daily States*, August 28, 1905; see also *Daily States*, January 2, 1906.
75. See *Daily Picayune*, January 15, 1906.
76. *Daily News*, March 30, 1906.
77. Ibid., August 20, 1906; see Conveyance Office Book (Orleans Parish Archives), 212/159.
78. Conveyance Office Book, 210/192.
79. Ibid., 272/443.
80. *Daily States*, January 2, 1906.

BIBLIOGRAPHY

A. PRIMARY SOURCES

1. Newspapers and Periodicals.

Bulletin of New Orleans Lodge of Elks, 1921 and 1924.
Chicago *Tribune*, 1883.
L'Abeille de la Nouvelle Orleans, 1863 and 1884.
Louisiana *Courier*, 1816 and 1818.
Moniteur de la Louisiane, 1806.
New Orleans *Daily News*, 1906.
New Orleans *Daily Picayune*, 1863-1906.
New Orleans *Daily States*, 1883-1906.
New Orleans *Daily True Delta*, 1861 and 1863.
New Orleans *Era*, 1863.
New Orleans *Evening Chronicle*, 1884-1886.
New Orleans *Item*, 1903.
New Orleans *Lantern*, 1887.
New Orleans *Mascot*, 1883-1888.
New Orleans *Times*, 1867.
New Orleans *Times-Democrat*, 1883-1905.
New Orleans *Times-Picayune*, 1924 and 1934.
New York Clipper, 1882-1889.
New York *Dramatic Mirror*, 1879.

2. Other Sources.

Acts of Charles E. Sel, N.P., 1/1473 (May 12, 1886). Orleans Parish Archives.
Acts of Marc Lafitte, N.P., 2/193 (October 9, 1812) and 8/72 (February 23, 1816). Orleans Parish Archives.
Acts of Philippe Pedesclaux, N.P., 73/585 (October 8, 1816). Orleans Parish Archives.
Acts of Robert Legier, N.P., 12 (1903). Orleans Parish Archives.
Acts of William O. Hart, N.P., 4 (1884-1885). Orleans Parish Archives.
Civil District Court, Parish of Orleans, No. 8505, June 5, 1883: "John H. Scott vs. Frederick W. Stemple." New Orleans Public Library.
Conveyance Office Book, 210/192, 212/159, and 272/443. Orleans Parish Archives.
New Orleans. *Proceedings of the City Council*, 1818 and 1884. New Orleans Public Library.
Passenger Lists of Vessels Arriving at New Orleans, 1820-1902. National Archives Microfilm. New Orleans Public Library.
Sanborn Map and Publishing Company. *Insurance Maps of New Orleans, 1885*. New York, 1885.
Soards, Lon (comp.). *Soards' New Orleans City Directory* (for the years 1884-1912). New Orleans, 1884-1912.

Theatre Program of the Pickwick Theatre, St. Louis, Missouri, September 29 and October 1 [1883]. Missouri Historical Society.

Vieux Carré Survey. Square 59. The Historic New Orleans Collection.

B. SECONDARY SOURCES

Ainsworth, William Harrison. "Jack Sheppard," *Bentley's Miscellany*, 5-7 (1839-1840).

Altick, Richard D. *The Shows of London.* Cambridge, Mass.: Harvard University Press, 1978.

Baroncelli, Joseph Gabriel de. *Le Théâtre-Francais, à la Nlle Orleans.* New Orleans: George Muller, 1906.

Chindahl, George L. *A History of the Circus in America.* Caldwell, Idaho: The Caxton Printers, Ltd., 1959.

Christopher, Milbourne. *Panorama of Magic.* New York: Dover Publications, 1962.

Coleman, Will H. (comp. and ed.). *Historical Sketch Book and Guide to New Orleans and Environs with Map.* New York: Will H. Coleman, 1885.

Fairall, Herbert S. *The World's Industrial and Cotton Centennial Exposition.* Iowa City: Republican Publishing Co., 1885.

Falk, Bernard. *The Naked Lady: A Biography of Adah Isaacs Menken.* London: Hutchinson, 1934.

Flynn, J.Q. *Flynn's Digest of the City Ordinances Together with the Constitutional Provisions, Acts of the General Assembly, and Decisions of the Courts Relative to the Government of the City of New Orleans.* New Orleans, 1896.

Ford, Ira W. *Traditional Music of America.* New York: De Capo Press, 1978.

Harris, Neil. *Humbug: The Art of P.T. Barnum.* Boston: Little, Brown and Co., 1973.

Harrison, Shirley Madeline. "The Grand Opera House (Third Varieties Theatre) of New Orleans, Louisiana, 1871 to 1906: A History and Analysis." Ph.D. dissertation, Louisiana State University, 1965.

Kendall, John S. *The Golden Age of the New Orleans Theater.* Baton Rouge: Louisiana State University Press, 1952.

_____. "'The World's Delight': The Story of Adah Isaacs Menken," *Louisiana Historical Quarterly*, 21 (1938), 846-868.

Kmen, Henry A. *Music in New Orleans: The Formative Years, 1791-1841.* Baton Rouge: Louisiana State University Press, 1966.

_____. "The Music of New Orleans," in Hodding Carter, ed., *The Past as Prelude: New Orleans, 1718-1968.* New Orleans: Tulane University Press [Pelican Publishing House], 1968.

Kunzog, John C. *The One-Horse Show.* Jamestown, N.Y.: John C. Kunzog, 1962.

Laurie, Joe, Jr. *Vaudeville: From the Honky-tonks to the Palace.* New York: Henry Holt & Co., 1953.

Le Gardeur, Rene J., Jr. *The First New Orleans Theatre, 1792-1803.* New Orleans: Leeward Books, 1963.

Lewis, Paul. *Queen of the Plaza: A Biography of Adah Isaacs Menken*. New York: Funk & Wagnalls, 1964.

Melebeck, Charles Bernard, Jr. "A History of the First and Second Varieties Theatres of New Orleans, Louisiana, 1849-1870." Ph.D. dissertation, Louisiana State University, 1973.

"New Orleans Stage," *Times-Democrat*, August 31, September 16, and September 23, 1894.

Newton, H. Chance. *Crime and Drama or Dark Deeds Dramatized*. London: Stanley Paul & Co., 1927.

O'Connor, Thomas (ed.). *The New Orleans Fire Department: From the Earliest Days to the Present Time; Including the Original Volunteer Department, the Firemen's Charitable Association, and the Paid Department down to 1895*. New Orleans, 1895.

Odell, George C.D. *Annals of the New York Stage*. 15 volumes. New York: Columbia University Press, 1927-1949.

Paskman, Daily. *"Gentlemen, Be Seated!": A Parade of the American Minstrels*. Rev. ed. New York: Clarkson N. Potter, Inc., 1976.

Shipley, Joseph T. *Guide to Great Plays*. Washington, D.C.: Public Affairs Press, 1956.

Shpall, Leo. "Adah Isaacs Menken," *Louisiana Historical Quarterly*, 26 (1943), 162-168.

Visitor's Guide to the World's Industrial and Cotton Centennial Exposition. Louisville, Ky.: Courier-Journal Job Printing Co., 1884.

Wallace, Irving. *The Fabulous Showman*. New York: Alfred A. Knopf, 1959.

Werner, Morris R. *Barnum*. New York: Harcourt, Brace and Company, 1923.

INDEX

Acting companies: Sargeant Aborn's Comedy Co., 80; Acme Dramatic Combination, 77-78; May Adams's Japanese Burlesque Co., 86; Arnold Stock Co., 116; Australian Novelty Show, 101; Avenue Theatre Stock Co., 90; I.W. Baird's Mammoth Minstrels, 79, 88; Barthold's Celebrated Liliputian Wonders, 95; Bayse-Davis Ideal Co., 88; Berland Combination, 92; Boston Ideal Co., 106; Nellie Boyd Dramatic Co., 94; John B. Brace's All Star Specialty Co., 89; Jennie Calef Combination, 79; California Minstrels, 68, 98; George Castle's Celebrities, 23-24; Castle's Comic Opera Co., 58; Hattie Bernard Chase Co., 112; George Christy's Minstrels, 6; Lottie E. Church Combination, 95; Edwin Clifford Dramatic Combination, 79; Combination Fraternal, 12; Criterion Opera Co., 24, 26; E.R. Dalton Drama Co., 42; E.R. Dalton's Sterling Comedy Co., 35; Davene's Allied Attractions, 81-82; Defossez French Opera Co., 33; Denier's Mammoth Humpty Dumpty Pantomime Troupe and European Specialty Co., 82; DePew-Burdette Co., 115; Devere's Great Carnival of Novelties, 80; Frank Dudley Co., 116; Elliot's Jolly Voyagers, 106; Elysium Stock Co., 113 ff.; English Royal Hand-Bell Ringers, 88; Erwood Combination, 95; Fisk Jubilee Singers and Plantation Shouters, 67; Foreman-Morton Combination, 103; Capitola Forrest's Novelty and Burlesque Co., 82; Fostelle Co., 68; French Opera Co., 50; A Friend Dramatic Co., 34; Georgia Minstrels, 116; Charles Gilday Comedy Co., 76, 86; Gilfoil & Bush Specialty Co., 86; Goodyear, Cook & Dillon Refined Minstrels, 101-103; Gorton's Mastadon Minstrels, 115; Great Blitz Combination, 27; Great World's Four Minstrels, 82; Grizzly Adams Combination, 97, 103; Harry Guion's Female Minstrel Combination, 31; Hall and Devoy Comedy Co., 92; Harris-Parkinson Stock Co., 116-117; Edward J. Hasson's Co., 104; Hawley's Magnets, 66; Howard & Whitney Ramblers, 69; Howard Dramatic Co., 102; Howe and Hummel Combination, 96-97; Hoyt Comedy Co., 114; Hume & Wesley's Big Specialty Co., 82; Huntley-Gilbert Co., 88-89; J.H. Huntley's Savoy Theater Co., 114; Billy Kersands Minstrels, 78, 128; George Lea's Variety Co., 8; Lester and Allen Early Birds Combination, 97; J.Z. Little Combination, 93; Little Muffets Combination, 79; McBride and Bryant Great Eastern Specialty Show, 106; McCabe & Young Refined Colored Operatic Minstrels, 102, 105; Majilton's Phenomenal Wonders, 103; Mastadon Monarchs, 89; Mexican Automaton Co., 56; Alfred Miaco's Humpty Dumpty Pantomime and Vaudeville Co., 114-115; Muldoon Picnic Co., 106, 108; Murphy and Mack Comedy Co., 68; New Orleans Juvenile Opera Co., 102, 103, 106; Our Goblins Co., 75; Palmer Company of Comics, 89; W.M. Paul Combination, 42-44, 52; W.M. Paul Comedy Co., 39; W.M. Paul Dramatic Co., 39; William Payne's Celebrities, 67; Payton Sisters Co., 115; Peerless Stock Co., 115; Ranch King Co., 104; Richards and Pringle Georgia Minstrels, 94; Richardson Dramatic Combination, 78; Riley and Fey Combination, 73-75; Riley and Wolf Specialty Co., 91-92; Walter S. Sanford Dramatic Co., 84, 86; Samuel S. Sanford's Opera Troupe, 3 ff., 119; Zera Semon's Novelty Combination, 97; Senegambian Minstrels, 21; Shield's Great Eastern Novelty Co., 95; Silbons Yellow Dwarf Co., 81; Sisson & Cawthorn Little Nuggets Comedy Co., 80; Will L. Smith's Swiss Bell Ringers, Comic Concert Co., and Humpty Dumpty Combination, 81; Spooner Dramatic Co., 116; Carrie Stanley Combination, 86, 87; J.C. Stewart Comedy Co., 87; Stranglers of Paris Co., 89; Charles Sturgis Comedy Co., 80; Dan Morris Sullivan Mirror of Ireland Combination Co., 97; George W. and William J. Thompson Troupe, 77, 88, 89; Thorne and Carleton Big Specialty Co., 95; Tyrolean National Concert Co., 21; Cora Van Tassel Co., 112; Harry Webber

Combination, 87; Weston Brothers Combination, 101; Georgia Woodthorpe Combination, 65.

Associations: American Benevolent & Mutual Aid Association, 95; American Red Cross, 102; Elks (B.P.O.E), 57-58, 79, 102, 117-118, 123, 128; Knights of Labor, 97; Knights of Pythias, 106; Louisiana State Society for the Prevention of Cruelty to Animals, 66; New Orleans Amateur League, 41; Odd Fellows, 83; Order of Railway Conductors, 90; Sons of Louisiana, 106, 107; Southern Rifle Club, 96, 106; Volunteer Fire Association, Philadelphia, 96; Young Pelican Mutual Benevolent Association, 91, 96.

Bidwell, David: 3-7, 31, 112, 119-120, 121.

Burlesque, modern: 11, 66.

Circuses: George F. Bailey & Co., 4, 8; P.T. Barnum's Circus, 32, 128; Batchelor & Doris Circus, 13; Buffalo Bill's Wild West Show, 58; W.W. Cole Circus, 86-87; Diefenbach's Great Transatlantic Shows, 112; Adam Forepaugh Circus, 87; Haight & Chambers Circus, 8; Howes' Great London Circus, 8; King, Burke & Co. Circus, 76, 87; Charles Lee's Great London Circus, 88; Lorrelaud's Circus, 78-79; Ryan & Robinson Circus, 8; Sands, Nathan & Co., 4; Sells Brothers Circus, 61, 87; Trans-Atlantic Circus, 63.

Expositions: Cotton Centennial, 31, 51, 62, 74; North Central and South American Exposition, 74; Paris, 1889, 111.

Faranta, Signor: With Academy of Music, 3 ff.; as "Mr. Stemple, the young American contortionist," 4; as "Ferranti," 6; his association with David Bidwell, 6-7; adopts "Signor Faranta," 6-7; his early years, 6, 8, 120; his marriage to Alva Lowe, 8; with Ryan & Robinson Circus, 12; with Combination Fraternal, 12; destitute in New Orleans, 12; leases Bourbon Street lot from Mary A. Roberts, 12, 40, 82, 108; his contract with John H. Scott, 13 ff., 22; erects mammoth pavilion, 12-13; arrested and jailed, 16; his public apologia, 17; in court, 16, 22, 57; opens and closes roller skating rink at Spanish Fort, 25; his life with Harry the sea lion, 35; his saloon "Tween the Acts," 39; sponsors baseball clubs, 41-42; his building contract with Cincinnati Corrugating Company of Ohio, 44-45, 65; opens his Iron Theatre, 54-55; his quarrel with W.M. Paul, 56; his connection with founding of Elks (B.P.O.E.) in New Orleans, 57-58; purchases circuses, 63, 78, 127; thwarts water filter swindle, 75-76; his last performance as contortionist, 83; aids earthquake victims, 83; purchases attractions from W.W. Cole Circus, 86-87; divorced from Alva Lowe, 82; marries Rose Marshall, 90; loses his iron theater to fire, 107-108; reopens his tent show, 108; in Paris, 111; a pallbearer at Bidwell's funeral, 112; moves to Chicago, 112; as manager of Elysium Theatre, 114-117; his retirement, 117-118.

Faranta's Pavilion, Signor: 11-45, 52-53, 108-112.

Fires, New Orleans: 14-16, 39, 50-51, 107-108, 119, 124, 127.

Gorman's Pavilion, Eugene: 18, 20, 21-22, 24, 31, 35, 36, 65.

Iron Buildings, New Orleans: Avenue Theatre, 52; "The Battle of Sedan," panorama, 51; Burke Hotel, 51; Cotton Centennial buildings, 51; Faranta's Iron Theatre, 51; Hotel Windsor, 52; Temple of Art, 51.

Iron Theatre, Faranta's: History of site, 49-50, 124; construction begun, 44-45; theater completed, 53; described, 53-54; cost and value, 44-45, 54, 130; staff, 73, 84, 129, 130; hosts meeting to ratify U.S. presidential nominations, 54; opens with *Mazeppa*, 54-55; proscenium boxes added, 58; dirt floor replaced with wood flooring, 73; gas fixtures replace electric lights, 73; William A. Miller appointed business manager, 73; boys borrow ladders and watch Faranta's show from theater's transoms, 74;

renamed "Faranta's Theatre," 77; new opera chairs added, 77, 78; new Babcock fire extinguisher added, 82; new incandescent lights added, 84; William A. Miller appointed manager of Faranta's Theatre, 84; tragedian Daniel E. Bandman defends theater's cheap prices, 87-88; balcony boxes added, 90; theater described, 90; new gas lights and new opera chairs added, 101; Faranta's Theatre destroyed by fire, 107-108; insurance companies, 130.

Lowe, Alva: 8, 12, 17, 21, 25, 26, 32, 35, 39, 42, 63, 73, 76, 82, 120.

Miller, William A.: 69, 73, 83, 84, 117.

Stempel, Ben: 12, 13, 22, 73, 101, 130.

Stempel, Edward: 101.

Stempel, Frank: 54.

Stempel, Frederick W., Jr.: 98, 117-118.

Stempel, Gus: 13, 22, 54, 73, 84, 101.

Stempel, Henry: 73.

Stempel, Isabelle Marie Lagarosse: 117-118.

Stempel, Mamie B.: 79.

Stempel, Rose: 79.

Stempel, Rose Marshall: 90, 98, 111, 117.

Theatres, New Orleans: Academy of Music, 3-8, 12, 31, 112, 119; Avenue Theatre, 52, 90, 96, 97, 106, 112, 124; Camp Street Theatre, 55; Eden Theatre, 96; Elysium Theatre, 113-117; Faranta's Iron Theatre, 44 ff.; Faranta's Theatre (Elysium), 114-117; French Opera House, 31, 54; Gaiety, 119; Grand Opera House, 31; Grunewald Opera House (Grunewald Hall), 58; Greenwall Theatre, 117; Orleans Theatre, 49-50; Park Theatre, 31; Dan Rice's Amphitheatre, 119; St. Charles Theatre, 12, 31, 50, 65, 112; Spalding and Rogers' Museum and Amphitheatre, 119; Spanish Fort, 18, 25, 121; Varieties Theatre, 3, 7, 50, 119; West End, 24, 26, 82, 90, 121.

Vaudeville: 11-12, 114.

Yellow Fever: 8, 12, 101-102.

LIST OF PLAYS

Ace of Spades, 66.
Across the Atlantic, 79.
Adonis in Cupid, 81.
After Seven Years; or, The Mystery of the Willows, 92.
The American Abroad, 79.
Among the Moonshiners, 117.
Around the World in Eighty Days, 93-94.
The Audition Parlor, 93.

Back From the Dead, 96.
Baked Alive, 27.
The Baron's Double, 104.
Because He Loved Her So, 116.
Ben Bolt, 116.
Beyond the Law, 114.
The Black Crook, 66.
The Black Flag, 105.
Black Hawks, 89.
The Black Statue, 3, 91.
The Boarding School, 69.
Bone Squash, 4.
The Boy Burglar, 40.
Brass Buttons, 82.
Braving the World, 104-105.
The Brigands of Calabria, 26.
Brother Against Brother, 96, 117.
A Brother's Oath, 86.

Camille, 116.
Capital Against Labor, 117.
Casey, the Piper, 40.
Cast Steel Seminary, 82.
Champion Jack, 80-81.
The Child Stealer, 116.
The Circus Girl, 116.
The Cobbler's Frolic, 6.
Collars and Cuffs, 76-77, 86.
The Collier's Daughter; or, A Coal Digger's Life in Pennsylvania Mines, 86.
Confusion, 69, 89.
The Convict's Daughter, 114.

The Corsican Brothers; or, The Duel in the Snow, 87.
Counterfeit, 106.
The Country Boy, 115.
Creme de la Creme of Ethiopia, 86.
The Cuban Spy, 104.

Damon and Pythias, 94.
The Danites, 78.
A Daughter of Satan, 116.
Davy Crockett, 42.
Dead or Alive, 88.
Dead to the World, 64.
Deadwood Dick, 114.
De Lillian's Duel, 88.
Delmonte, 96.
A Desert Bride, 114.
Diamond Dick, 116.
Dr. Jekyll and Mr. Hyde, 106, 116.
The Dog Spy, 96.
Don Caesar de Bazan, 88.
The Doomed Bride; or, The Jealous Mute, 4.
Dora, 88.
Duchesse du Barry, 113.
The Dumb Man of Manchester; or, The Murder at the Mill, 39.

East Lynne, 87, 88, 116.
Elsie, the Mountain Waif, 69.

The Factory Assistant, 39.
Fanchon, the Cricket, 41, 80.
Fatinitza, 102.
Faust, 26, 66.
The Five Black Noses, 91.
Fogarty's Racket, 66.
A Fool and His Money, 116.
For a Life, 88.
Forget Me Not, 112.
The Four Lovers, 3.
Fraud and Its Victims, 42, 67.
The French Spy, 41, 56, 57.
A Friend, 34.

Fun in a Boarding School, 34-35, 69, 92.
Fun on the Rhine, 75.

A Game of Life, 86.
A Gigantic Liar, 116.
Giroflé-Girofla, 102.
Going to the Ball, 40.
The Gold King; or, The Life Prisoner,
    77, 88.
Good as Gold, 79.

Hamlet, 87, 94.
Hauled Back, 66.
The Haunted House of Lafayette, 4.
Hearts of the Blue Ridge, 116-117.
Heege's Bad Boy, 82, 83.
The Hermit, 103.
A Hot Time, 115.
Humpty Dumpty, 32, 105, 114.
Humpty Dumpty No. 2, 25.
Humpty Dumpty's Picnic, 25.
A Husband on Salary, 115.

The Idle Apprentice, 40.
In Darkest Russia, 116.
In His Power, 116.
Inshavogue; or, The Fenian Chief of
    '98, 88, 95.
In the Rockies, 116.
In the Web, 64.

Jack Ketch, the London Apprentice, 40.
Jack Sheppard, 39-40, 44.
The James Boys, 63-64.
The James Boys in Kentucky, 117.
The James Boys in Missouri, 116.
Jean de Paris, 50.
Joshua Whitcomb, 35, 44.
Just in Time, 106.

Kitty's Luck; or, Sight-Seeing in the
    Emerald Isles, 97.
A Knight of Labor; or, The Master
    Workman's Vow, 96-97.

The Lady of Lyons, 87-88.
Lafitte; or, The Pirates of the Gulf, 36.
Lafitte, the Pirate, 44.
The Lighthouse Robbery, 115, 116.

The Lights of Gotham, 115-116.
The Lights of New Orleans, 34.
Little Barefoot, 79-80.
Little Butterfly, 65.
The Little Coquette, 112.
The Little Mother, 116.
Little Muffets, 79.
Little Nuggets, 80.
Little Red Riding Hood, 116.
The Little Sinner, 112.
A Living Lie, 106.
The Long Strike, 52-53.
Lost in Boston, 116.
The Lost Paradise, 114.
The Lucky Ranche, 35, 44.

Macbeth, 87.
The Magic Flute, 26.
The Magic Talisman, 96, 105.
Man and Master, 116.
The Man From Mexico, 115.
Mardo, the Hunter, 96.
Marked for Life, 61-62.
The Married Bachelors, 50.
La Mascotte, 102.
May's Devotion, 96.
Mazeppa; or, The Wild Horse of
    Tartary, 54, 125.
The Merchant of Venice, 87.
Mexico, 57.
Midnight in Chinatown, 116.
The Midnight Special, 115.
The Mikado, 102.
The Miner's Oath, 115.
M'liss, Child of the Sierras, 69.
Monte Cristo, 79, 86, 87, 105-106, 116.
Mother Goose and the Golden Egg, 116.
Mrs. Partington, 68.
Muldoon's Picnic, 40, 69, 106-107.
The Mummy, 3.
My Old Kentucky Home, 116.
Les Mystères de Paris, 65.

Narcisse, 87.
Nature's Nobleman, 116.
Neck and Neck, 94.
Nell Gwynne, 116.
Never Say Die, 87.
New York by Gaslight, 88.
Nip and Tuck, 87.
Nobody's Claim, 87.

Old London, 40.
Oliver Twist, 39, 44.
One of the Finest, 104.
Only a Country Girl, 95.
The Opium Fiend, 117.
Othello, 87, 88, 94.
Our Bachelors, 78.
Our Boarding House, 89.
Our School Girls, 86.
The Outlaw Prince, 66.

Pa-Pe-To, 95.
Passion's Slave, 94.
Les Pauvres de Paris, 67.
The Pavements of Paris, 102.
Peaceful Valley, 115, 116.
The Pearl of Savoy; or, A Mother's
    Blessing, 116.
Peck's Bad Boy, 97, 116.
Peril, or Life by the Sea Side, 39.
The Phantom Avenger, 36, 44.
A Piece of Pie in 3 Slices, 86.
Pink Dominos, 88-89.
The Planter's Child, 96.
A Plum Pudding, 93.
Pluto; or, The Seven Daughters of
    Satan, 36, 66.
The Poor of London, 67.
The Poor of New York, 67.
A Practical Joke, 86.
The Price of Silence, 116.
The Princess of Trebizonde, 58, 61.

Ragged Jack, the Vagabond, 73-74, 86.
The Ranch King, 104.
Resurrection, 116.
Richard III, 4, 58, 88, 94.
Richelieu, 87, 94.
Rip Van Winkle, 68, 89, 115, 117.
Roanoke, 114.
Robbers of the Devil's Gulch, 86.
Robert Macaire, 26.
Romeo and Juliet, 3, 87.
Rooms to Rent, 68.
Rosedale; or, The Rifle Ball, 36.
A Royal Rival, 115.

The Scout's Revenge, 114.
Seeing the Elephant, 90.
The Senator From Kentucky, 116.

The Seven Daughters of Satan, 36, 66.
The Seven Sisters, 36, 66-67.
The Shadow Detective; or, Leonie the
    Waif, 92.
The Siege of the Alamo, 115.
The Sightless Bride, 77.
Siskyon; or, For a Brother's Crime, 77.
Si Slocum, 96.
Slaves of the Orient, 116.
The Sleeping City, 116.
A Soldier's Honor, 115.
A Southern Romance, 116, 117.
The Spectre Guest, 4.
Sports of the Mines, 66.
Storm Beaten, 93.
The Storm in the Thames, 40.
The Stranglers of Paris, 89-90.
The Streets of London, 67.
The Streets of New York, 67, 89.
Success, 88.

A Tale of Enchantment, 66.
Ten Nights in a Barroom, 106, 116.
Texas, or the Siege of the Alamo, 116.
That Bad Boy; or, Fun in a Grocery, 75.
Thomas Darrell, 40.
The Thunderbolt, 89.
The Ticket-of-Leave Man, 42-43.
Timour the Tartar; or, The Captive
    Prince, 56, 57.
La Tour de Nesle, 50.
Tourists in a Pullman Palace Car, 80.
The Tradesman, 116.
The Trail of Blood, 90.
The Travelers, 74.
Trix, 80.
Turn Him Out, 88.
The Two Johns, 87.
The Two Orphans, 42.

Uncle Tom's Cabin, 67, 106.
Under the Gaslight; or, Life and Love
    in These Times, 68-69.
Under the Gas Pipes, 81.
Under the Lash, 84.
Unknown, 80, 95.
Up the Spout, 80.
Utah, 115.

The Way of the World, 92, 101.
The Whippoorwill, 89.

Wild Violet, 89.
Woman Against Woman, 114.
The World, 93.
The World Against Him, 117.
Worse and Worse, 77.

Yankee in Cuba, 116.
Yawcup; or, The Peddler's Story, 77.
The Yellow Dwarf, 81.
The Young Housebreaker, 40.

Zao, 82.

Board of Directors

Benjamin W. Yancey, *President*

Ernest C. Villeré
Mrs. William K. Christovich

G. Henry Pierson, Jr.
Fred M. Smith

The body of this book is set on a Penta-driven APS Micro-5 in Caledonia, designed by William Addison Dwiggins (1880-1956), primary developer of the Knopf typographic style.

Director of Publications, The Historic New Orleans Collection, Patricia Brady Schmit.

Jacket and book design are by Michael Ledet of Ledet Mann Productions, New Orleans.

Typography and production are by Impressions, Inc., Madison, Wisconsin.

DATE DUE

GAYLORD | | | PRINTED IN U.S.A.

VERMONT STATE COLLEGES

0 00003 0522640 9

Souvenir--Press Night.

FARANTA'S IRON THEATRE.

BOURBON & ORLEANS STS.

NEW ORLEANS, LA.,

PROGRAMME:

FRIDAY EVENING, DECEMBER 26

MR. SID. C. FRANCE

In the Great Sensational Drama, entitled

THE JAMES BOYS,

In Five Acts.

CAST OF CHARACTERS.

BUCKSKIN............................MR. SID. FRANCE
Jessie James.........................R. Hamilton Nicholls
F........ ....es.......................Harry Melmer
Chas. Quantrell.......................Al. Hensley
Bob Ford............................Ja..... Guzette
Dr. Samuels..........................W. Kline
Ted Cross...........................R. French
Cashier.............................H. Miller
Sheriff.............................W. Green
Jennie Somers.......................Miss Emily Walton
Mrs. Samuels........................Miss Benham
Lizzie Jane Green....................Larry Darley

Soldiers, Outlaws, Police, Highwaymen.

Incidental to the action of the piece, the following

THRILLING SITUATIONS.

THE HANGING OF DR. SAMUELS............
            THE BURNING OF THE HOUSE
THE SP.....